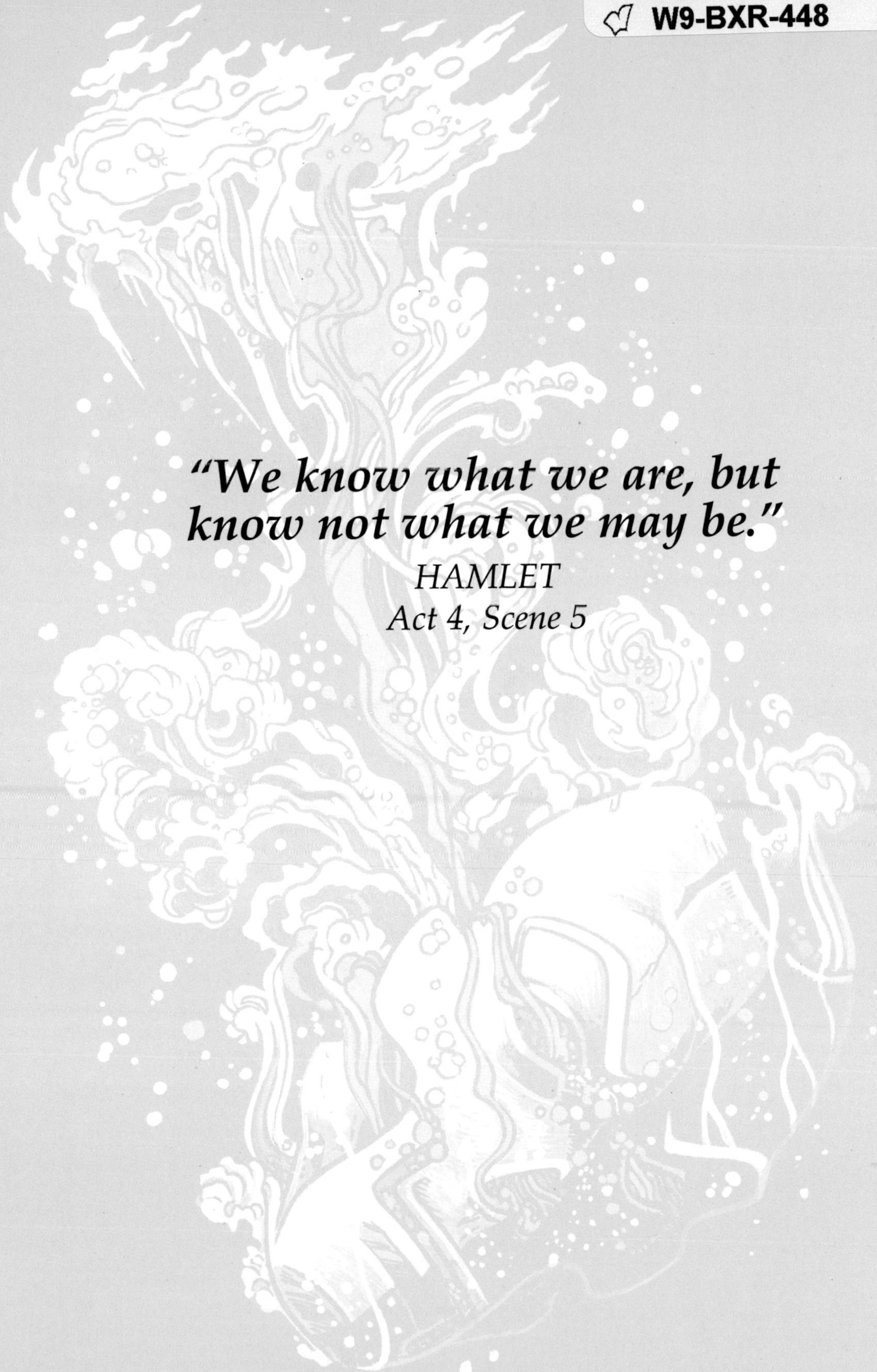

"We know what we are, but know not what we may be."

HAMLET

Act 4, Scene 5

"I can no other answer make but thanks,
And thanks."

Lisa Newal, Anna Del Col, Andy Zvanitajs, Jim and Marianne Del Col, Crystal Luxmore, Peregrine Luxmore, Owen and Elizabeth McCreery, Brian McCreery, Bonnie Belanger, Paul Belanger.

Everyone at IDW Publishing and Diamond Books — they continue to amaze us with their dedication to making great books. We wish to single out the contribution of Chris Mowry, who went above and beyond the call of duty on this book.

Keith Morris, Sam Zimmerman, Dr. Toby Malone, Martha Cornog, Paola Paulino, Vaneda Vireak, Kelsie Yoshida, PIE, Karl Kerschl, Stephanie Mah, Beata Shih, Ciaran McElvoy, Ryan North, Vicky Anderson, Carole-Ann Perron, Dominique Poitras, Neil Gibson, Fred Kennedy, Steve Paugh, Gabriel Rodriguez, Marc Andreyko, Francis Manapul, David Petersen, Mike Carey, Bryan J.L. Glass, Stephanie Cooke, Clement Wan, Serena Obhrai, Lisa Girard, Ben Sokolowski, Michael Ball, Kevin Cox, Tony Kramreither, Ryan Nord, Jeff Okin, Ari Greenburg, Jethro Bushenbaum, Dawn Douglas, Chris Smith, Sharon Fleming, Ted Fleming, Frank Galea, Andrew Apangu, Al Bugeja, Rob Chiasson, Steve Lawlor, Katie Musgrave.

And finally, the most masked man of them all, Mr. William Shakespeare.

ISBN: 978-1-63140-058-2

17 16 15 14   1 2 3 4

IDW®
www.IDWPUBLISHING.com
IDW founded by Ted Adams, Alex Garner, Kris Oprisko, and Robbie Robbins

Ted Adams, CEO & Publisher
Greg Goldstein, President & COO
Robbie Robbins, EVP/Sr. Graphic Artist
Chris Ryall, Chief Creative Officer/Editor-in-Chief
Matthew Ruzicka, CPA, Chief Financial Officer
Alan Payne, VP of Sales
Dirk Wood, VP of Marketing
Lorelei Bunjes, VP of Digital Services
Jeff Webber, VP of Digital Publishing & Business Development

Facebook: facebook.com/idwpublishing
Twitter: @idwpublishing
YouTube: youtube.com/idwpublishing
Instagram: instagram.com/idwpublishing
deviantART: idwpublishing.deviantart.com
Pinterest: pinterest.com/idwpublishing/idw-staff-faves

Originally published as KILL SHAKESPEARE: THE MASK OF NIGHT issues #1-4.

KILL SHAKESPEARE
THE MASK OF NIGHT

CREATED AND WRITTEN BY
Conor McCreery
and
Anthony Del Col

ART BY
Andy Belanger

COLORS BY
Shari Chankhamma

LETTERING BY
Chris Mowry

ORIGINAL SERIES EDITS BY
Tom Waltz

COLLECTION COVER BY
Andy Belanger

COLLECTION DESIGN BY
Chris Mowry

COLLECTION EDITS BY
**Justin Eisinger
& Alonzo Simon**

The Story So Far...

It is four months since the armies of Richard III and Lady Macbeth were defeated on the fields of Shrewsbury by Juliet Capulet's Prodigal rebellion and the appearance of the Wizard-God William Shakespeare.

It is four weeks since Hamlet, Juliet, Othello, and Romeo travelled to the island of Prospero, where they were met with madness, the blind wizard Prospero, and the cunning witch Lady Macbeth, who coaxed Romeo to turn against his friends, forcing Juliet to kill her former lover to protect her new one, Hamlet.

It is four days since Hamlet, Juliet, Othello, and William Shakespeare have gone missing in a sea of troubles...

HAMLET:

The Shadow King of prophesy, Hamlet succeeded in bringing Shakespeare back from his self-imposed exile and helped lead the Prodigal army to victory over Richard III. In his quest for the Bard, Hamlet fell in love with Juliet, but their bond was smashed when he witnessed Romeo's death at the hands of his new love. Lost on the waves, the Dane has still not recovered from this seeming murder.

JULIET:

The leader of the Prodigal rebels, Juliet spearheaded the victory over Lady Macbeth and Richard III's forces at the battle of Shrewsbury. But Juliet was a victim of the poisonous nature of Prospero's Island as she was driven mad, leading to her and Romeo re-consummating their relationship. Juliet then killed Romeo when he became pathologically bent on her and Hamlet's destruction.

OTHELLO:

Othello again donned the mantle of General as he played a major role in the Prodigal victory in Shrewsbury. Othello was able to overcome his hatred for his old nemesis Iago, but was forced to kill his former friend when Iago proved to still be a villain. However, Prospero's Island brought Othello to his knees with visions of his dead wife Desdemona, and he has lost all touch with reality as she continues to whisper to him in his dreams.

SHAKESPEARE:

The controller of the quill and creator of the world, Shakespeare has proven himself to be neither the evil wizard his detractors claimed, nor the benevolent God his followers believed him to be. He reluctantly travelled to the island to face off against his former protégé, Prospero, but in the process of stopping the sorcerer from unmaking all of creation his energy was drained from him and he has slipped into a coma.

ROMEO (DECEASED?):

A man once sworn to kill Hamlet the Shadow King, Romeo had reformed and joined the Prodigals but lost his purpose in life when Shakespeare proved not to be an infallible God and Juliet found comfort in Hamlet's arms. Looking for purpose, he led the mission to Prospero's Island but manipulated by Lady Macbeth and driven insane with anger by the island, he attempted to kill Hamlet and Juliet before being killed in turn. He seemingly has been resurrected by Lady Macbeth.

LADY MACBETH:

The mistress of dark magic, Lady Macbeth hungers for the power of the quill and seeks revenge on Shakespeare for the tragedies that befell her in her past. A former protégé of Prospero, she used her old teacher's island as a stage to woo Shakespeare back to the world and in the process turned Romeo against his friends. She now possesses Prospero's staff and, with Romeo as her loyal lieutenant, she lies in wait plotting her next move.

DESDEMONA:

Othello's former wife, who died at his hands due to betrayal by Othello's lieutenant, Iago. Thought dead, she somehow manages to haunt her former husband and killer though her purpose is unclear – if she even exists.

CAPTAIN CESARIO:

The fabled pirate of the seas, Cesario is known to be wearing his gold and obsidian mask that fuses together the faces of Comedy and Tragedy. Reckless and daring, he has developed a reputation as someone who cannot be killed. What is not known to his rivals on the seas is the love that he and Viola share, a secret held only by the crew of *The Boreas*.

VIOLA:

The first mate of Captain Cesario's ship *The Boreas*, Viola is a pirate in the same vein as Cesario – quick with sword, temper and wit. She escaped from Richard's armies, but her twin brother Sebastian was not so lucky. Viola wandered Illyria, seeking her brother for months before hiding herself aboard *The Boreas*. She was discovered but surprised her pirate captors, and herself, by being a natural at sea. She also discovered something else in the process – love with Cesario.

YOUNG LUCIUS:

The captain of one of Titus Andronicus' capital ships, *The Lavinia*, Lucius is known across Illyria for his quick temper and his terrifying cannibalistic appetites. The grandson of Titus, he has been assigned the task of destroying the remnants of the Prodigal fleet, crushing any attempts to resupply the Prodigal army by sea, and stopping all piracy. He has been hunting Cesario for months.

TITUS ANDRONICUS:

Though he has yet to appear on our stage, Titus quickly seized the void left after the defeat of Richard III and Lady Macbeth. The cunning warrior and strategist is known for his desire to conquer all that lies before him, and now, with Shakespeare and Richard both defeated he has turned his sights on Illyria. In the first major battle his armies massacred the fledgling Prodigal forces and put Illyria's new government to flight.

Behind the Mask...

Two stories about pirates and sailors, *Treasure Island* and *The Odyssey*, are works of fiction that deeply marked my childhood. Despite the fact that I read both books at very different times (R.L. Stevenson's adventure when I was a child, and Homer's epic in my university years), my introduction to both was through unconventional channels.

In South America in the mid-'80s, an anime TV series based on *Treasure Island* (*Takarajima*, 1978) fascinated me, and not just because of its great visuals. With an extended cast of compelling characters, the thrilling and sometimes dark adventures of Jim Hawkins and Long John Silver showed how a boy's quest for treasure turned into an unforgettable journey to adulthood. *The Odyssey*, on the other hand, came to me as a 52-page comic book beautifully drawn by Jess Jodloman (*Marvel Classics Comics* #18, 1977) and in Odysseus, I immediately found a favorite hero. A guy who confronted sea monsters, witches, giants, and even the gods' wrath, armed only with the sharpness of his intellect and the strength of his will to prevail and return home? Awesome.

As the years passed, I recognized in both tales elements that were relevant in many stories that became meaningful to me: vivid and humanly gifted and flawed characters; no iconic absolutes but instead shaded heroes and enlightened villains; imaginative and entertaining plots, founded in conflicts driven by intimately appealing motivations; the promise of journeys to the unknown; the challenge to explore both new worlds and our own hidden, inner boundaries…

Expanding the *Kill Shakespeare* saga, *The Mask of Night* invites us to sail alongside fascinating and complex characters in an open sea of thrilling pirate adventures. A masked pirate who never dies and a fierce woman who fears nothing invite us to their world of blood, iron, and tumultuous waters, into a life of lights and shades that's driven by passion and thirst for adventure. They're blessed in that they're allowed to share love and adventure, but cursed by being denied their dream of enduring happiness. We face in their enemies the most horrible monsters, which rise from the bottomless pit that lies deep in the darkness of the human heart. And we meet again an awkward band (a lady general, a raging Moor, a wandering prince, and a particularly mysterious old man) who are trying to sort a doomed fate to succeed in a mission tied to the destiny of their world.

As in any proper pirate's tale, McCreery, Del Col, Belanger, and Chankhamma invite us along on a treasure hunt. We dig through these pages to find solid gold characters, fully and deeply shaped, with vivid voices and heartfelt conflicts. Anthony Del Col and Conor McCreery capture the soul of iconic characters like Juliet, Hamlet, Cesario or Viola, successfully breathing into them new life with refreshing contemporary charm. Meanwhile, Andy Belanger and Shari Chankhamma flesh out overwhelmingly rich portraits of the cast and the world that frames their adventures and travels. We sail through mind-blowing action sequences in beautifully rendered landscapes to face thrilling and gut-wrenching surprises.

And there's even another treasure to discover: the remarkable accomplishment of offering the legacy of the Bard's mythology to a new generation of readers. They remind us once again how important it is to open new doors and windows to the essence of these milestones of all-time storytelling, alternative paths to explore new horizons in those creative territories. Share dreams and ideas that readers can likewise revisit or discover for the first time, while giving a creative testimony of love and respect to classic works that keep inspiring new generations of writers and artists.

Kill Shakespeare? Ha! I can't think of a funnier and more provocative way to remind us how alive he is and how much we owe him for expanding the frontiers of the realms of imagination.

Gabriel Rodríguez
(*Locke & Key, Little Nemo: Adventures in Slumberland*)
Santiago, Chile
September 2014

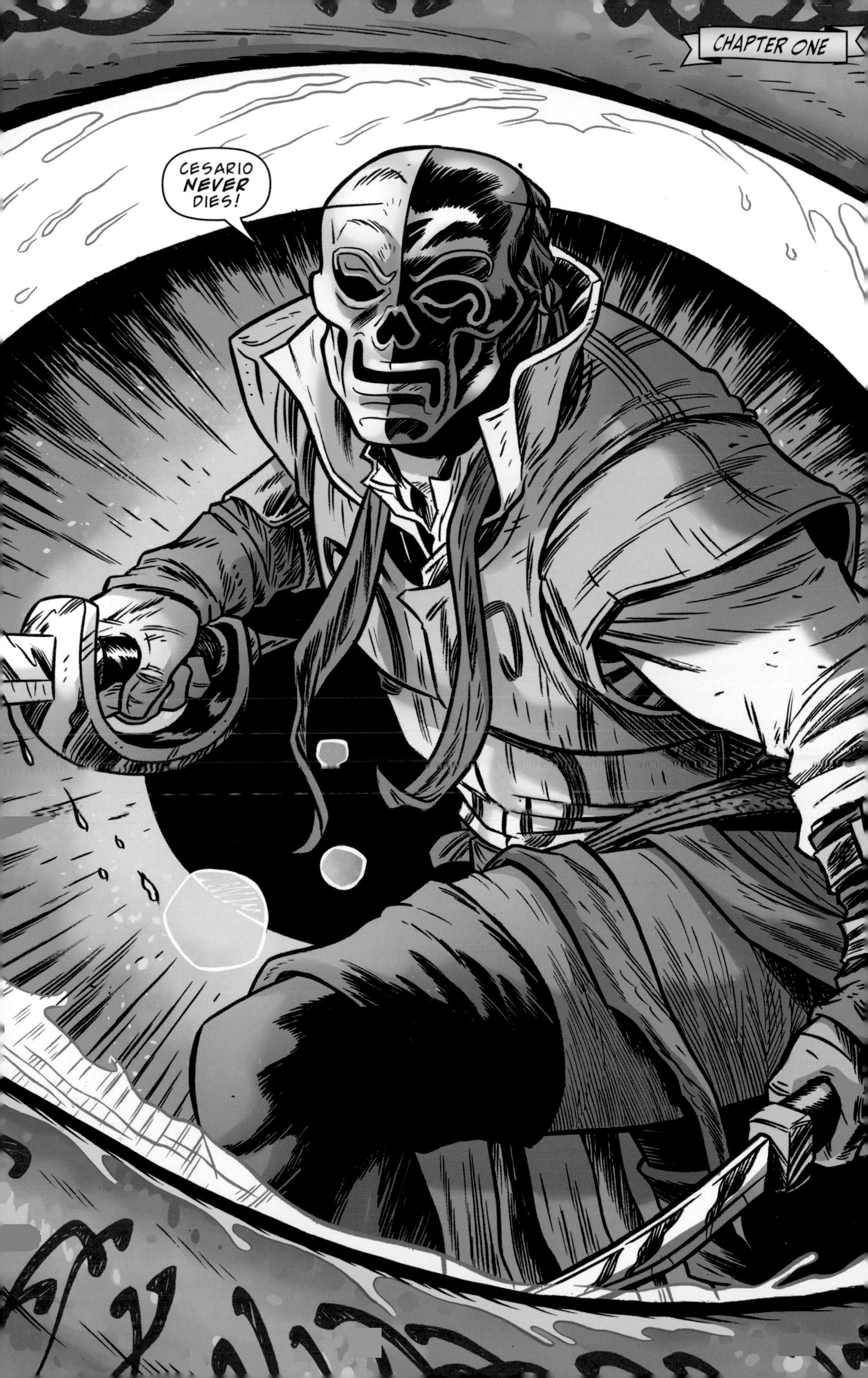
CHAPTER ONE
CESARIO NEVER DIES!

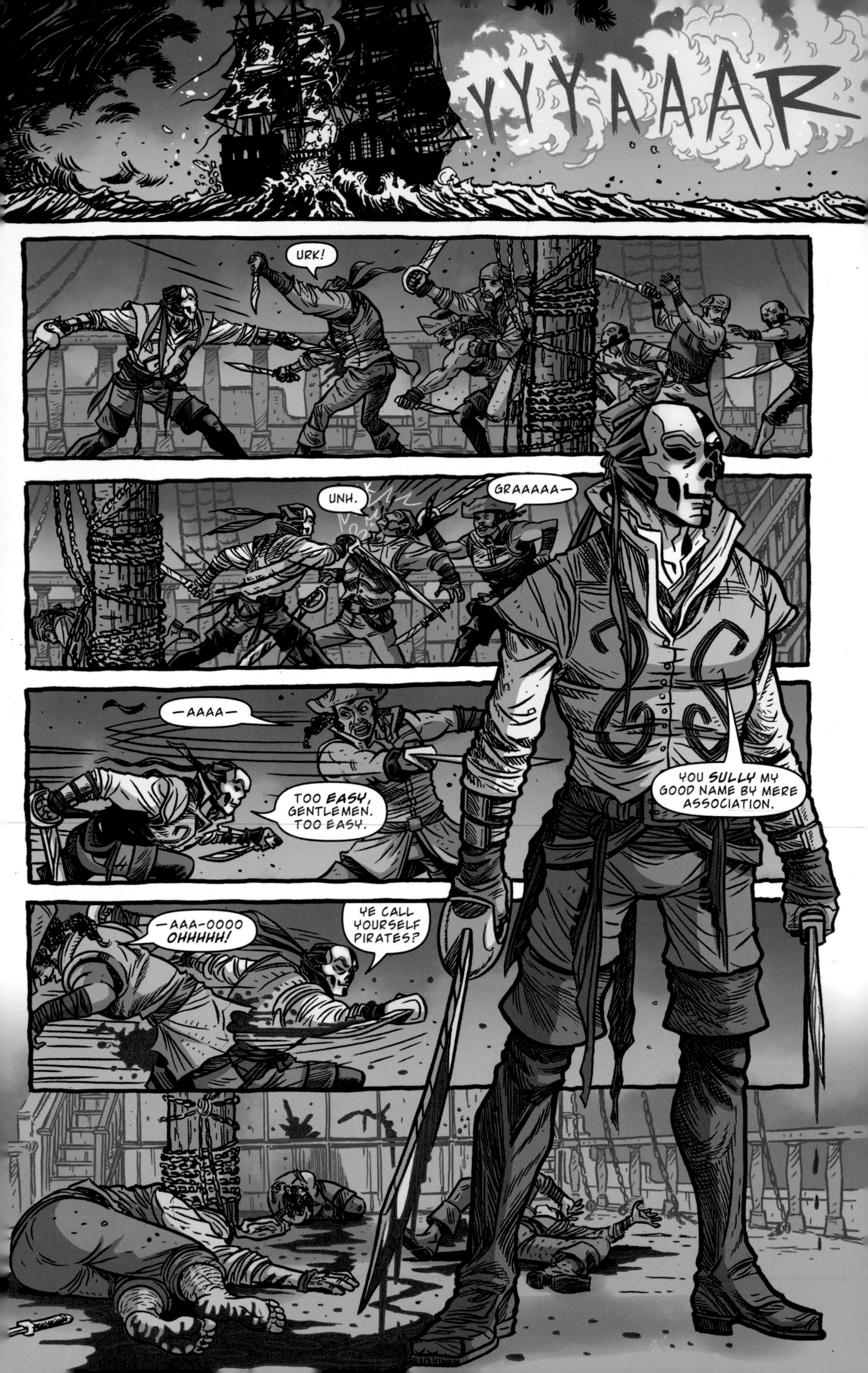
YYYAAAR
URK!
UNH.
GRAAAAA—
—AAAA—
TOO EASY, GENTLEMEN. TOO EASY.
—AAA-OOOO OHHHHH!
YE CALL YOURSELF PIRATES?
YOU SULLY MY GOOD NAME BY MERE ASSOCIATION.

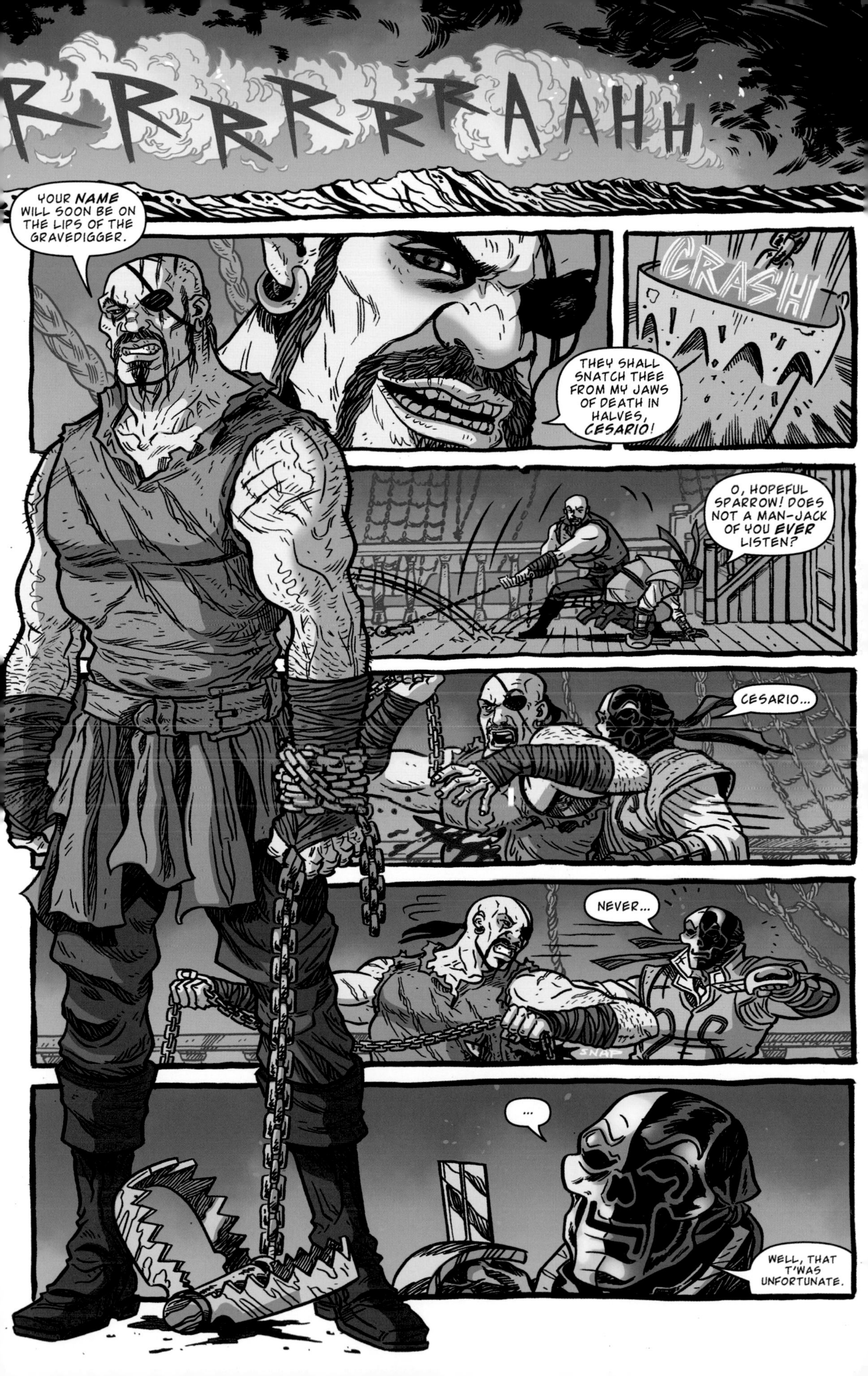
RRRRRRAAHH
YOUR NAME WILL SOON BE ON THE LIPS OF THE GRAVEDIGGER.
THEY SHALL SNATCH THEE FROM MY JAWS OF DEATH IN HALVES, CESARIO!
CRASH
O, HOPEFUL SPARROW! DOES NOT A MAN-JACK OF YOU EVER LISTEN?
CESARIO...
NEVER...
SNAP
...
WELL, THAT T'WAS UNFORTUNATE.

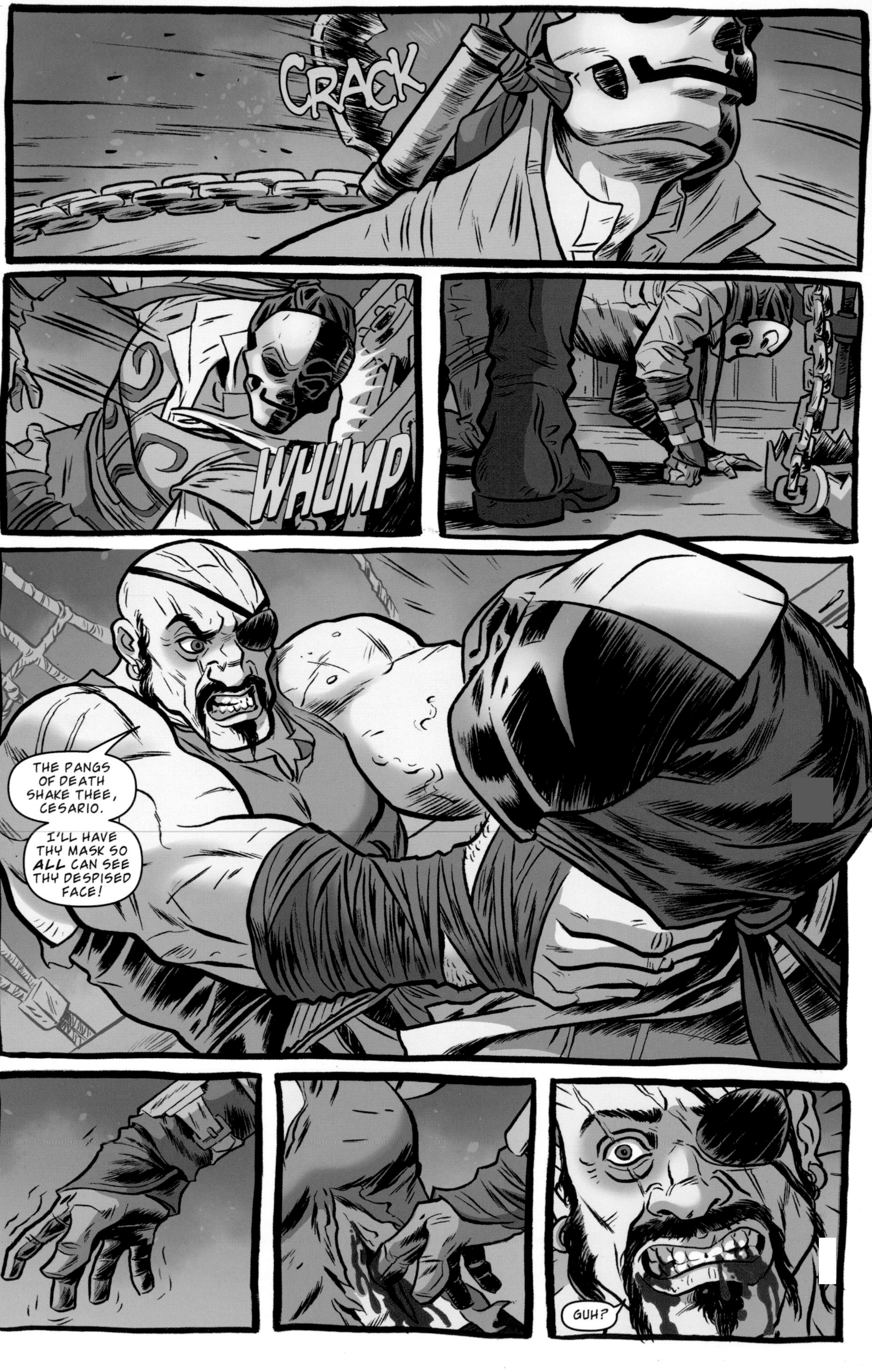
CRACK
WHUMP
THE PANGS OF DEATH SHAKE THEE, CESARIO.
I'LL HAVE THY MASK SO **ALL** CAN SEE THY DESPISED FACE!
GUH?

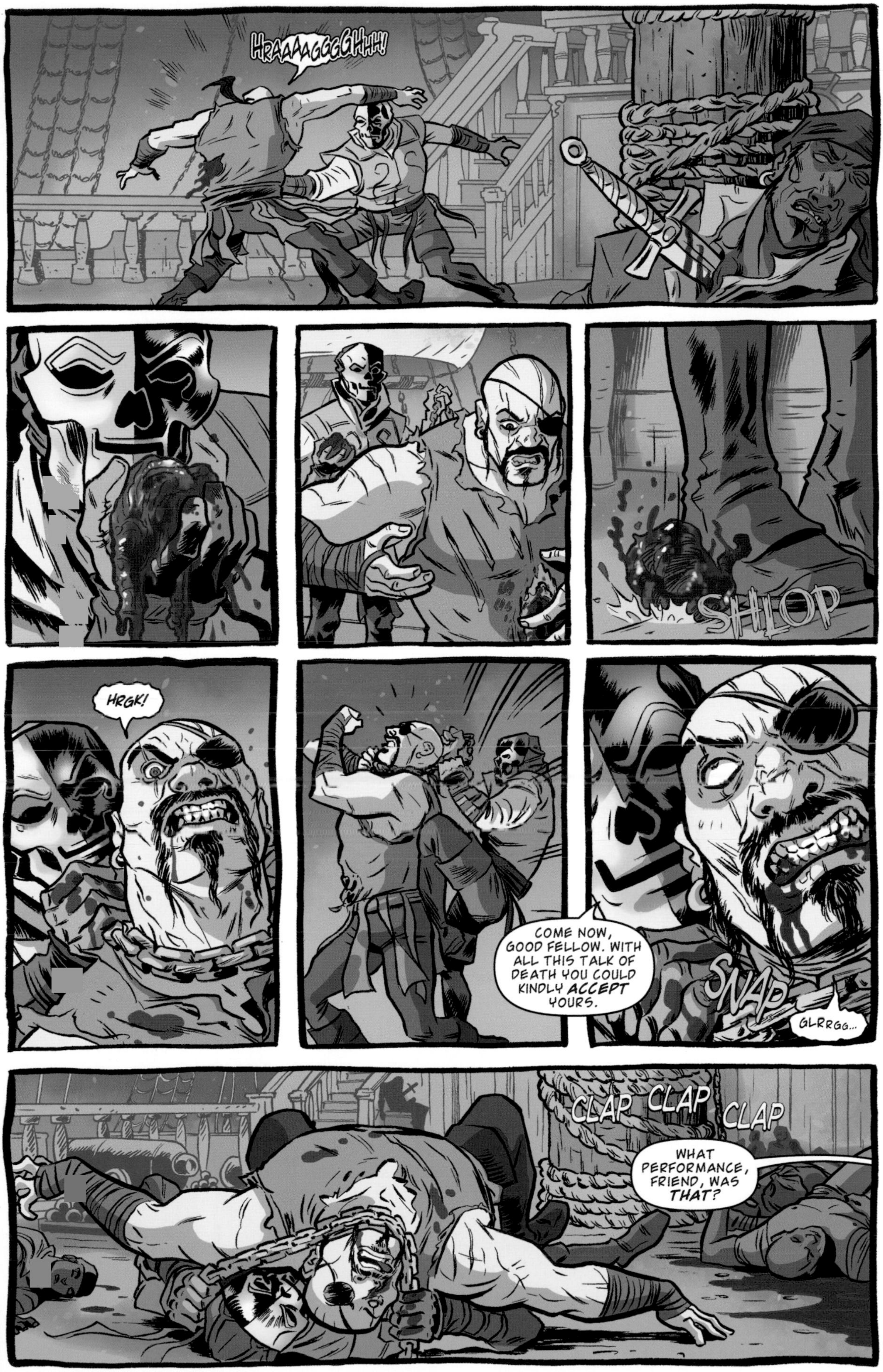
HRAAAAGGGHHH!
SHLOP
HRGK!
COME NOW, GOOD FELLOW. WITH ALL THIS TALK OF DEATH YOU COULD KINDLY ACCEPT YOURS.
SNAP
GLRRGG...
CLAP CLAP CLAP
WHAT PERFORMANCE, FRIEND, WAS THAT?

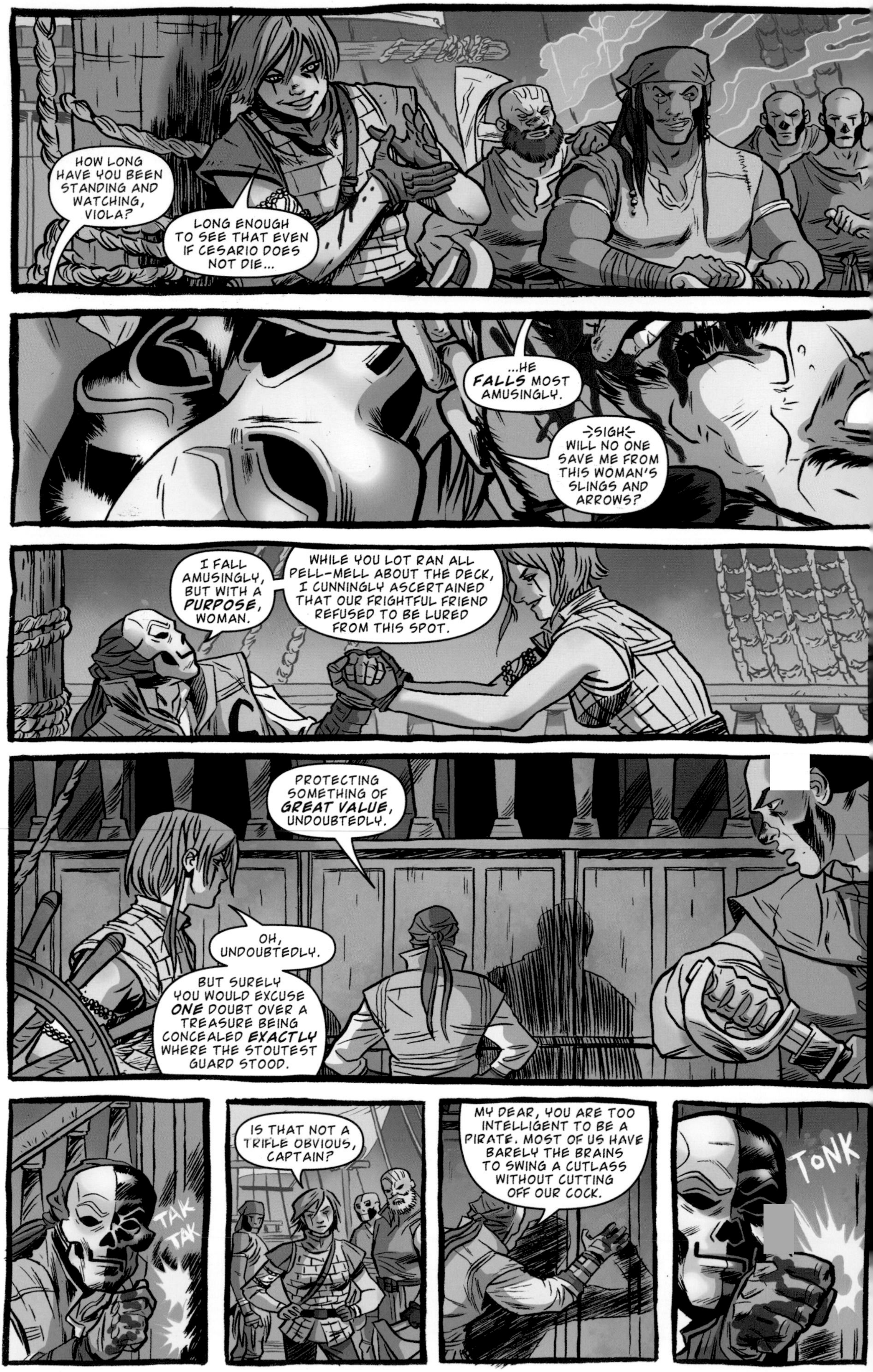

HOW LONG HAVE YOU BEEN STANDING AND WATCHING, VIOLA?
LONG ENOUGH TO SEE THAT EVEN IF CESARIO DOES NOT DIE...
...HE **FALLS** MOST AMUSINGLY.
SIGH WILL NO ONE SAVE ME FROM THIS WOMAN'S SLINGS AND ARROWS?
I FALL AMUSINGLY, BUT WITH A **PURPOSE**, WOMAN.
WHILE YOU LOT RAN ALL PELL-MELL ABOUT THE DECK, I CUNNINGLY ASCERTAINED THAT OUR FRIGHTFUL FRIEND REFUSED TO BE LURED FROM THIS SPOT.
PROTECTING SOMETHING OF **GREAT VALUE**, UNDOUBTEDLY.
OH, UNDOUBTEDLY.
BUT SURELY YOU WOULD EXCUSE **ONE** DOUBT OVER A TREASURE BEING CONCEALED **EXACTLY** WHERE THE STOUTEST GUARD STOOD.
TAK TAK
IS THAT NOT A TRIFLE OBVIOUS, CAPTAIN?
MY DEAR, YOU ARE TOO INTELLIGENT TO BE A PIRATE. MOST OF US HAVE BARELY THE BRAINS TO SWING A CUTLASS WITHOUT CUTTING OFF OUR COCK.
TONK

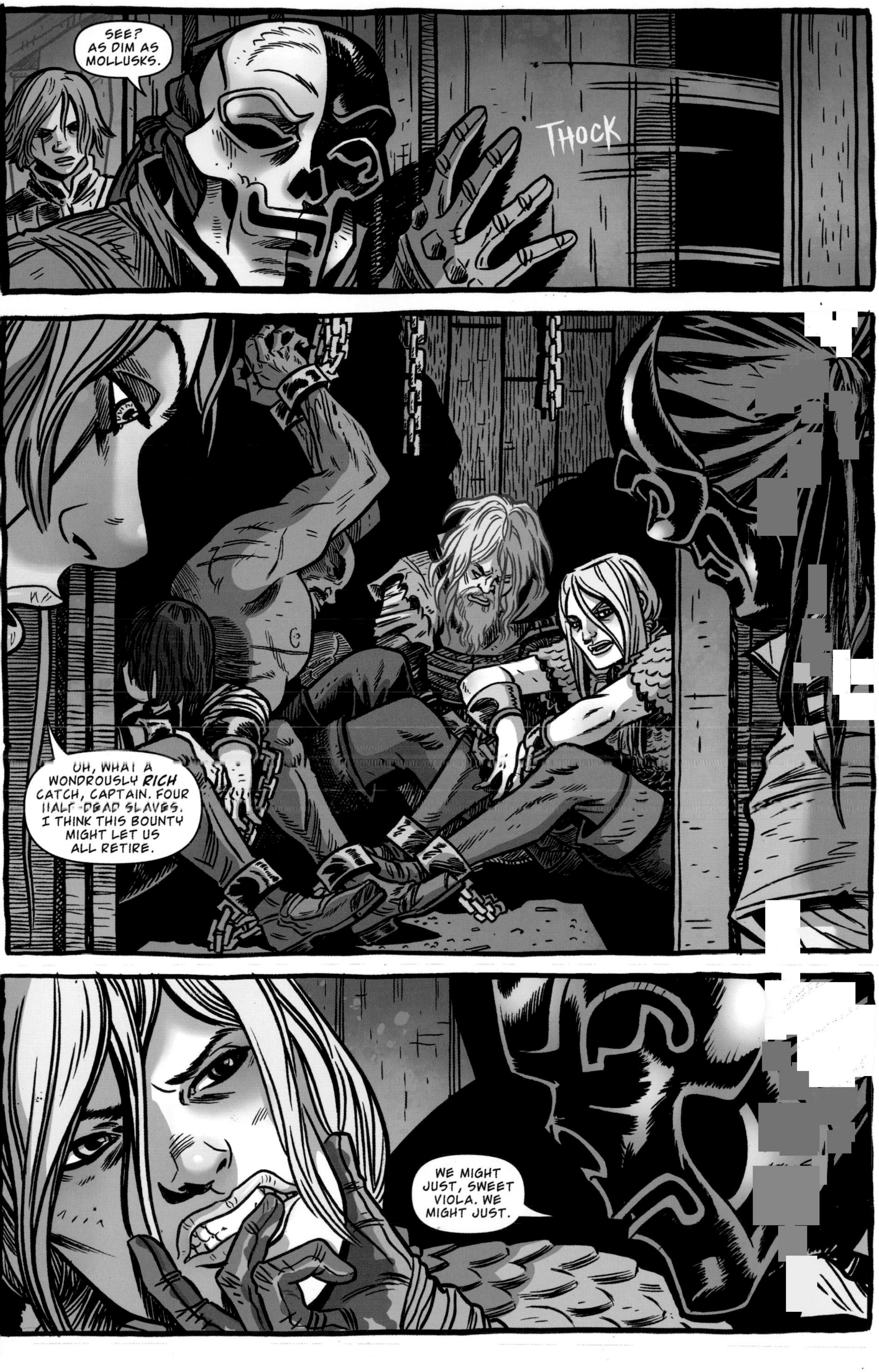
SEE? AS DIM AS MOLLUSKS.
THOCK
OH, WHAT A WONDROUSLY RICH CATCH, CAPTAIN. FOUR HALF-DEAD SLAVES. I THINK THIS BOUNTY MIGHT LET US ALL RETIRE.
WE MIGHT JUST, SWEET VIOLA. WE MIGHT JUST.

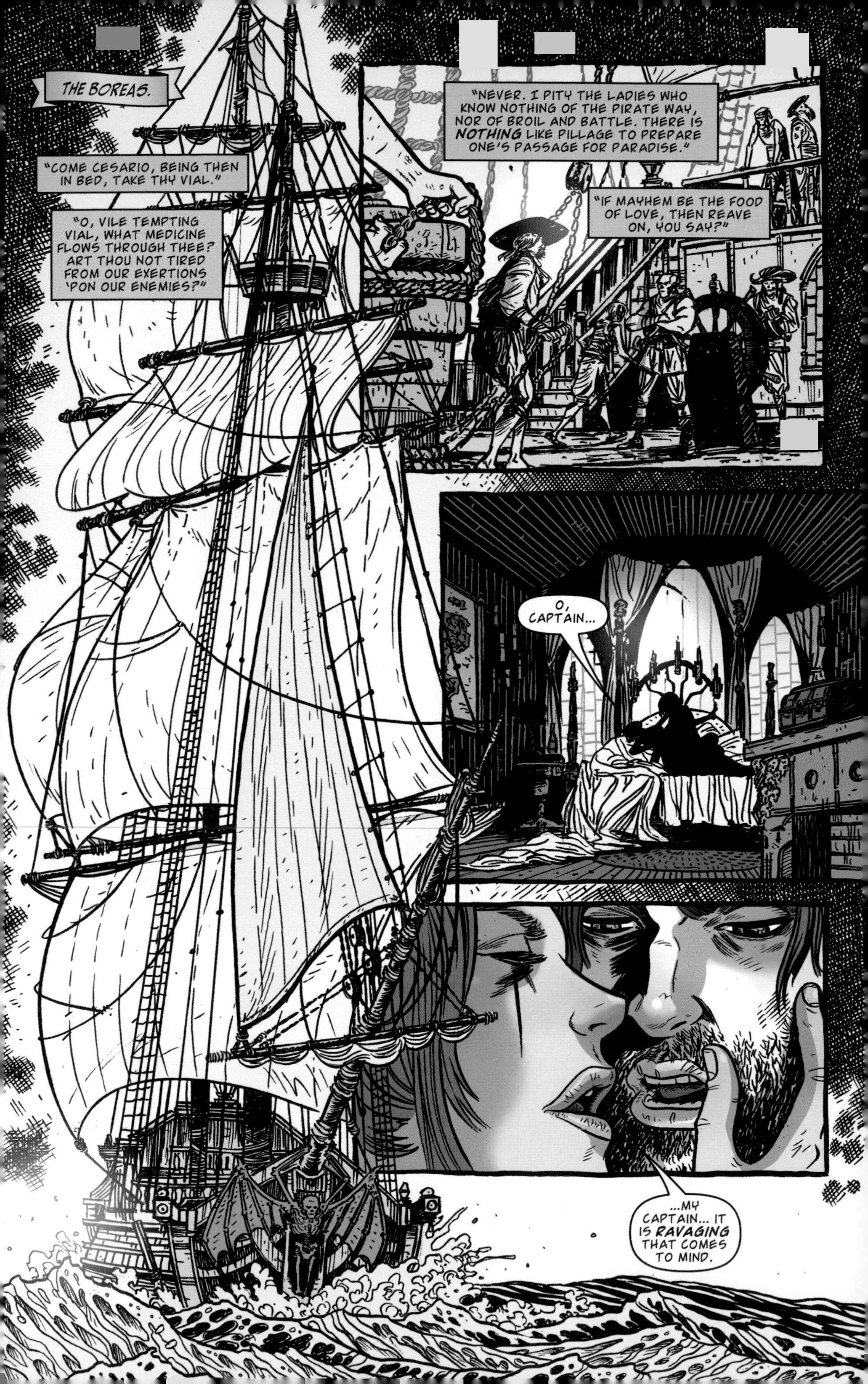
THE BOREAS.
"COME CESARIO, BEING THEN IN BED, TAKE THY VIAL."
"O, VILE TEMPTING VIAL, WHAT MEDICINE FLOWS THROUGH THEE? ART THOU NOT TIRED FROM OUR EXERTIONS 'PON OUR ENEMIES?"
"NEVER. I PITY THE LADIES WHO KNOW NOTHING OF THE PIRATE WAY, NOR OF BROIL AND BATTLE. THERE IS NOTHING LIKE PILLAGE TO PREPARE ONE'S PASSAGE FOR PARADISE."
"IF MAYHEM BE THE FOOD OF LOVE, THEN REAVE ON, YOU SAY?"
O, CAPTAIN...
...MY CAPTAIN... IT IS RAVAGING THAT COMES TO MIND.

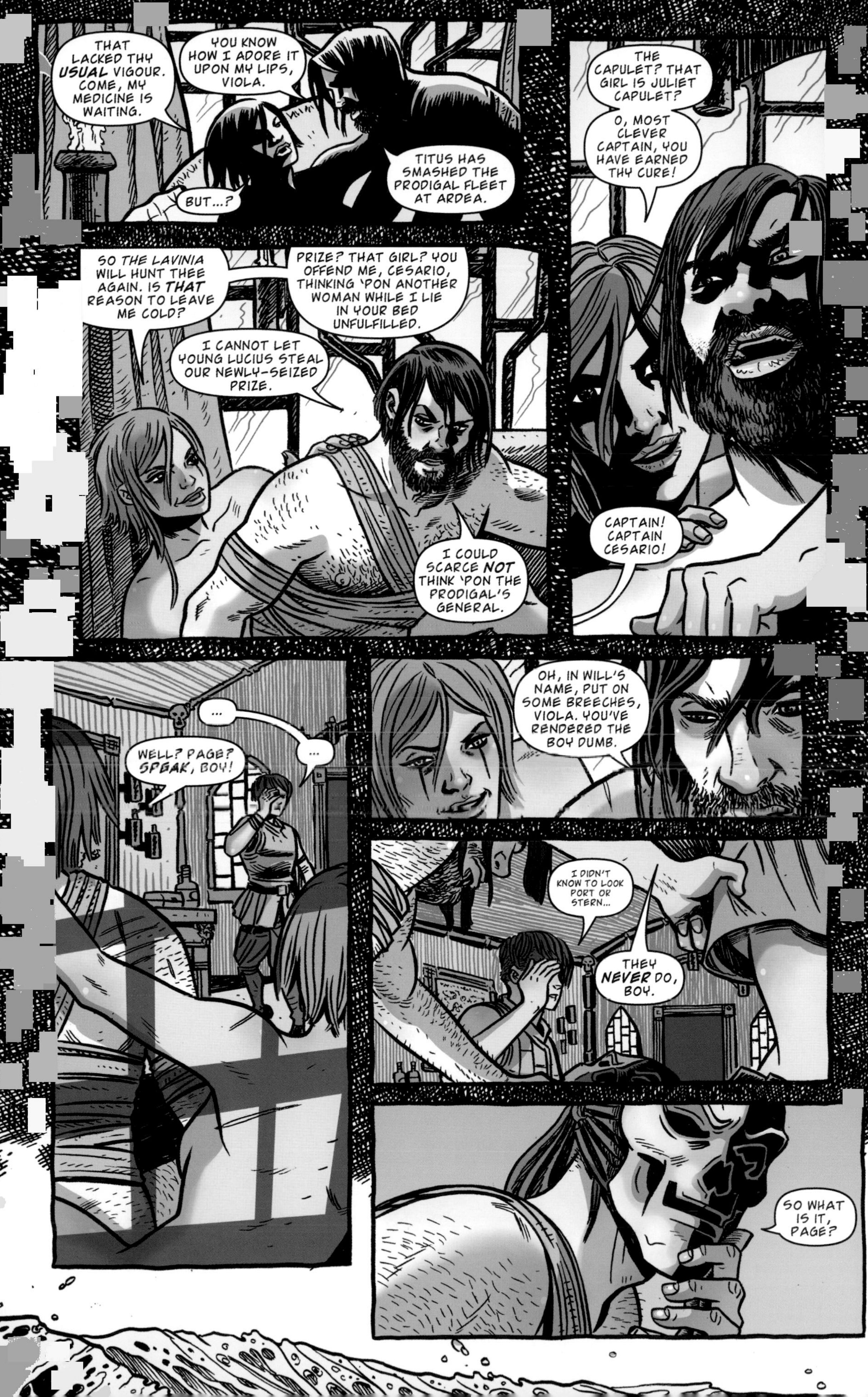
THAT LACKED THY USUAL VIGOUR. COME, MY MEDICINE IS WAITING.
YOU KNOW HOW I ADORE IT UPON MY LIPS, VIOLA.
BUT...?
TITUS HAS SMASHED THE PRODIGAL FLEET AT ARDEA.
SO THE LAVINIA WILL HUNT THEE AGAIN. IS THAT REASON TO LEAVE ME COLD?
I CANNOT LET YOUNG LUCIUS STEAL OUR NEWLY-SEIZED PRIZE.
PRIZE? THAT GIRL? YOU OFFEND ME, CESARIO, THINKING 'PON ANOTHER WOMAN WHILE I LIE IN YOUR BED UNFULFILLED.
I COULD SCARCE NOT THINK 'PON THE PRODIGAL'S GENERAL.
THE CAPULET? THAT GIRL IS JULIET CAPULET?
O, MOST CLEVER CAPTAIN, YOU HAVE EARNED THY CURE!
CAPTAIN! CAPTAIN CESARIO!
...
WELL? PAGE? SPEAK, BOY!
...
OH, IN WILL'S NAME, PUT ON SOME BREECHES, VIOLA. YOU'VE RENDERED THE BOY DUMB.
I DIDN'T KNOW TO LOOK PORT OR STERN...
THEY NEVER DO, BOY.
SO WHAT IS IT, PAGE?

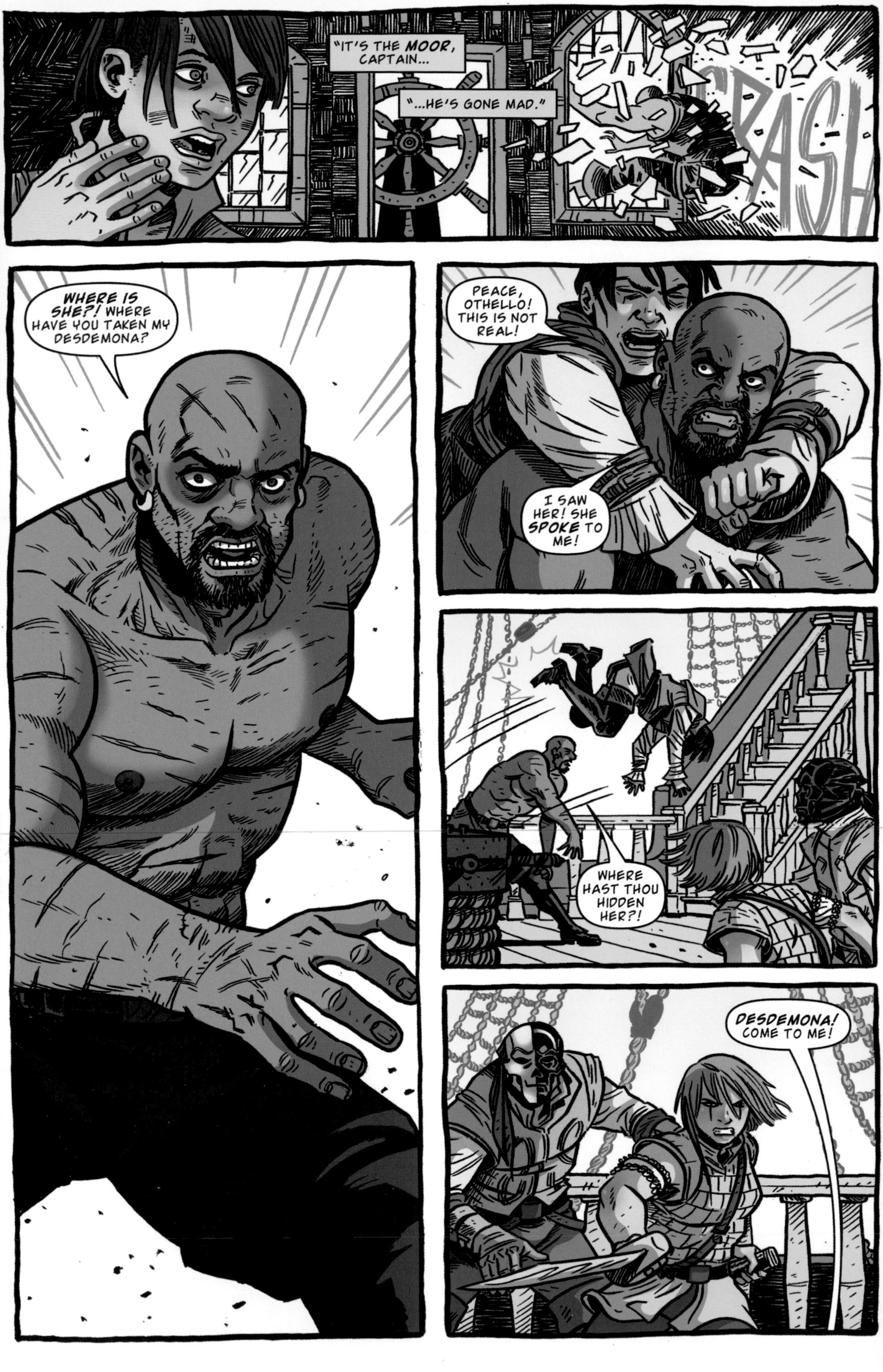
"IT'S THE MOOR, CAPTAIN...
"...HE'S GONE MAD."
CRASH
WHERE IS SHE?! WHERE HAVE YOU TAKEN MY DESDEMONA?
PEACE, OTHELLO! THIS IS NOT REAL!
I SAW HER! SHE SPOKE TO ME!
WHERE HAST THOU HIDDEN HER?!
DESDEMONA! COME TO ME!

HOLD! OTHELLO IS SICK, BUT IT WILL PASS.

STAND ASIDE, CAPULET! THE MOOR WILL MURDER US ALL!

IT IS A FEVER OF THE MIND. I CAN CALM IT.

STAND ASIDE!

STAY THY HAND, VIOLA!

I HOPE THE CAPULET'S WORTH AS MUCH DEAD AS SHE IS ALIVE.

OTHELLO, DESDEMONA IS NOT HERE. SHE IS GONE. YOU *KNOW* THIS.

YOU LIE...

YOU KNOW I DO NOT.

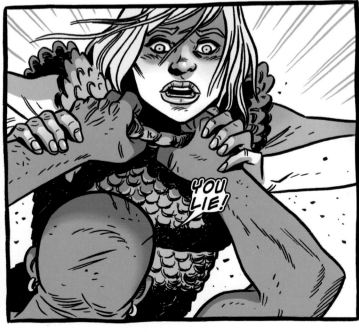

YOU LIE!

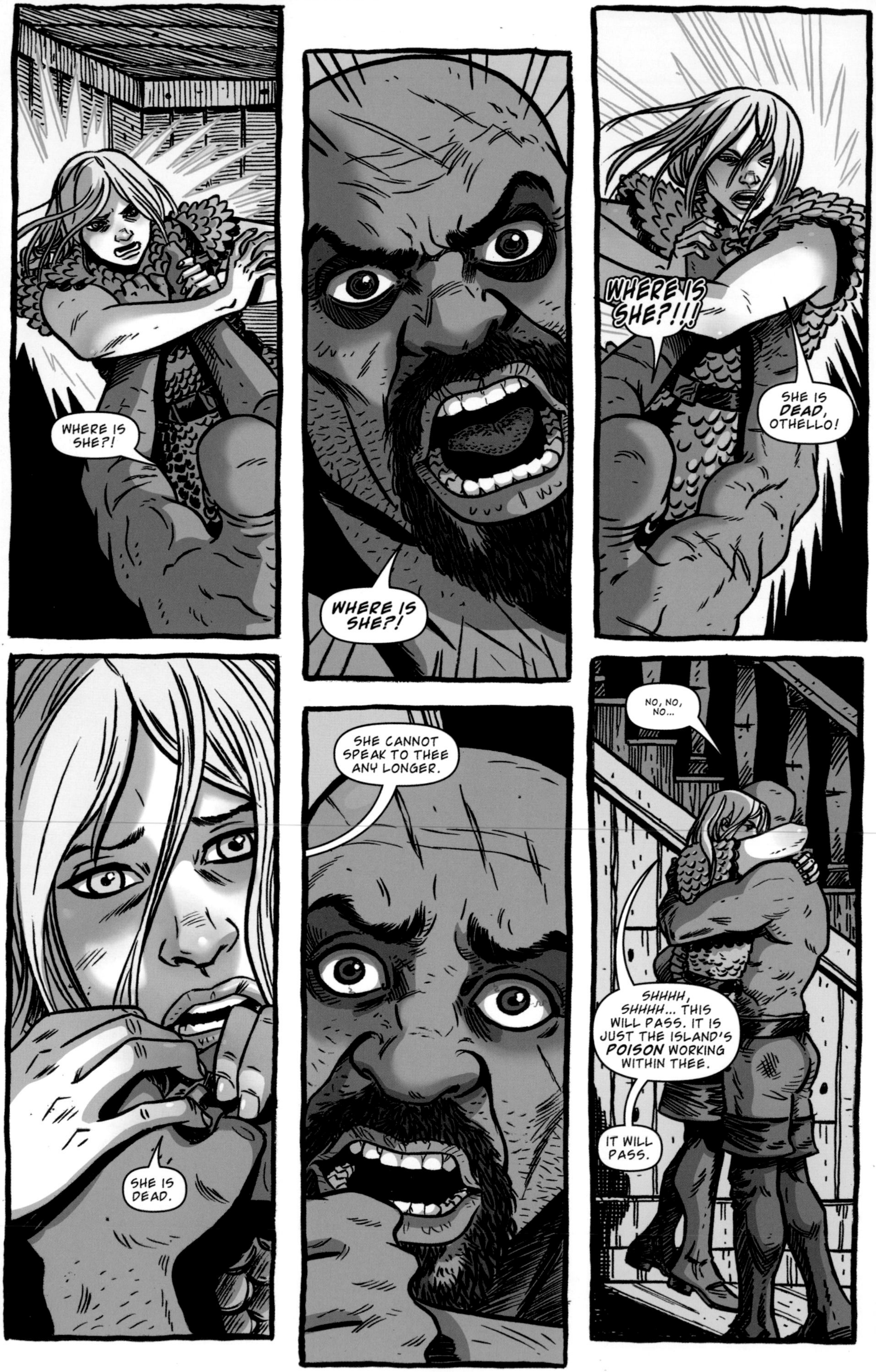
WHERE IS SHE?!
WHERE IS SHE?!
WHERE IS SHE?!!!
SHE IS DEAD, OTHELLO!
SHE IS DEAD.
SHE CANNOT SPEAK TO THEE ANY LONGER.
NO, NO, NO...
SHHHH, SHHHH... THIS WILL PASS. IT IS JUST THE ISLAND'S POISON WORKING WITHIN THEE.
IT WILL PASS.

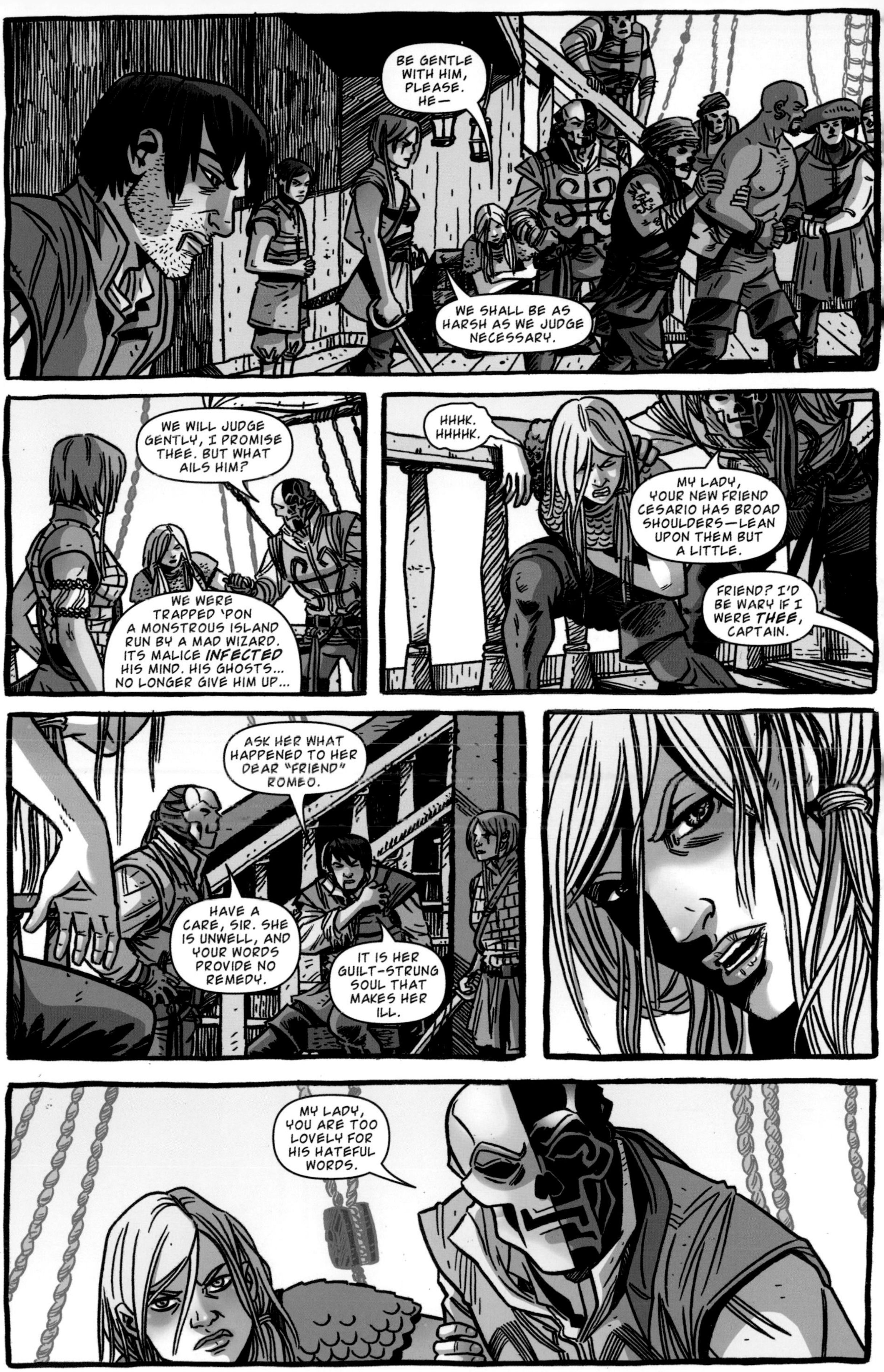
BE GENTLE WITH HIM, PLEASE. HE—
WE SHALL BE AS HARSH AS WE JUDGE NECESSARY.
WE WILL JUDGE GENTLY, I PROMISE THEE. BUT WHAT AILS HIM?
WE WERE TRAPPED 'PON A MONSTROUS ISLAND RUN BY A MAD WIZARD. ITS MALICE INFECTED HIS MIND. HIS GHOSTS... NO LONGER GIVE HIM UP...
HHHK. HHHHK.
MY LADY, YOUR NEW FRIEND CESARIO HAS BROAD SHOULDERS—LEAN UPON THEM BUT A LITTLE.
FRIEND? I'D BE WARY IF I WERE THEE, CAPTAIN.
ASK HER WHAT HAPPENED TO HER DEAR "FRIEND" ROMEO.
HAVE A CARE, SIR. SHE IS UNWELL, AND YOUR WORDS PROVIDE NO REMEDY.
IT IS HER GUILT-STRUNG SOUL THAT MAKES HER ILL.
MY LADY, YOU ARE TOO LOVELY FOR HIS HATEFUL WORDS.

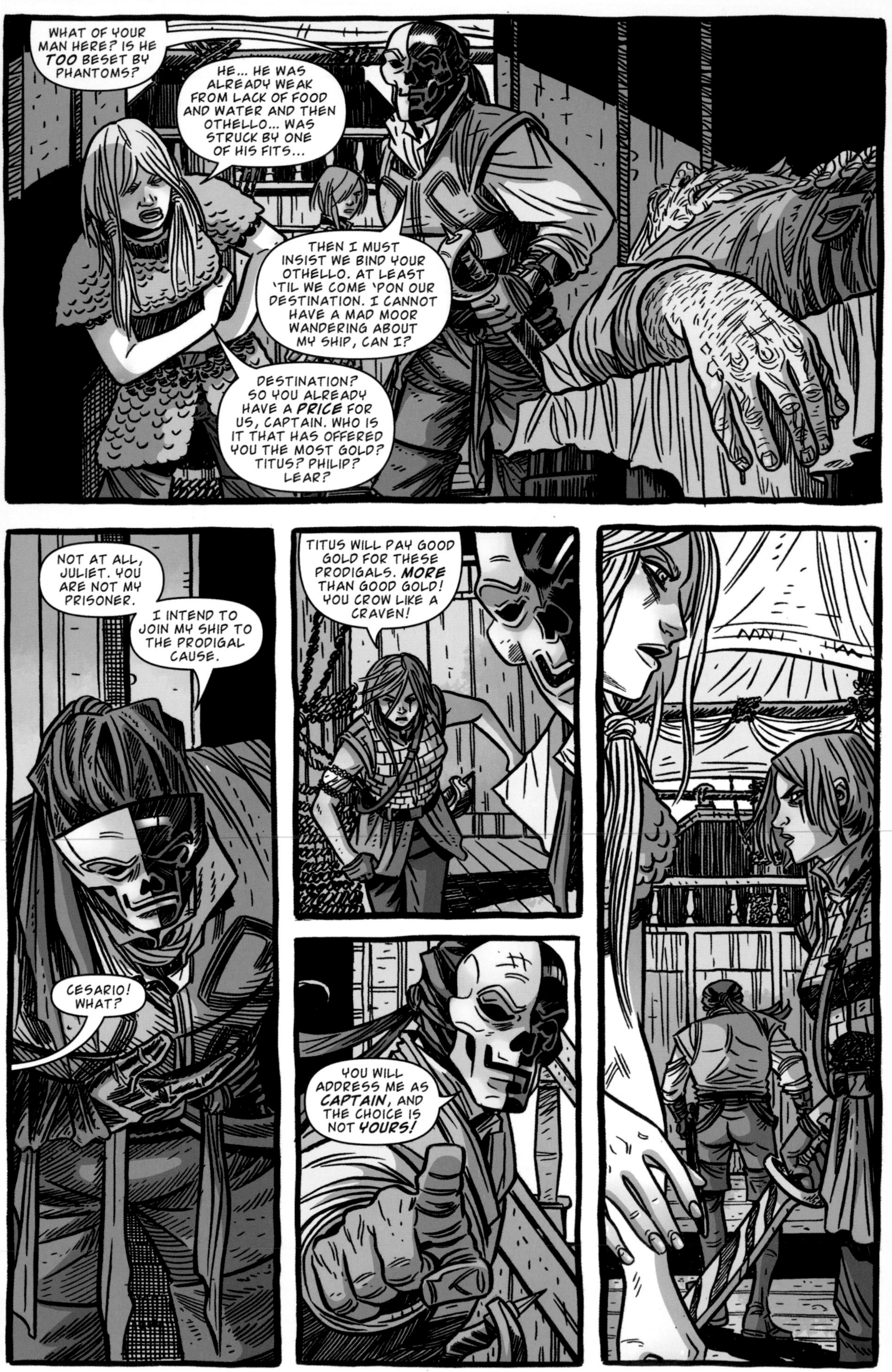
WHAT OF YOUR MAN HERE? IS HE TOO BESET BY PHANTOMS?
HE... HE WAS ALREADY WEAK FROM LACK OF FOOD AND WATER AND THEN OTHELLO... WAS STRUCK BY ONE OF HIS FITS...
THEN I MUST INSIST WE BIND YOUR OTHELLO. AT LEAST 'TIL WE COME 'PON OUR DESTINATION. I CANNOT HAVE A MAD MOOR WANDERING ABOUT MY SHIP, CAN I?
DESTINATION? SO YOU ALREADY HAVE A PRICE FOR US, CAPTAIN. WHO IS IT THAT HAS OFFERED YOU THE MOST GOLD? TITUS? PHILIP? LEAR?
NOT AT ALL, JULIET. YOU ARE NOT MY PRISONER.
I INTEND TO JOIN MY SHIP TO THE PRODIGAL CAUSE.
CESARIO! WHAT?
TITUS WILL PAY GOOD GOLD FOR THESE PRODIGALS. MORE THAN GOOD GOLD! YOU CROW LIKE A CRAVEN!
YOU WILL ADDRESS ME AS CAPTAIN, AND THE CHOICE IS NOT YOURS!

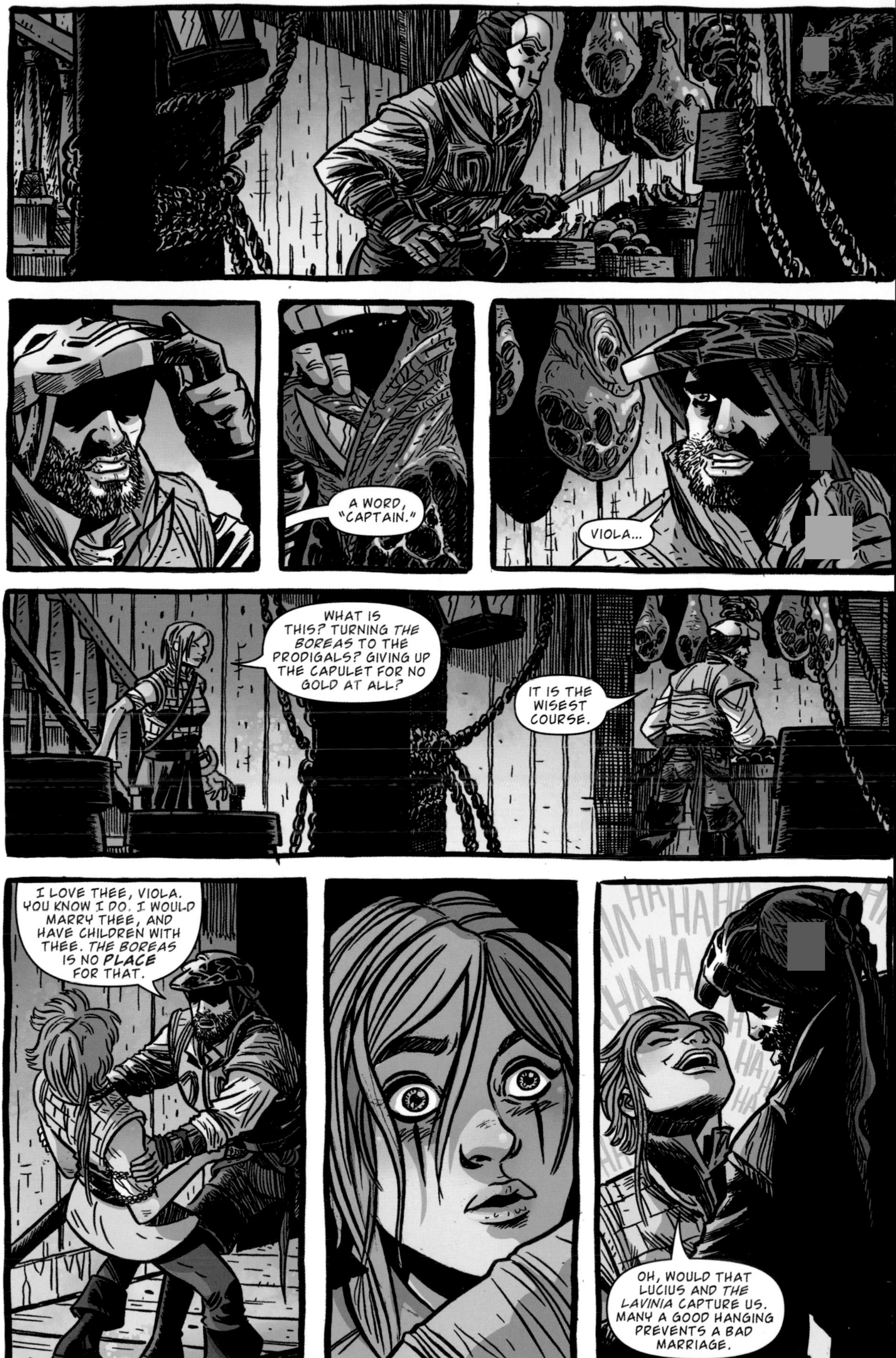
A WORD, "CAPTAIN."
VIOLA...
WHAT IS THIS? TURNING *THE BOREAS* TO THE PRODIGALS? GIVING UP THE CAPULET FOR NO GOLD AT ALL?
IT IS THE WISEST COURSE.
I LOVE THEE, VIOLA. YOU KNOW I DO. I WOULD MARRY THEE, AND HAVE CHILDREN WITH THEE. *THE BOREAS* IS NO ***PLACE*** FOR THAT.
HA HA HA HA HA HA HA
OH, WOULD THAT LUCIUS AND *THE LAVINIA* CAPTURE US. MANY A GOOD HANGING PREVENTS A BAD MARRIAGE.

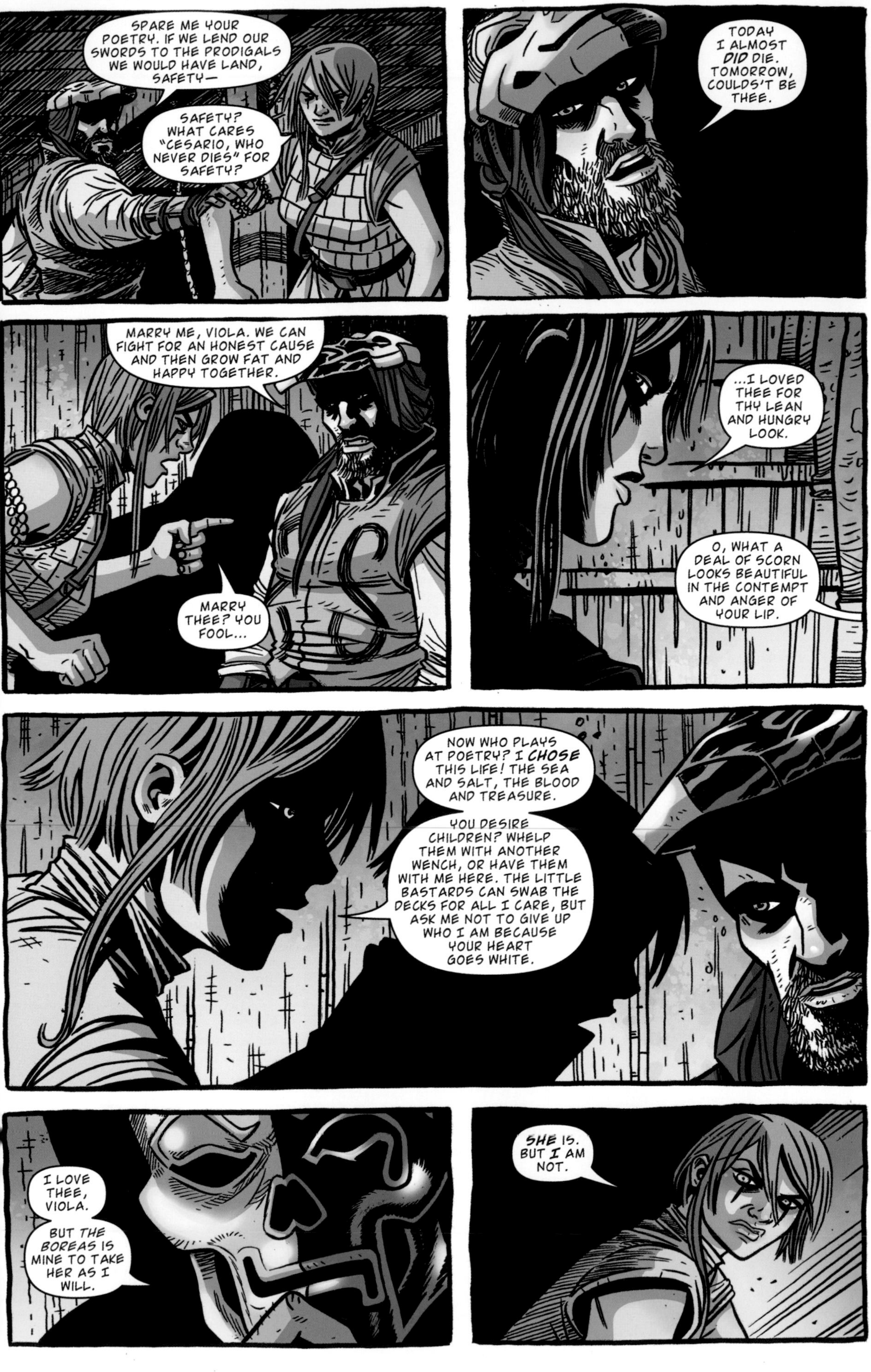
SPARE ME YOUR POETRY. IF WE LEND OUR SWORDS TO THE PRODIGALS WE WOULD HAVE LAND, SAFETY—
SAFETY? WHAT CARES "CESARIO, WHO NEVER DIES" FOR SAFETY?
TODAY I ALMOST DID DIE. TOMORROW, COULDS'T BE THEE.
MARRY ME, VIOLA. WE CAN FIGHT FOR AN HONEST CAUSE AND THEN GROW FAT AND HAPPY TOGETHER.
MARRY THEE? YOU FOOL...
...I LOVED THEE FOR THY LEAN AND HUNGRY LOOK.
O, WHAT A DEAL OF SCORN LOOKS BEAUTIFUL IN THE CONTEMPT AND ANGER OF YOUR LIP.
NOW WHO PLAYS AT POETRY? I CHOSE THIS LIFE! THE SEA AND SALT, THE BLOOD AND TREASURE.
YOU DESIRE CHILDREN? WHELP THEM WITH ANOTHER WENCH, OR HAVE THEM WITH ME HERE. THE LITTLE BASTARDS CAN SWAB THE DECKS FOR ALL I CARE, BUT ASK ME NOT TO GIVE UP WHO I AM BECAUSE YOUR HEART GOES WHITE.
I LOVE THEE, VIOLA.
BUT THE BOREAS IS MINE TO TAKE HER AS I WILL.
SHE IS. BUT I AM NOT.

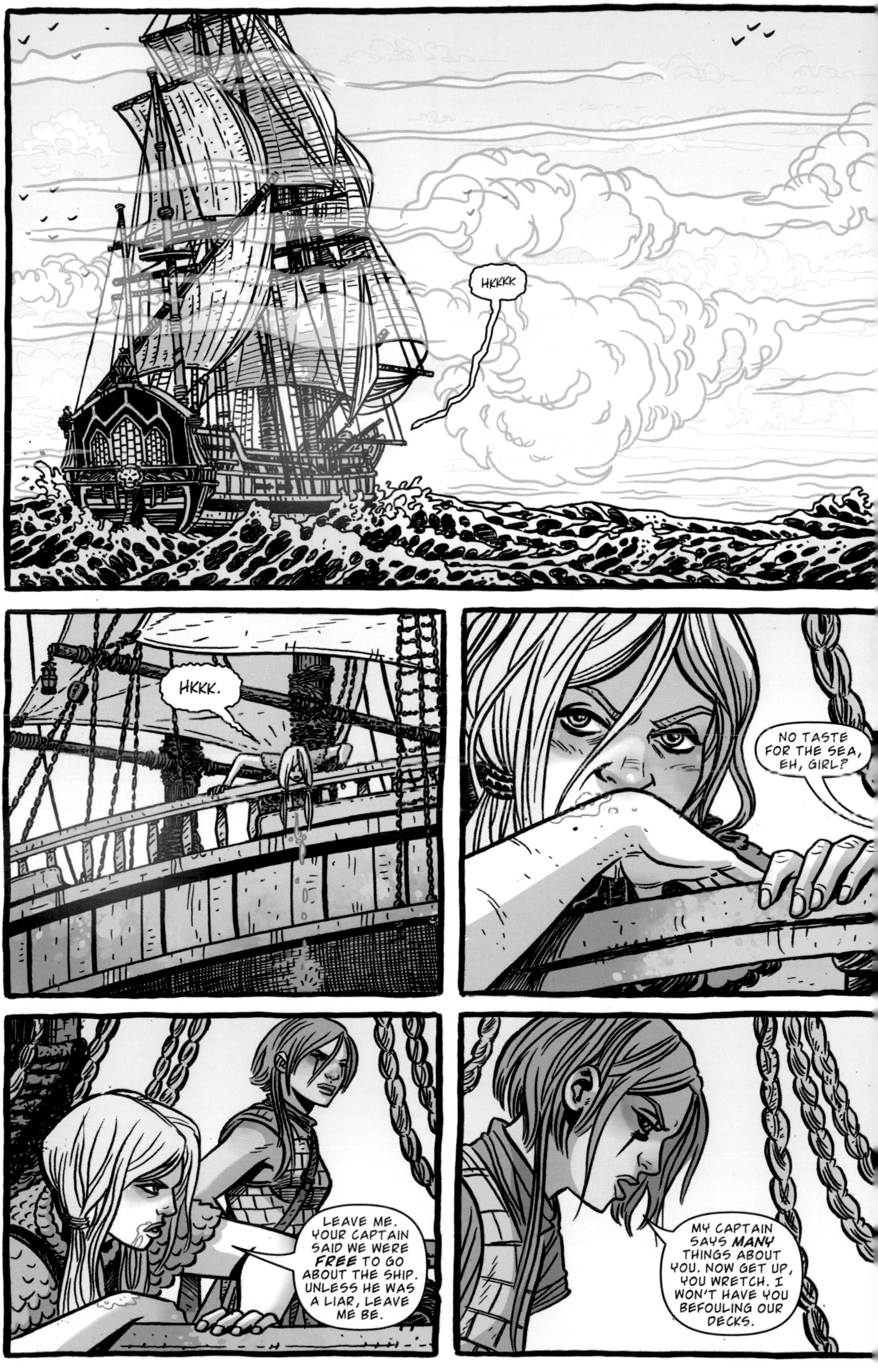
HKKKK
HKKK.
NO TASTE FOR THE SEA, EH, GIRL?
LEAVE ME. YOUR CAPTAIN SAID WE WERE FREE TO GO ABOUT THE SHIP. UNLESS HE WAS A LIAR, LEAVE ME BE.
MY CAPTAIN SAYS MANY THINGS ABOUT YOU. NOW GET UP, YOU WRETCH. I WON'T HAVE YOU BEFOULING OUR DECKS.

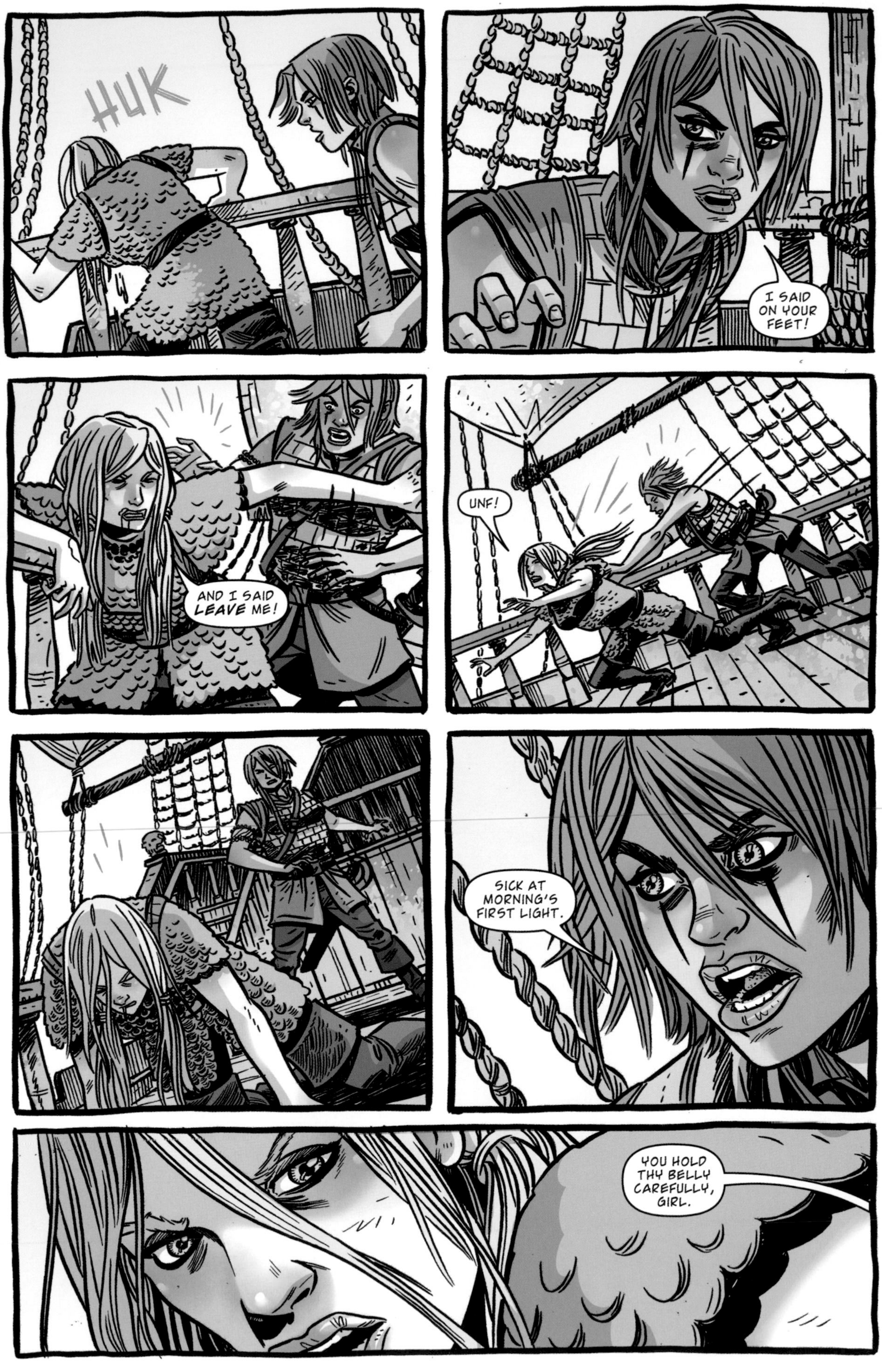
HUK
I SAID ON YOUR FEET!
AND I SAID LEAVE ME!
UNF!
SICK AT MORNING'S FIRST LIGHT.
YOU HOLD THY BELLY CAREFULLY, GIRL.

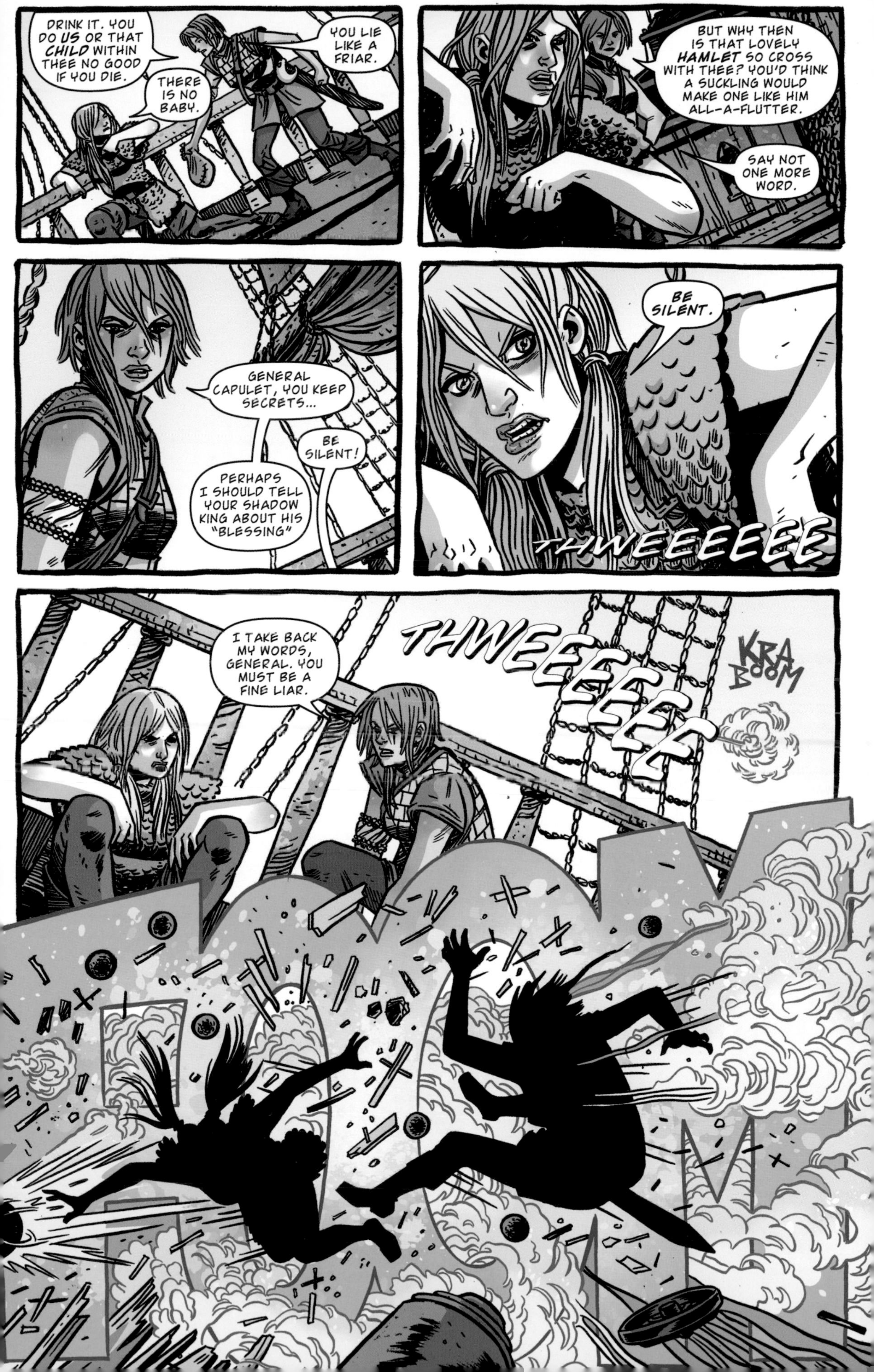
DRINK IT. YOU DO US OR THAT CHILD WITHIN THEE NO GOOD IF YOU DIE.
THERE IS NO BABY.
YOU LIE LIKE A FRIAR.
BUT WHY THEN IS THAT LOVELY HAMLET SO CROSS WITH THEE? YOU'D THINK A SUCKLING WOULD MAKE ONE LIKE HIM ALL-A-FLUTTER.
SAY NOT ONE MORE WORD.
GENERAL CAPULET, YOU KEEP SECRETS...
PERHAPS I SHOULD TELL YOUR SHADOW KING ABOUT HIS "BLESSING"
BE SILENT!
BE SILENT.
THWEEEEEEE
I TAKE BACK MY WORDS, GENERAL. YOU MUST BE A FINE LIAR.
THWEEEEEEE
KRA BOOM

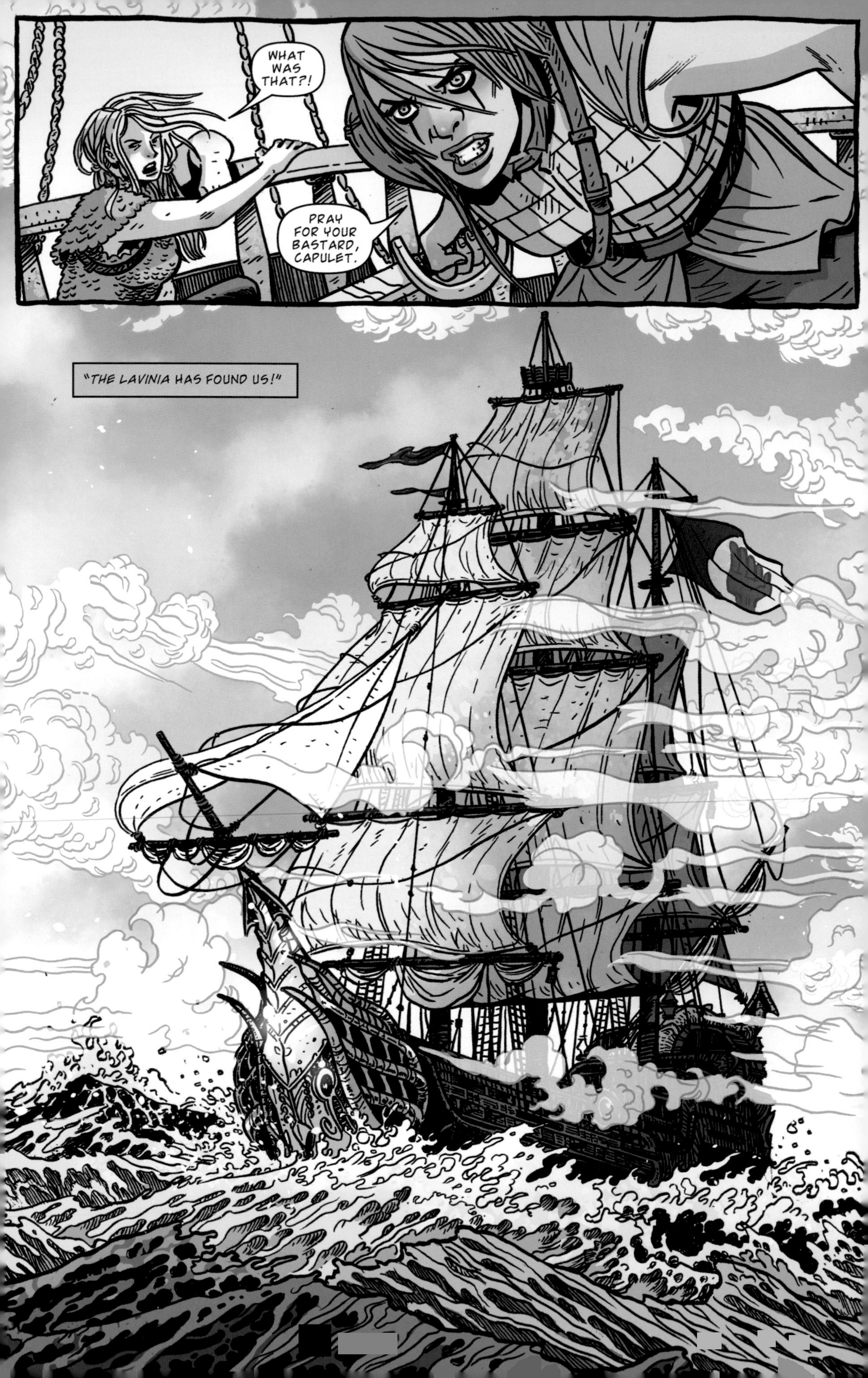
WHAT WAS THAT?!
PRAY FOR YOUR BASTARD, CAPULET.
"THE LAVINIA HAS FOUND US!"

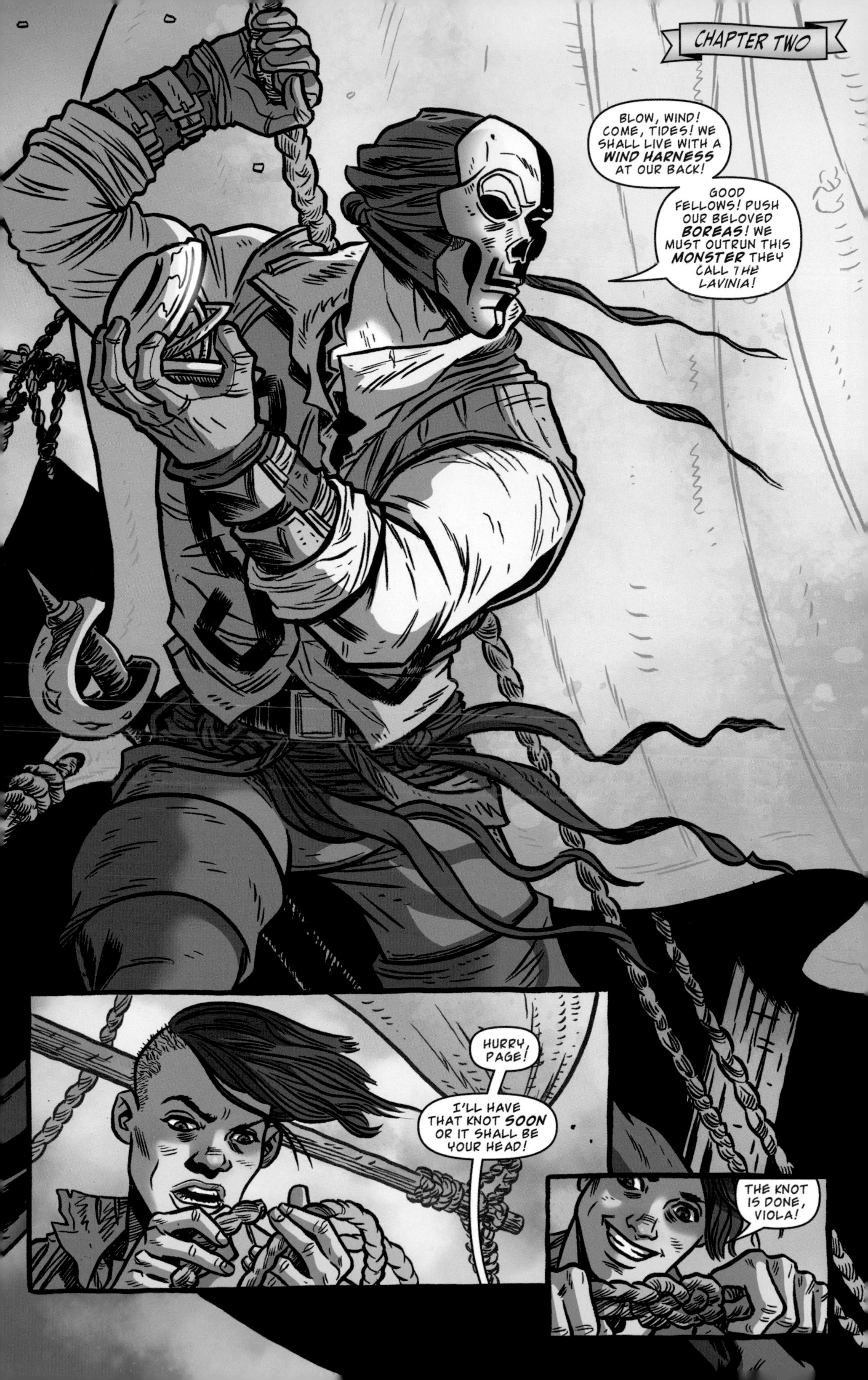
CHAPTER TWO
BLOW, WIND! COME, TIDES! WE SHALL LIVE WITH A WIND HARNESS AT OUR BACK!
GOOD FELLOWS! PUSH OUR BELOVED BOREAS! WE MUST OUTRUN THIS MONSTER THEY CALL THE LAVINIA!
HURRY, PAGE!
I'LL HAVE THAT KNOT SOON OR IT SHALL BE YOUR HEAD!
THE KNOT IS DONE, VIOLA!

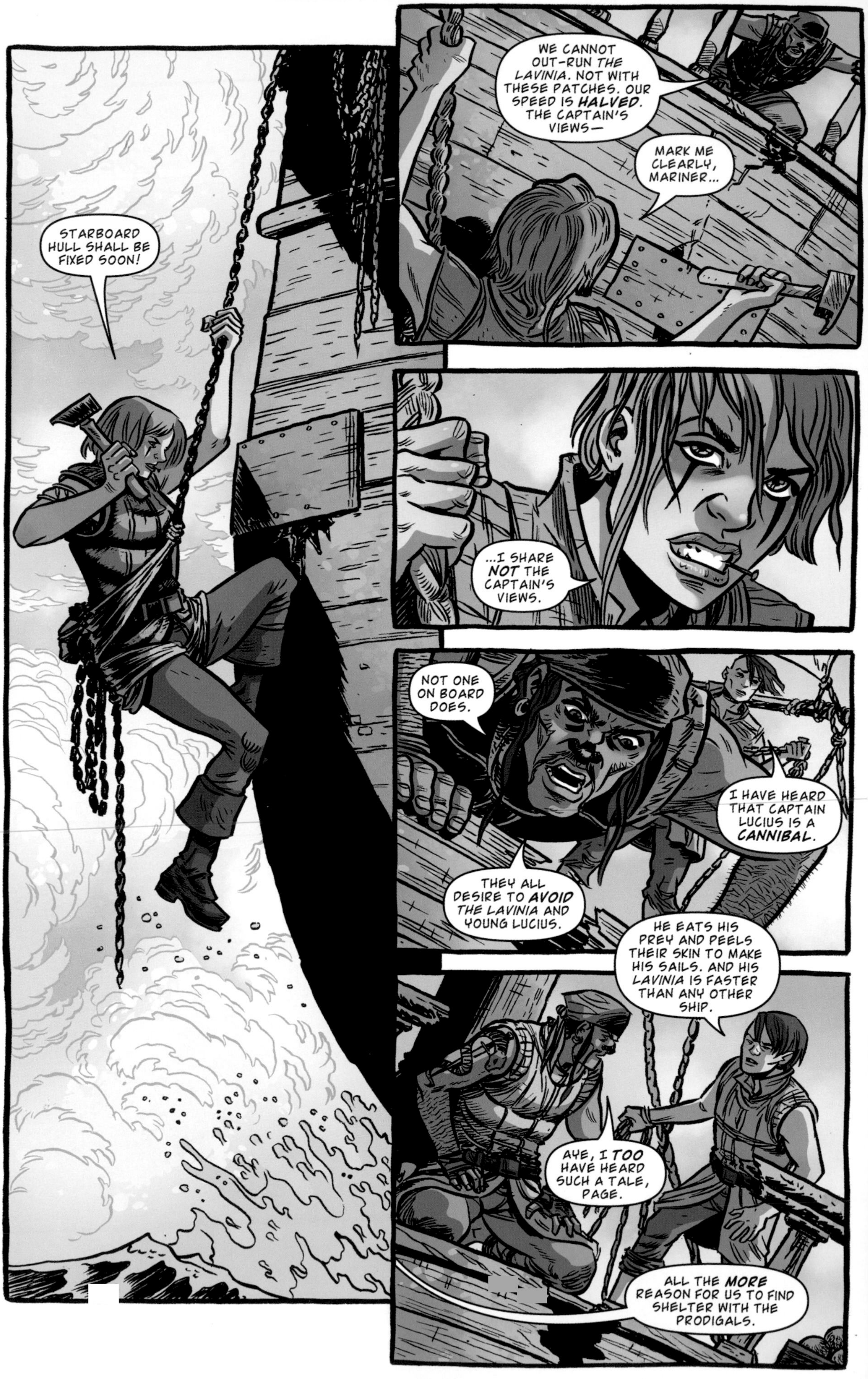
STARBOARD HULL SHALL BE FIXED SOON!
WE CANNOT OUT-RUN THE LAVINIA. NOT WITH THESE PATCHES. OUR SPEED IS HALVED. THE CAPTAIN'S VIEWS—
MARK ME CLEARLY, MARINER...
...I SHARE NOT THE CAPTAIN'S VIEWS.
NOT ONE ON BOARD DOES.
I HAVE HEARD THAT CAPTAIN LUCIUS IS A CANNIBAL.
THEY ALL DESIRE TO AVOID THE LAVINIA AND YOUNG LUCIUS.
HE EATS HIS PREY AND PEELS THEIR SKIN TO MAKE HIS SAILS. AND HIS LAVINIA IS FASTER THAN ANY OTHER SHIP.
AYE, I TOO HAVE HEARD SUCH A TALE, PAGE.
ALL THE MORE REASON FOR US TO FIND SHELTER WITH THE PRODIGALS.

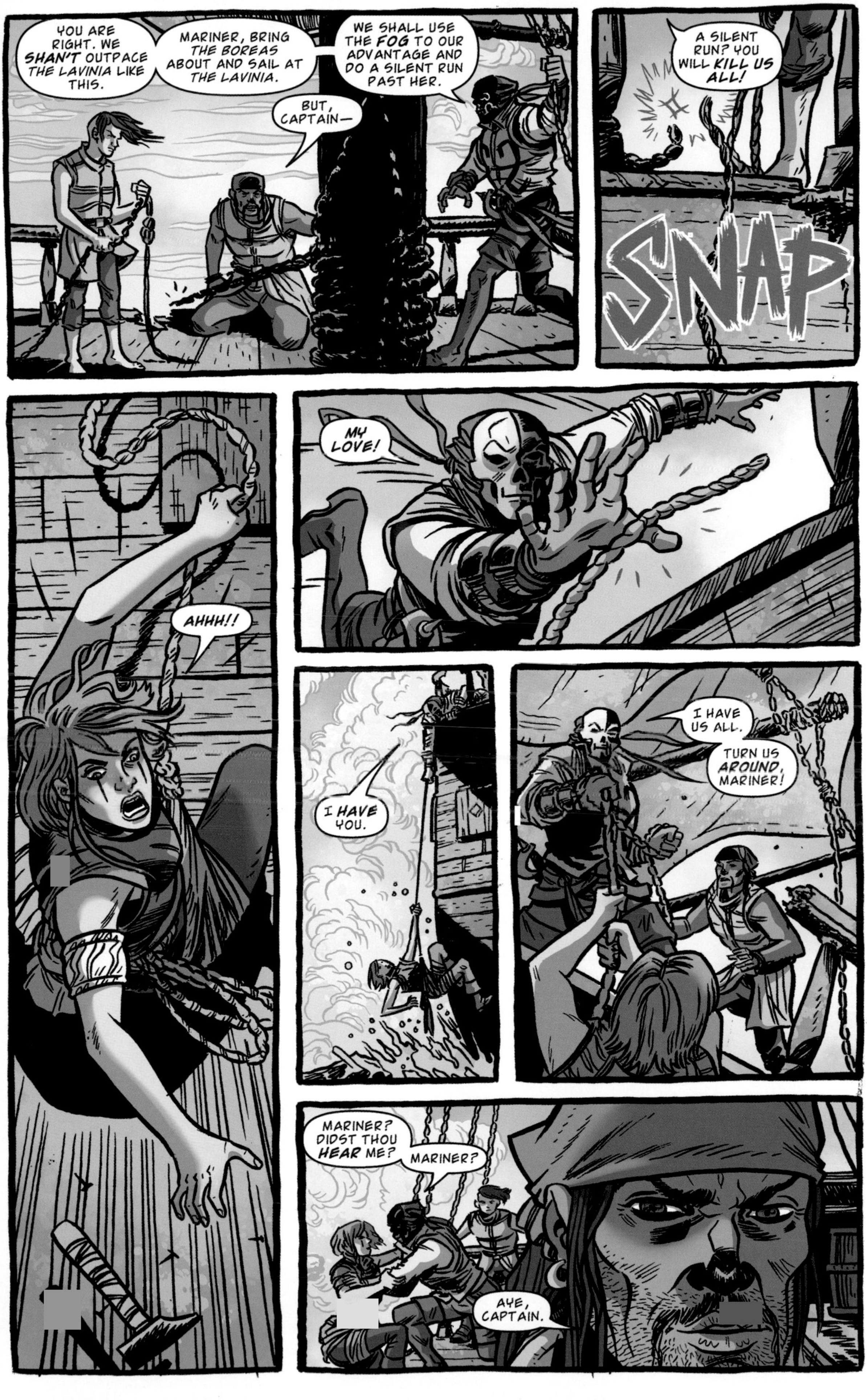
YOU ARE RIGHT. WE SHAN'T OUTPACE THE LAVINIA LIKE THIS.
MARINER, BRING THE BOREAS ABOUT AND SAIL AT THE LAVINIA.
WE SHALL USE THE FOG TO OUR ADVANTAGE AND DO A SILENT RUN PAST HER.
BUT, CAPTAIN—
A SILENT RUN? YOU WILL KILL US ALL!
SNAP
AHHH!!
MY LOVE!
I HAVE YOU.
I HAVE US ALL.
TURN US AROUND, MARINER!
MARINER? DIDST THOU HEAR ME?
MARINER?
AYE, CAPTAIN.

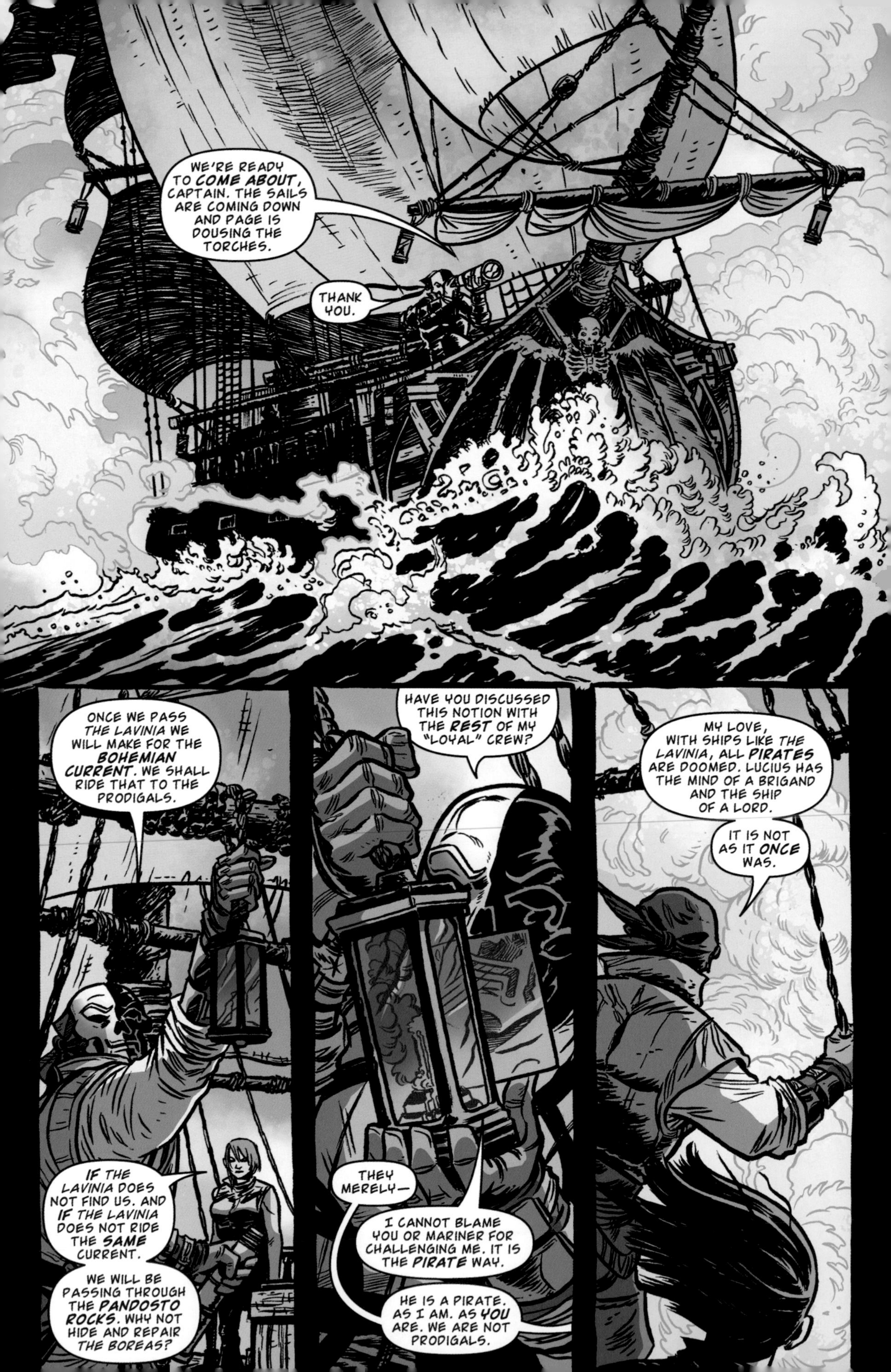
WE'RE READY TO COME ABOUT, CAPTAIN. THE SAILS ARE COMING DOWN AND PAGE IS DOUSING THE TORCHES.
THANK YOU.
ONCE WE PASS THE LAVINIA WE WILL MAKE FOR THE BOHEMIAN CURRENT. WE SHALL RIDE THAT TO THE PRODIGALS.
IF THE LAVINIA DOES NOT FIND US. AND IF THE LAVINIA DOES NOT RIDE THE SAME CURRENT.
WE WILL BE PASSING THROUGH THE PANDOSTO ROCKS. WHY NOT HIDE AND REPAIR THE BOREAS?
HAVE YOU DISCUSSED THIS NOTION WITH THE REST OF MY "LOYAL" CREW?
THEY MERELY—
I CANNOT BLAME YOU OR MARINER FOR CHALLENGING ME. IT IS THE PIRATE WAY.
HE IS A PIRATE. AS I AM. AS YOU ARE. WE ARE NOT PRODIGALS.
MY LOVE, WITH SHIPS LIKE THE LAVINIA, ALL PIRATES ARE DOOMED. LUCIUS HAS THE MIND OF A BRIGAND AND THE SHIP OF A LORD.
IT IS NOT AS IT ONCE WAS.

THEN LET US PERISH AS PIRATES! I WAS **BORN** A PIRATE, AND I DESIRE TO **DIE** AS ONE.

AYE, A PIRATE YOU HAVE BEEN SINCE I **FIRST** LAID MY EYES UPON THEE.

A YOUNG WOMAN, HOMELESS, LOOKING FOR A BED AND A MEAL AND HAVING **SNUCK** ABOARD MY SHIP, POUNCING AND THREATENING ME WITH YOUR LITTLE KNIFE.

I WELCOMED YOU IMMEDIATELY. AND FELL IN **LOVE** WITH YOU AS WELL.

I WAS SO HUNGRY. I HAD WAITED FOR DAYS. THE LOOK OF **SURPRISE** ON YOUR FACE...

IS THAT—?

'TIS. I HAVE **KEPT** IT ALL THESE YEARS.

YOU TRY TO **WOO** ME WITH SENTIMENTAL OBJECTS?

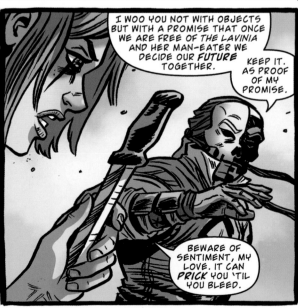

I WOO YOU NOT WITH OBJECTS BUT WITH A PROMISE THAT ONCE WE ARE FREE OF **THE LAVINIA** AND HER MAN-EATER WE DECIDE OUR **FUTURE** TOGETHER.

KEEP IT. AS PROOF OF MY PROMISE.

BEWARE OF SENTIMENT, MY LOVE. IT CAN **PRICK** YOU 'TIL YOU BLEED.

WE'RE READY, CAPTAIN.

THANK YOU, PAGE.

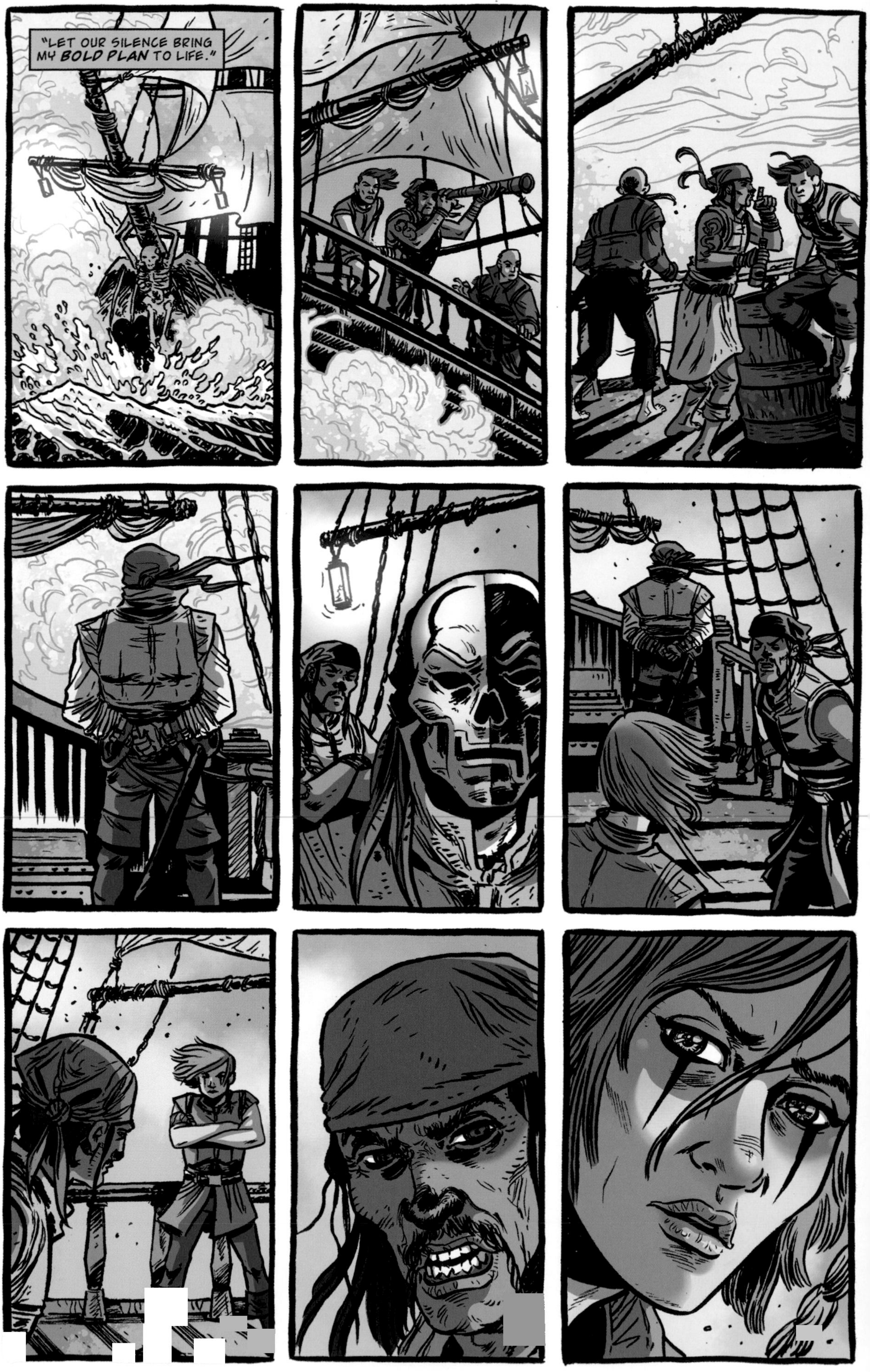
"LET OUR SILENCE BRING MY BOLD PLAN TO LIFE."

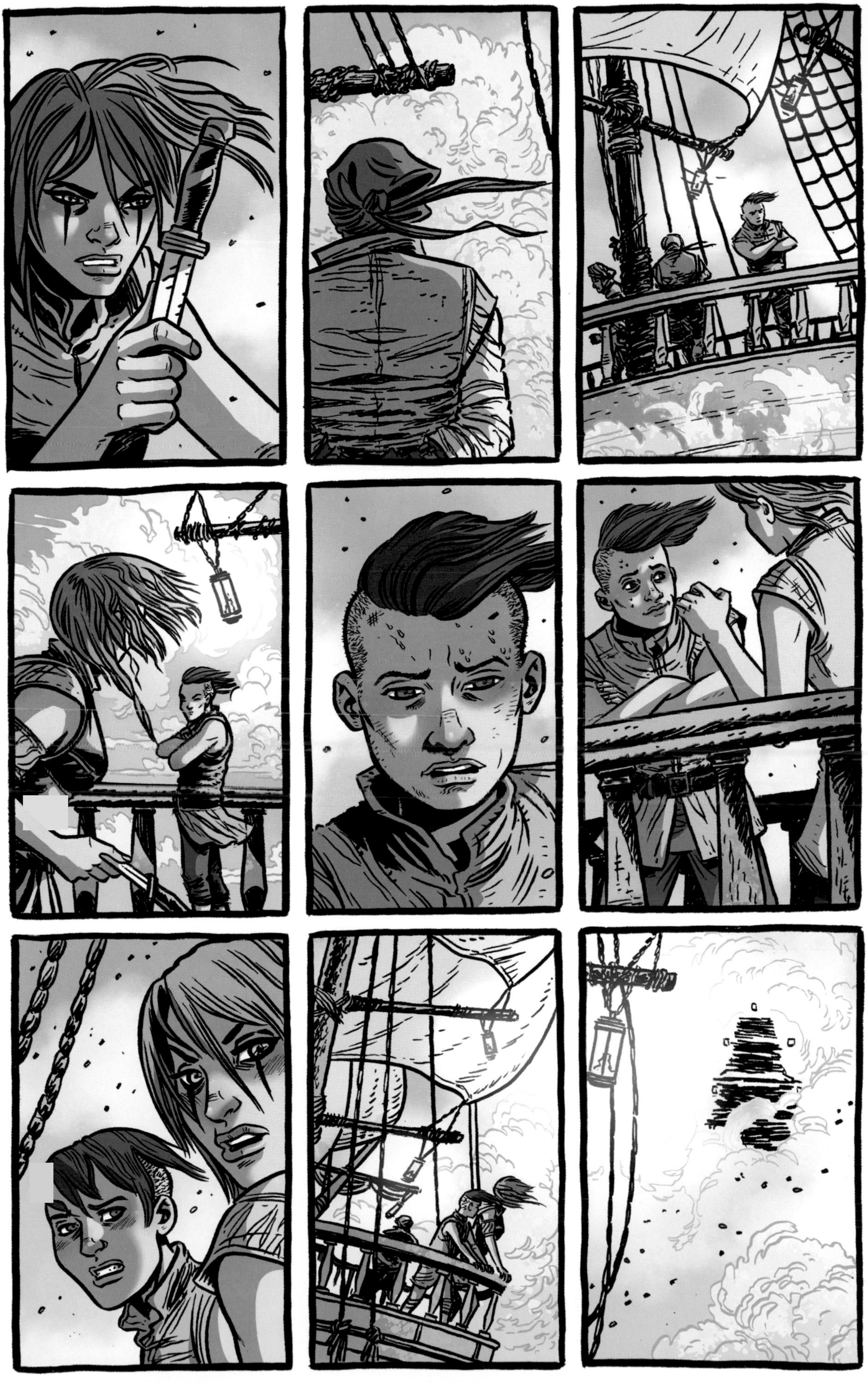

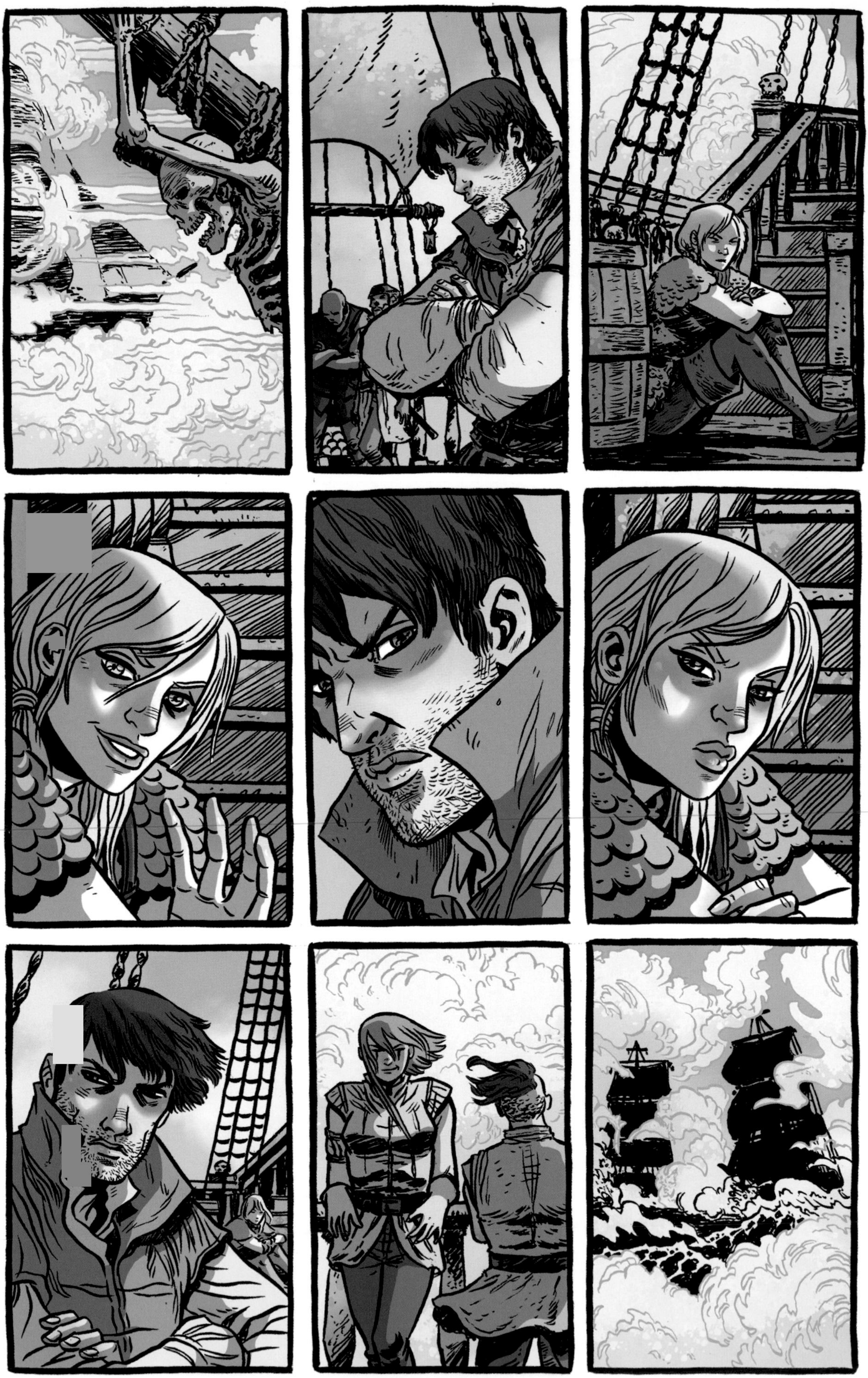

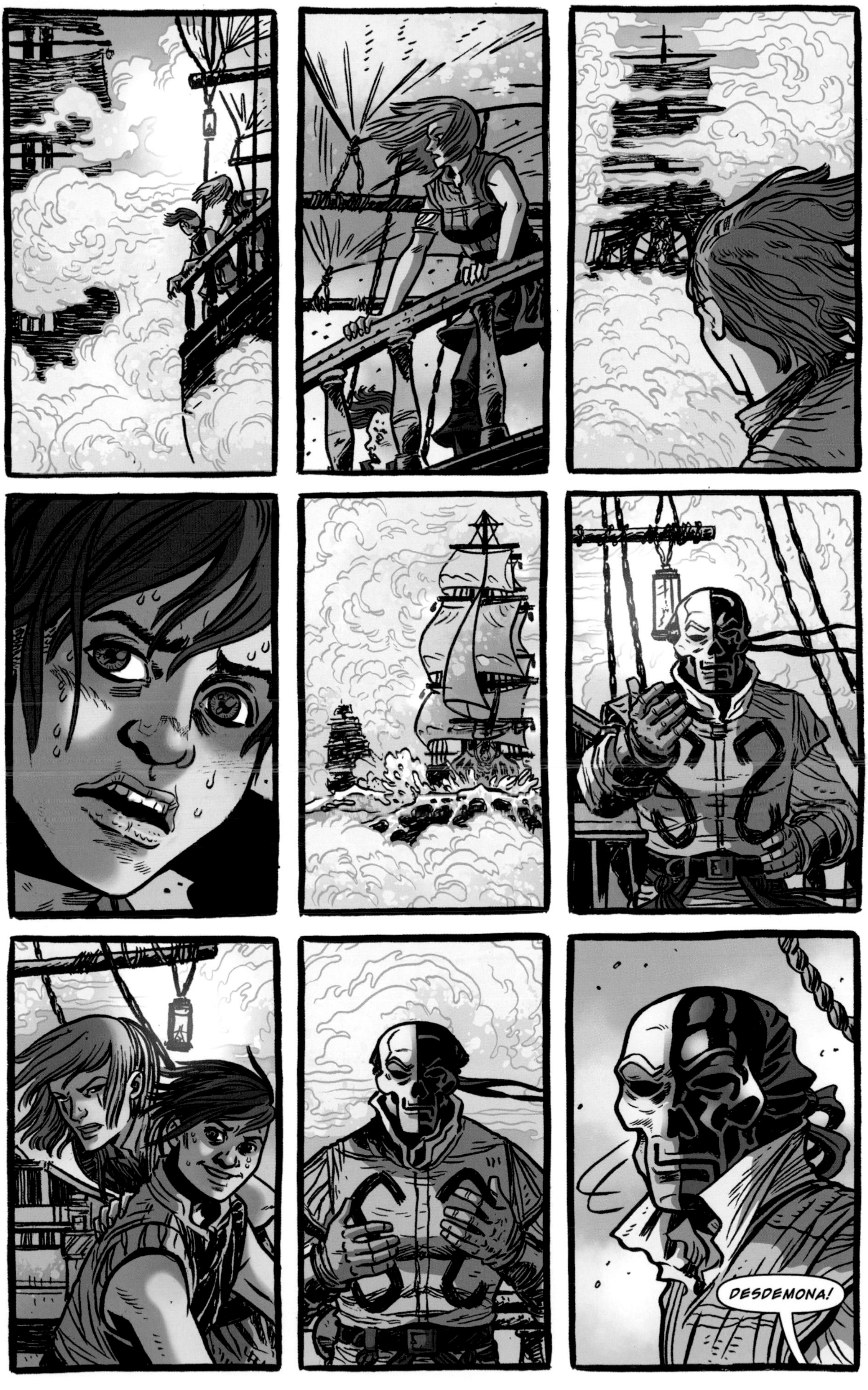
DESDEMONA!

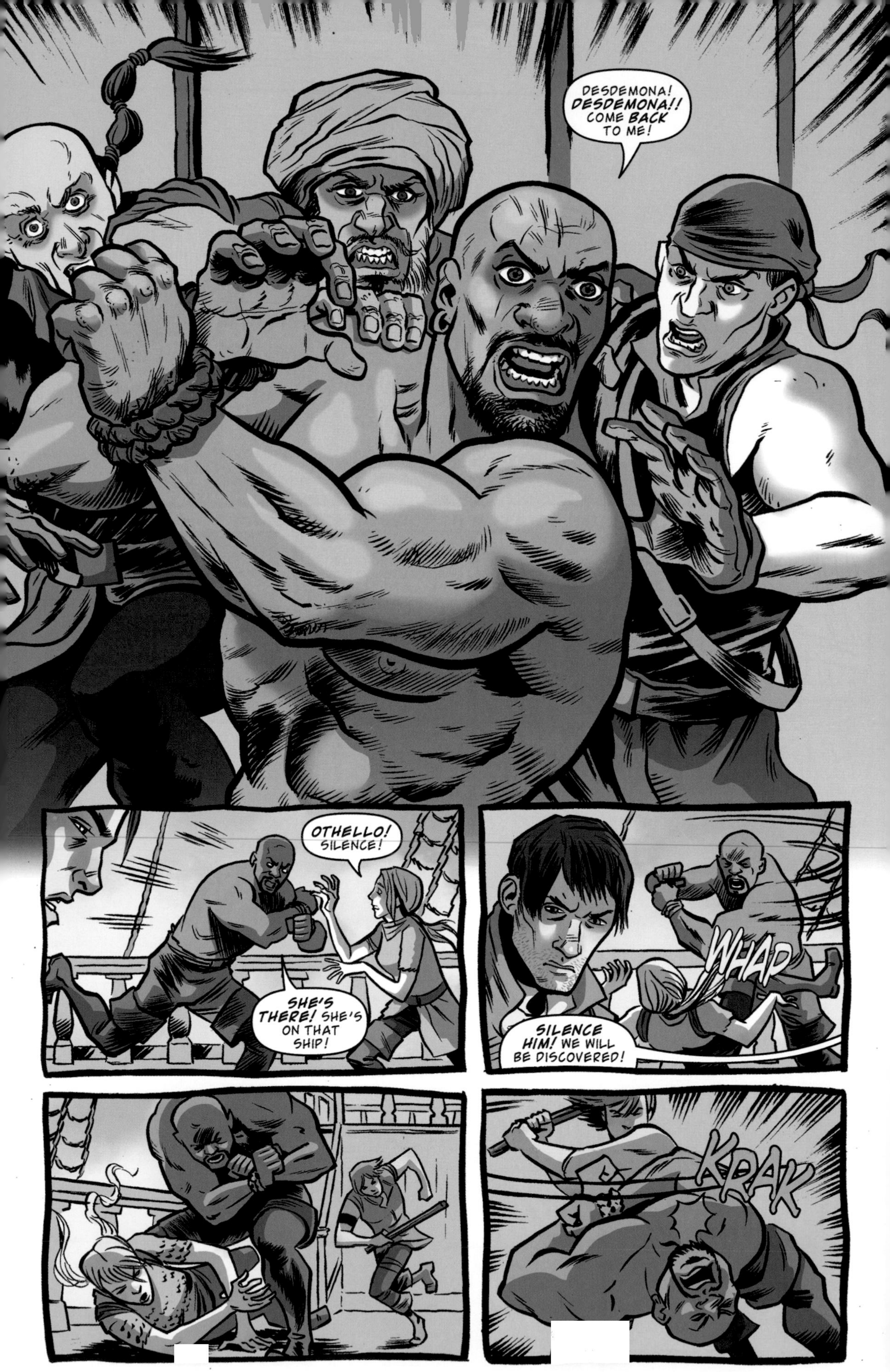
DESDEMONA! DESDEMONA!! COME BACK TO ME!
OTHELLO! SILENCE!
SHE'S THERE! SHE'S ON THAT SHIP!
WHAP
SILENCE HIM! WE WILL BE DISCOVERED!
KRAK

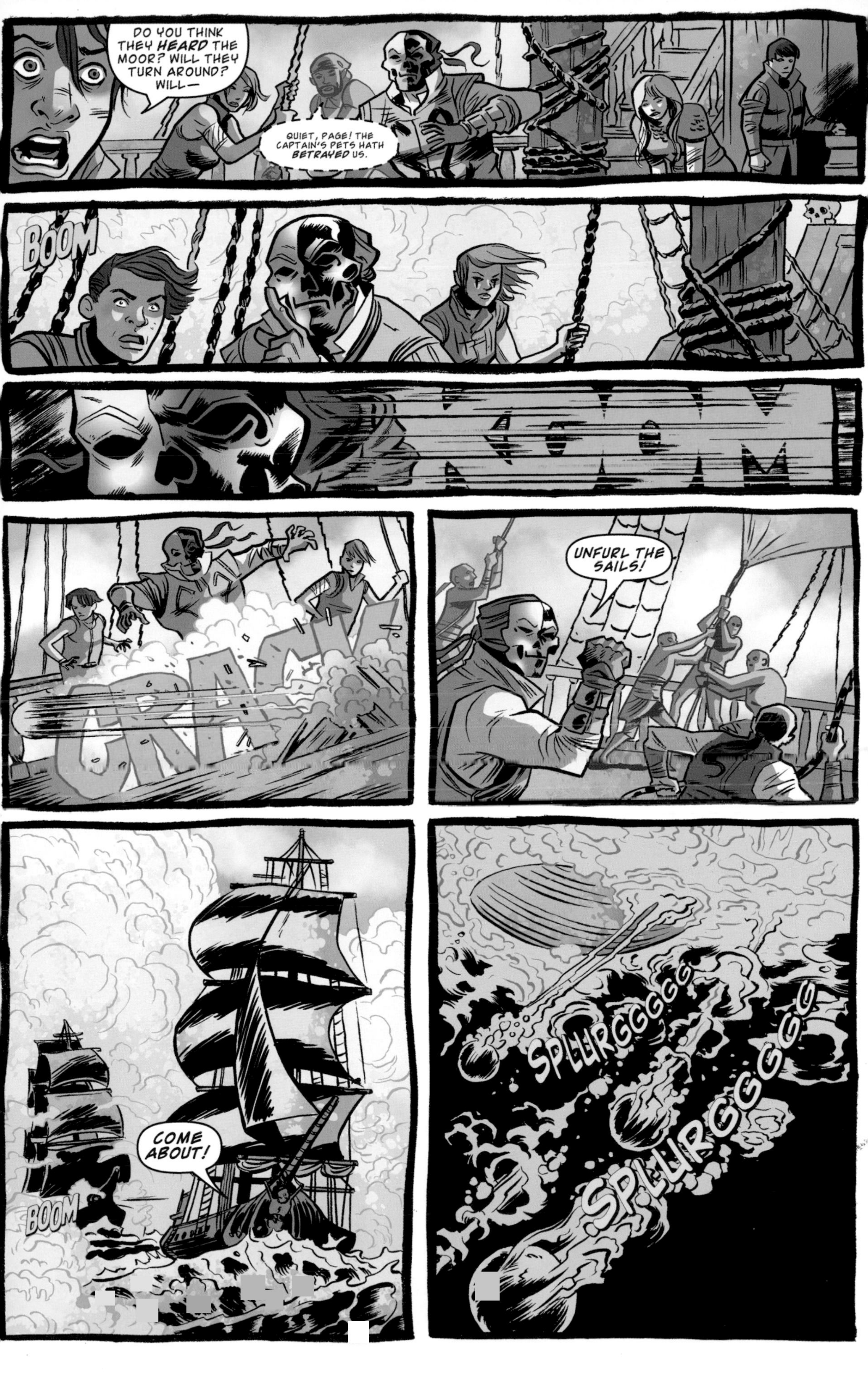
DO YOU THINK THEY HEARD THE MOOR? WILL THEY TURN AROUND? WILL—
QUIET, PAGE! THE CAPTAIN'S PETS HATH BETRAYED US.
BOOM
UNFURL THE SAILS!
COME ABOUT!
BOOM
SPLURGGGGG
SPLURGGGGGG

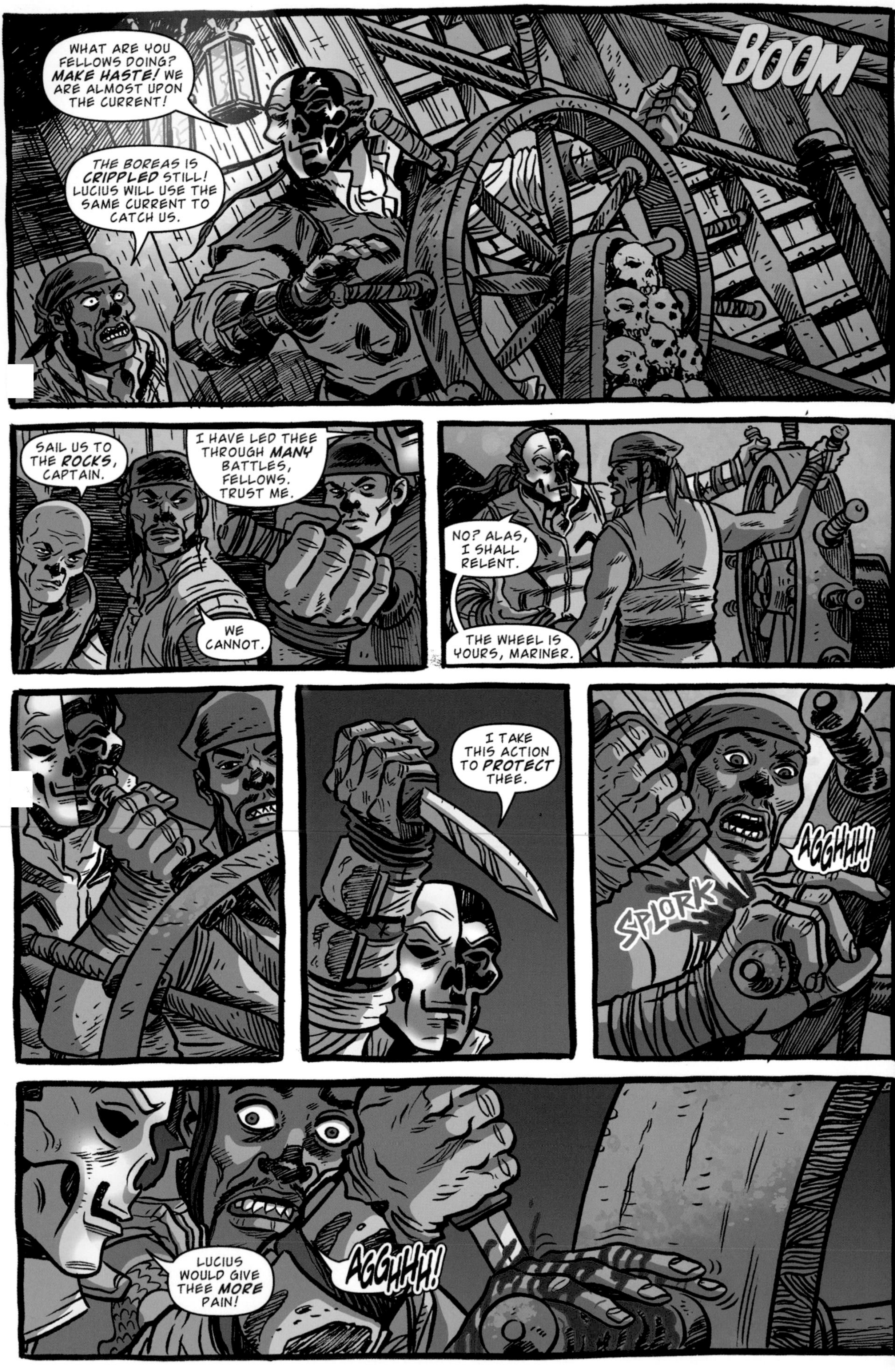
BOOM
WHAT ARE YOU FELLOWS DOING? MAKE HASTE! WE ARE ALMOST UPON THE CURRENT!
THE BOREAS IS CRIPPLED STILL! LUCIUS WILL USE THE SAME CURRENT TO CATCH US.
SAIL US TO THE ROCKS, CAPTAIN.
I HAVE LED THEE THROUGH MANY BATTLES, FELLOWS. TRUST ME.
WE CANNOT.
NO? ALAS, I SHALL RELENT.
THE WHEEL IS YOURS, MARINER.
I TAKE THIS ACTION TO PROTECT THEE.
AGGHHH!
SPLORK
LUCIUS WOULD GIVE THEE MORE PAIN!
AGGHHH!

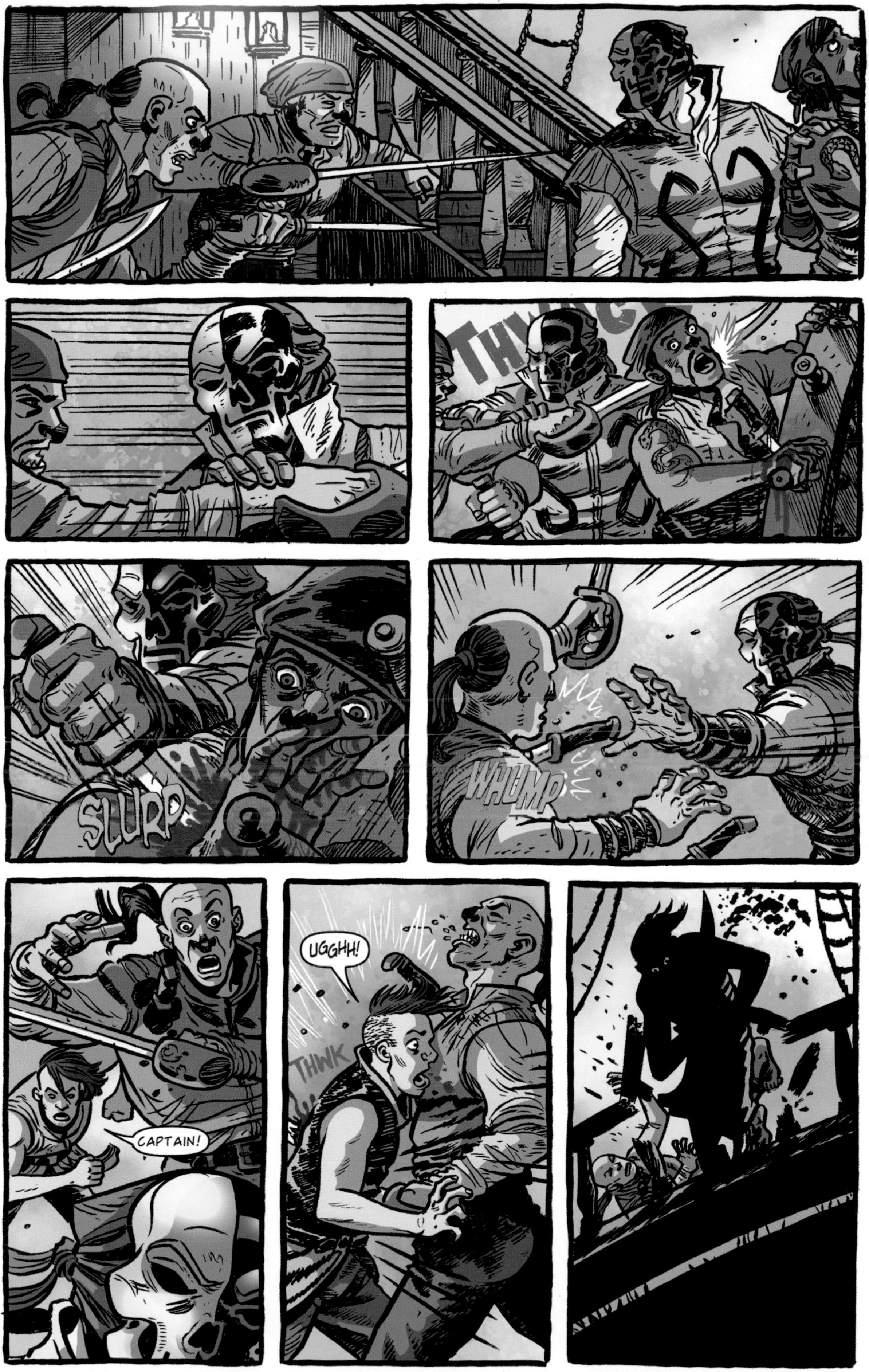
SLURP
WHUMP
CAPTAIN!
UGGHH!
THWK

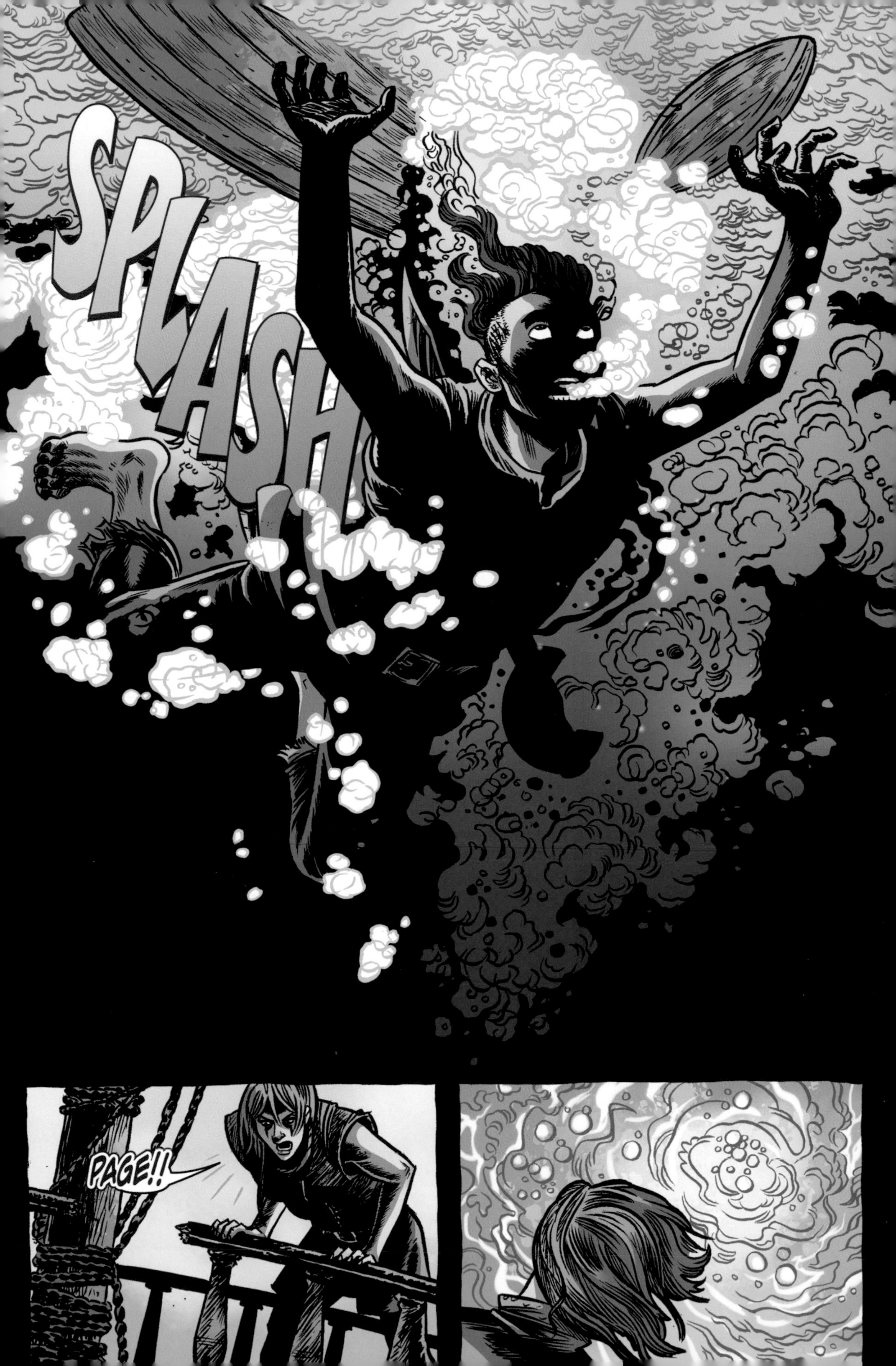
SPLASH
PAGE!!

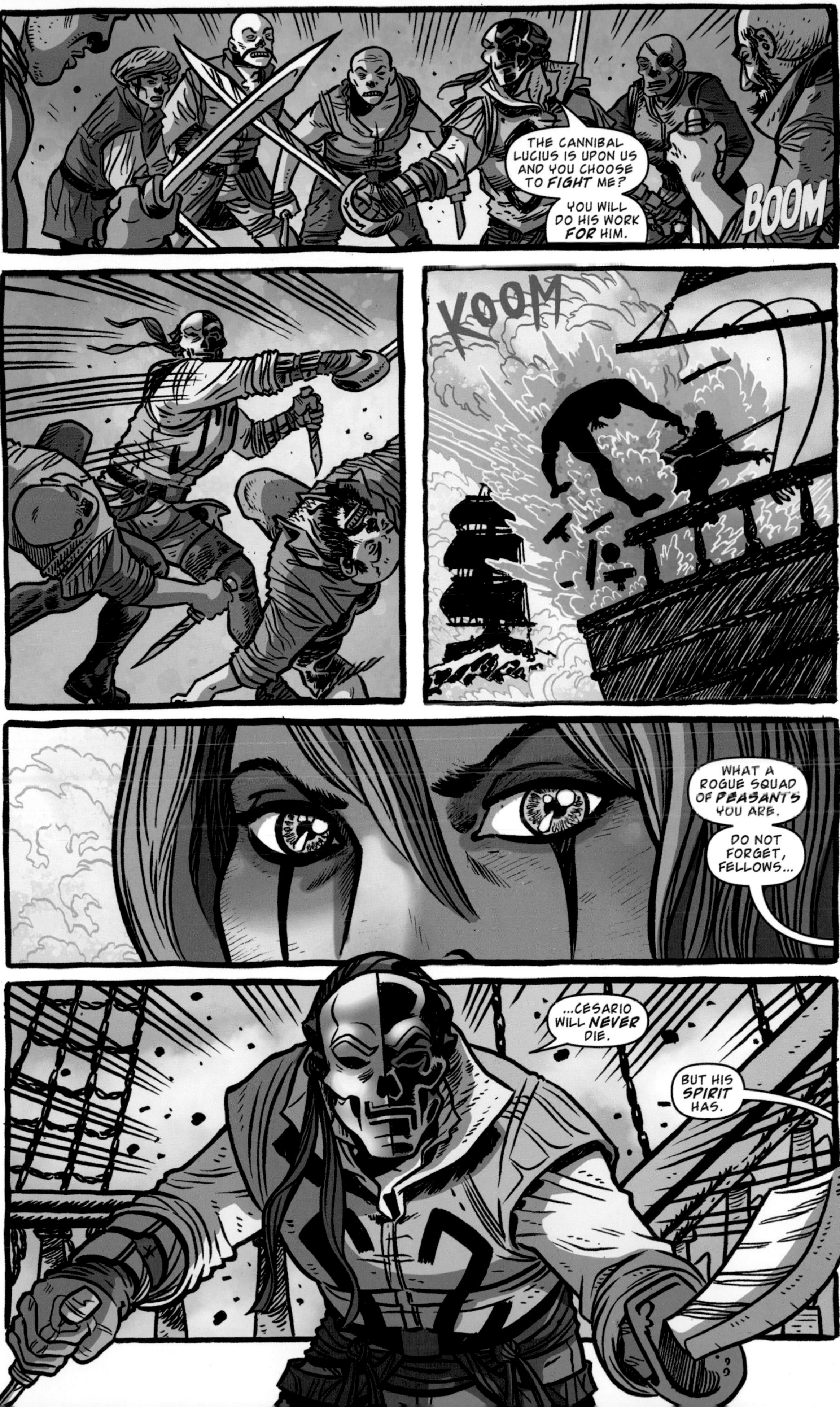
THE CANNIBAL LUCIUS IS UPON US AND YOU CHOOSE TO FIGHT ME?
YOU WILL DO HIS WORK FOR HIM.
BOOM
KOOM
WHAT A ROGUE SQUAD OF PEASANTS YOU ARE.
DO NOT FORGET, FELLOWS...
...CESARIO WILL NEVER DIE.
BUT HIS SPIRIT HAS.

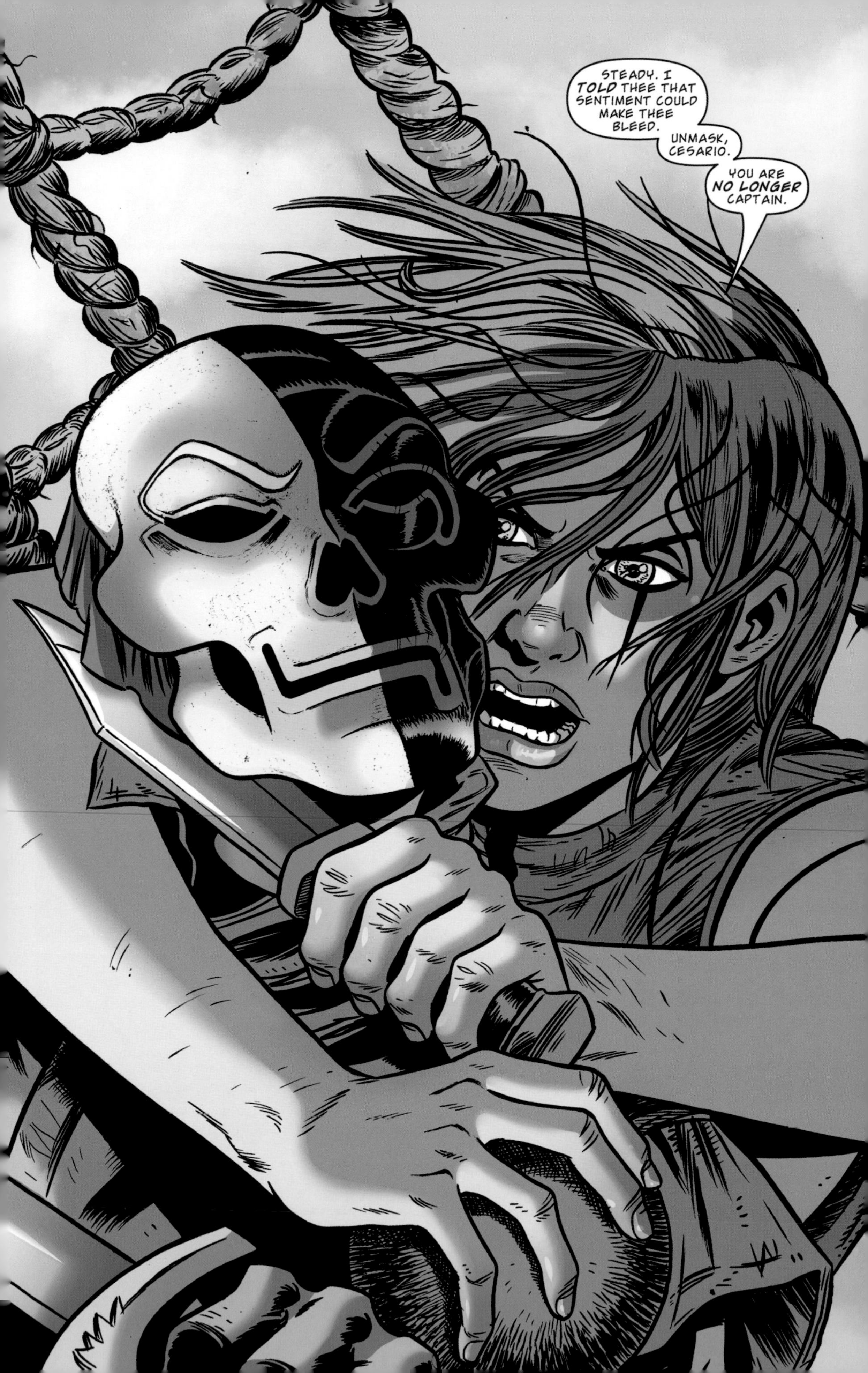
STEADY. I TOLD THEE THAT SENTIMENT COULD MAKE THEE BLEED.
UNMASK, CESARIO.
YOU ARE NO LONGER CAPTAIN.

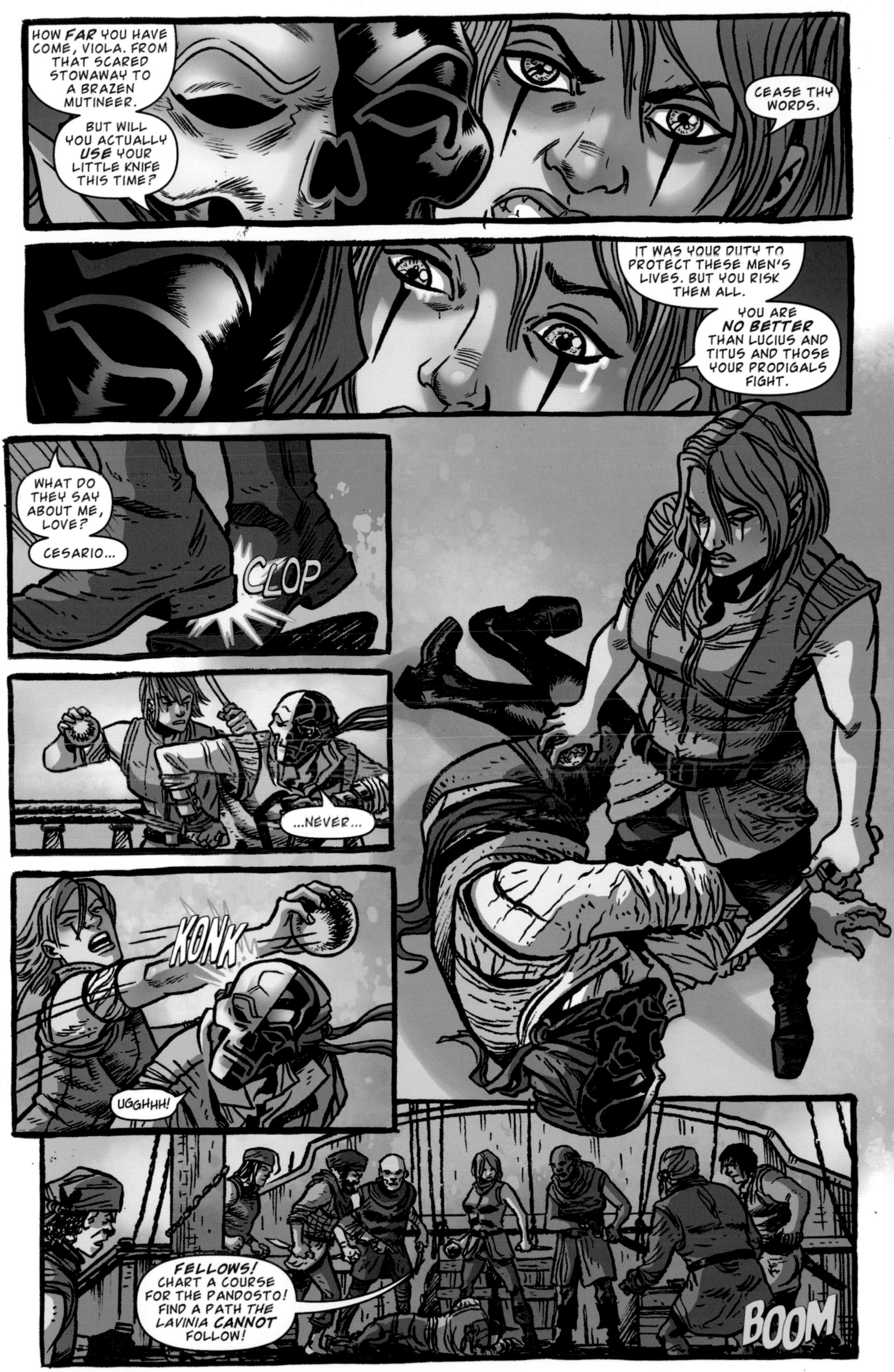
HOW FAR YOU HAVE COME, VIOLA. FROM THAT SCARED STOWAWAY TO A BRAZEN MUTINEER.
BUT WILL YOU ACTUALLY USE YOUR LITTLE KNIFE THIS TIME?
CEASE THY WORDS.
IT WAS YOUR DUTY TO PROTECT THESE MEN'S LIVES. BUT YOU RISK THEM ALL.
YOU ARE NO BETTER THAN LUCIUS AND TITUS AND THOSE YOUR PRODIGALS FIGHT.
WHAT DO THEY SAY ABOUT ME, LOVE?
CESARIO...
CLOP
...NEVER...
KONK
UGGHHH!
FELLOWS! CHART A COURSE FOR THE PANDOSTO! FIND A PATH THE LAVINIA CANNOT FOLLOW!
BOOM

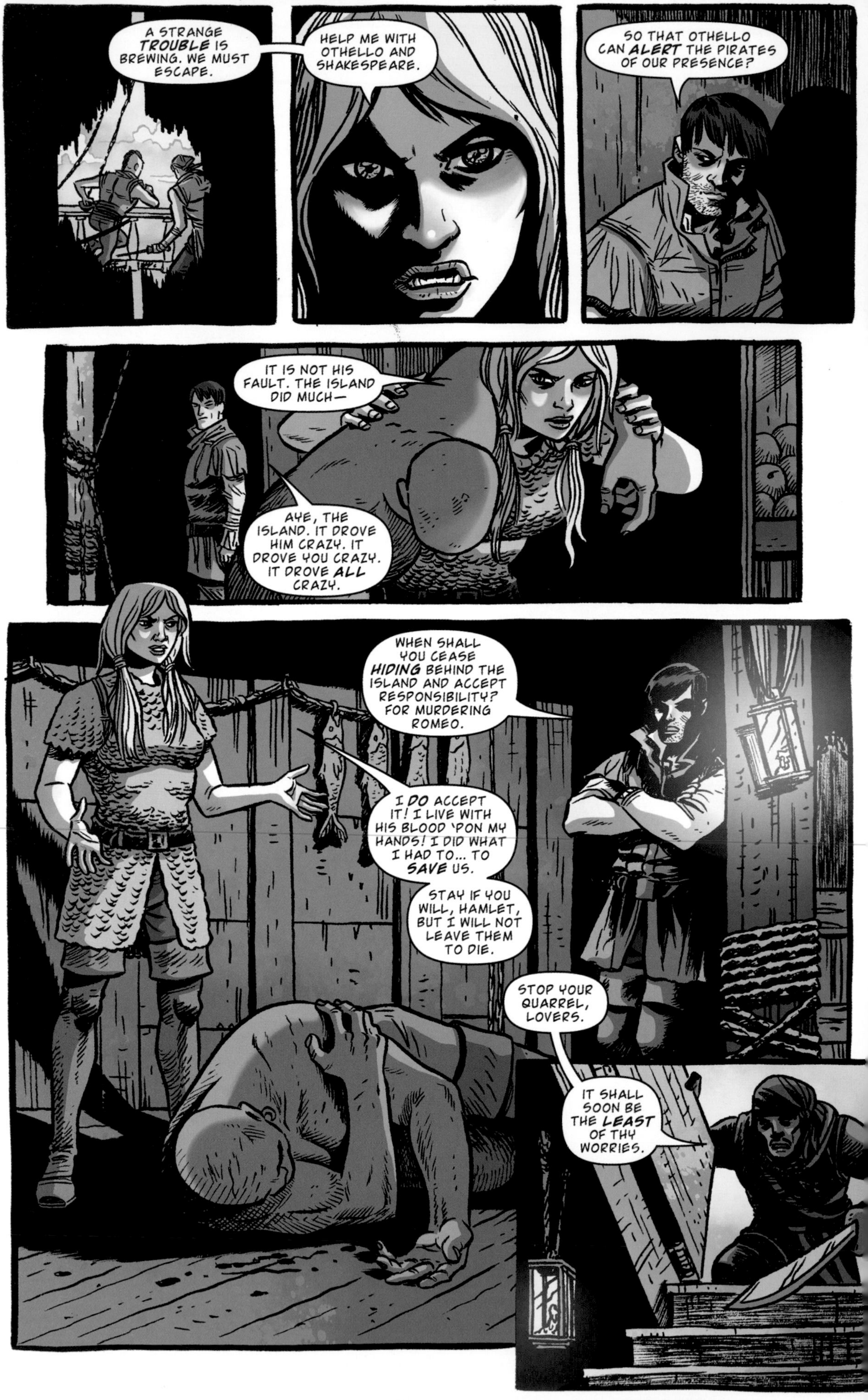
A STRANGE TROUBLE IS BREWING. WE MUST ESCAPE.
HELP ME WITH OTHELLO AND SHAKESPEARE.
SO THAT OTHELLO CAN ALERT THE PIRATES OF OUR PRESENCE?
IT IS NOT HIS FAULT. THE ISLAND DID MUCH—
AYE, THE ISLAND. IT DROVE HIM CRAZY. IT DROVE YOU CRAZY. IT DROVE ALL CRAZY.
WHEN SHALL YOU CEASE HIDING BEHIND THE ISLAND AND ACCEPT RESPONSIBILITY? FOR MURDERING ROMEO.
I DO ACCEPT IT! I LIVE WITH HIS BLOOD 'PON MY HANDS! I DID WHAT I HAD TO... TO SAVE US.
STAY IF YOU WILL, HAMLET, BUT I WILL NOT LEAVE THEM TO DIE.
STOP YOUR QUARREL, LOVERS.
IT SHALL SOON BE THE LEAST OF THY WORRIES.

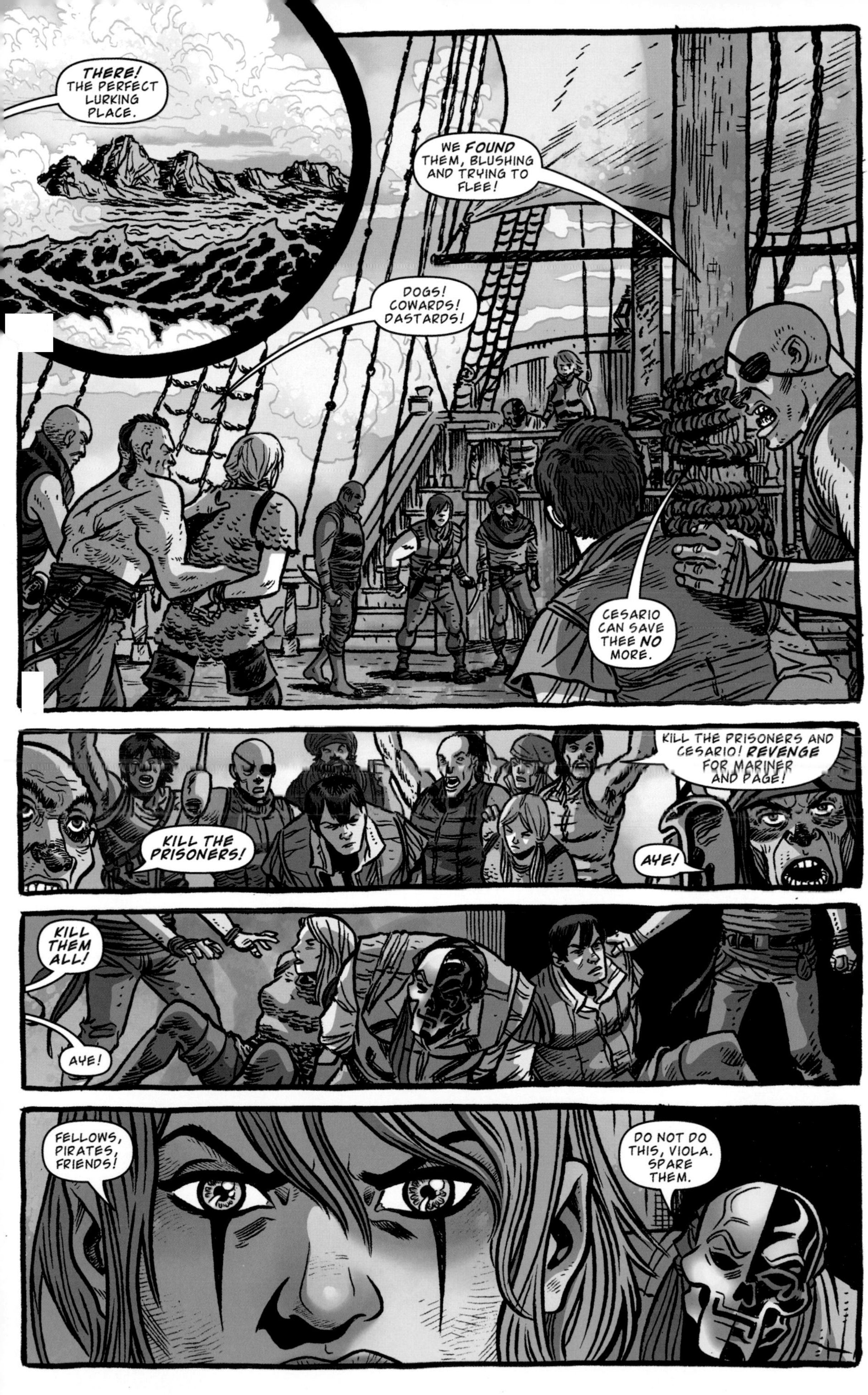
THERE! THE PERFECT LURKING PLACE.
WE FOUND THEM, BLUSHING AND TRYING TO FLEE!
DOGS! COWARDS! DASTARDS!
CESARIO CAN SAVE THEE NO MORE.
KILL THE PRISONERS!
KILL THE PRISONERS AND CESARIO! REVENGE FOR MARINER AND PAGE!
AYE!
KILL THEM ALL!
AYE!
FELLOWS, PIRATES, FRIENDS!
DO NOT DO THIS, VIOLA. SPARE THEM.

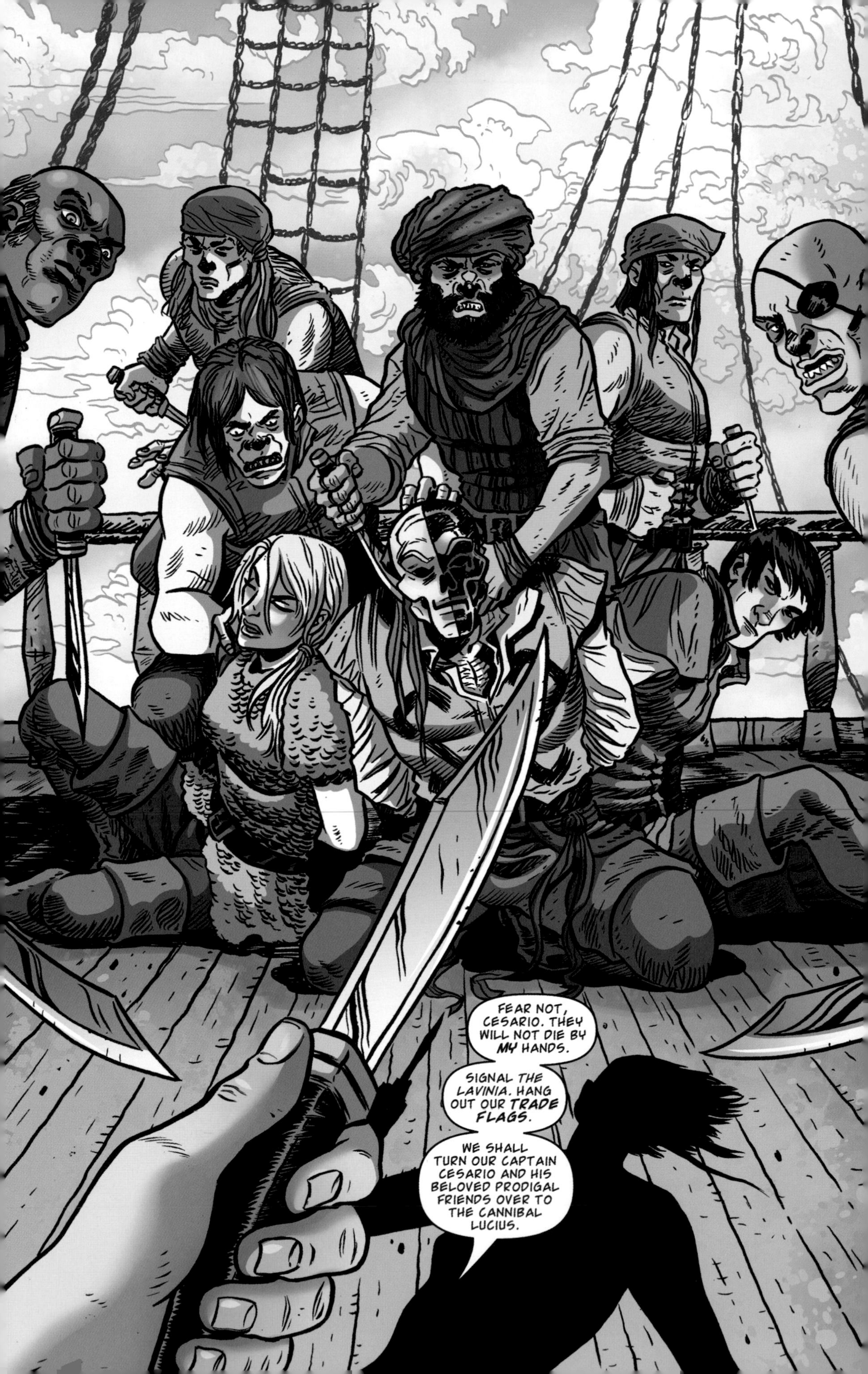

FEAR NOT, CESARIO. THEY WILL NOT DIE BY *MY* HANDS.
SIGNAL *THE LAVINIA*. HANG OUT OUR ***TRADE FLAGS***.
WE SHALL TURN OUR CAPTAIN CESARIO AND HIS BELOVED PRODIGAL FRIENDS OVER TO THE CANNIBAL LUCIUS.

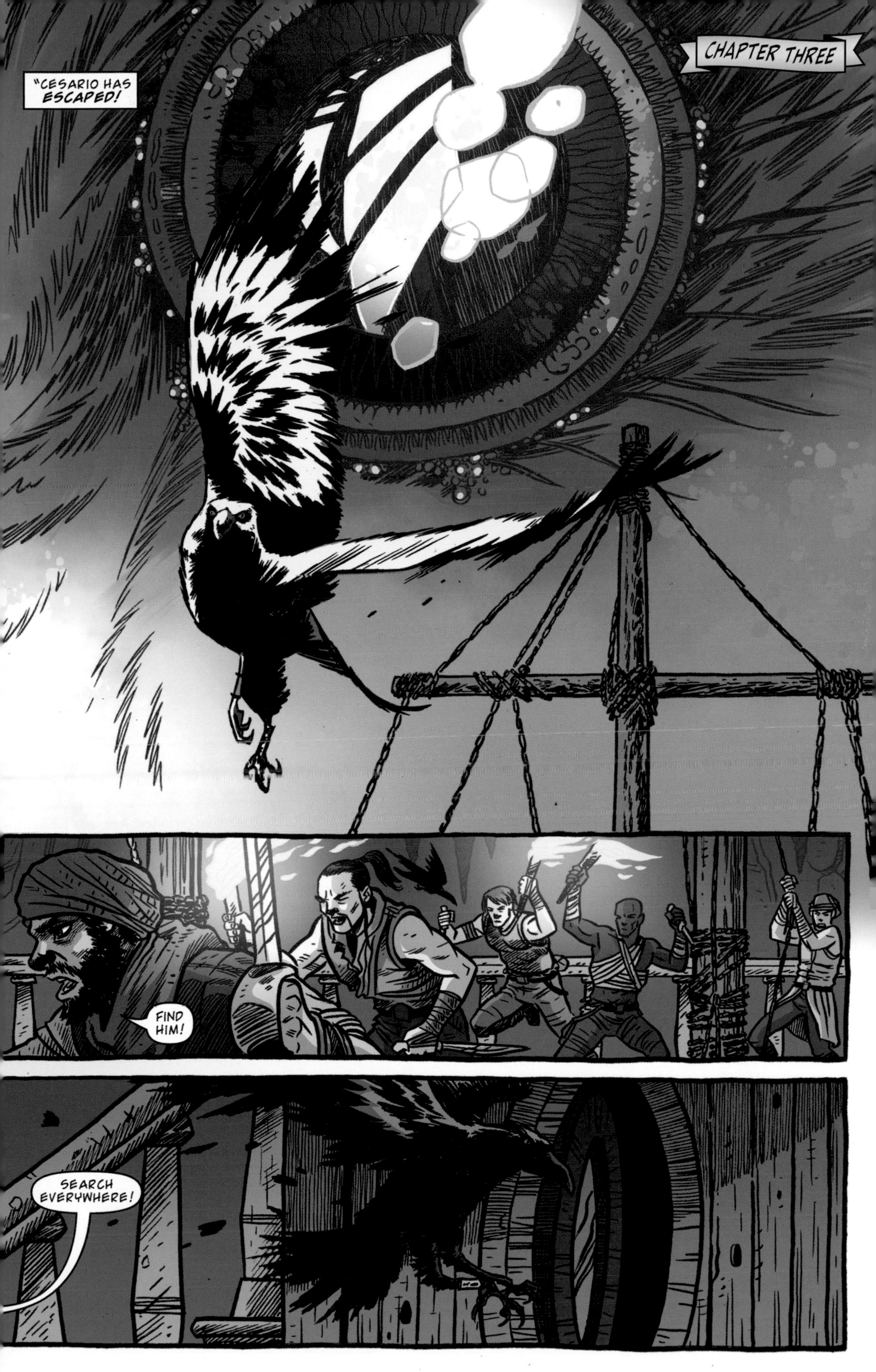
CHAPTER THREE
"CESARIO HAS ESCAPED!
FIND HIM!
SEARCH EVERYWHERE!

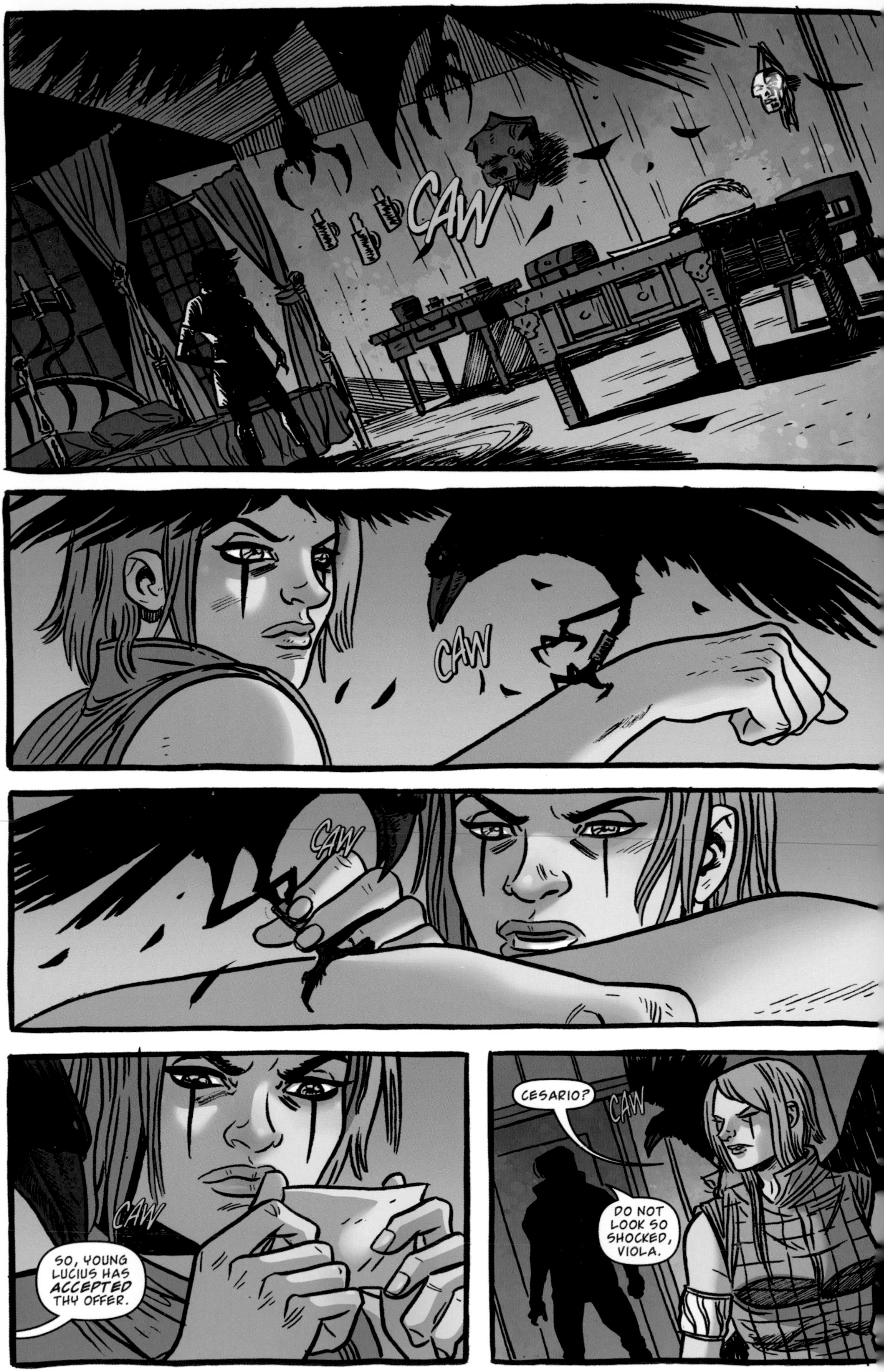
CAW
CAW
CAW
CAW
SO, YOUNG LUCIUS HAS ACCEPTED THY OFFER.
CESARIO?
CAW
DO NOT LOOK SO SHOCKED, VIOLA.

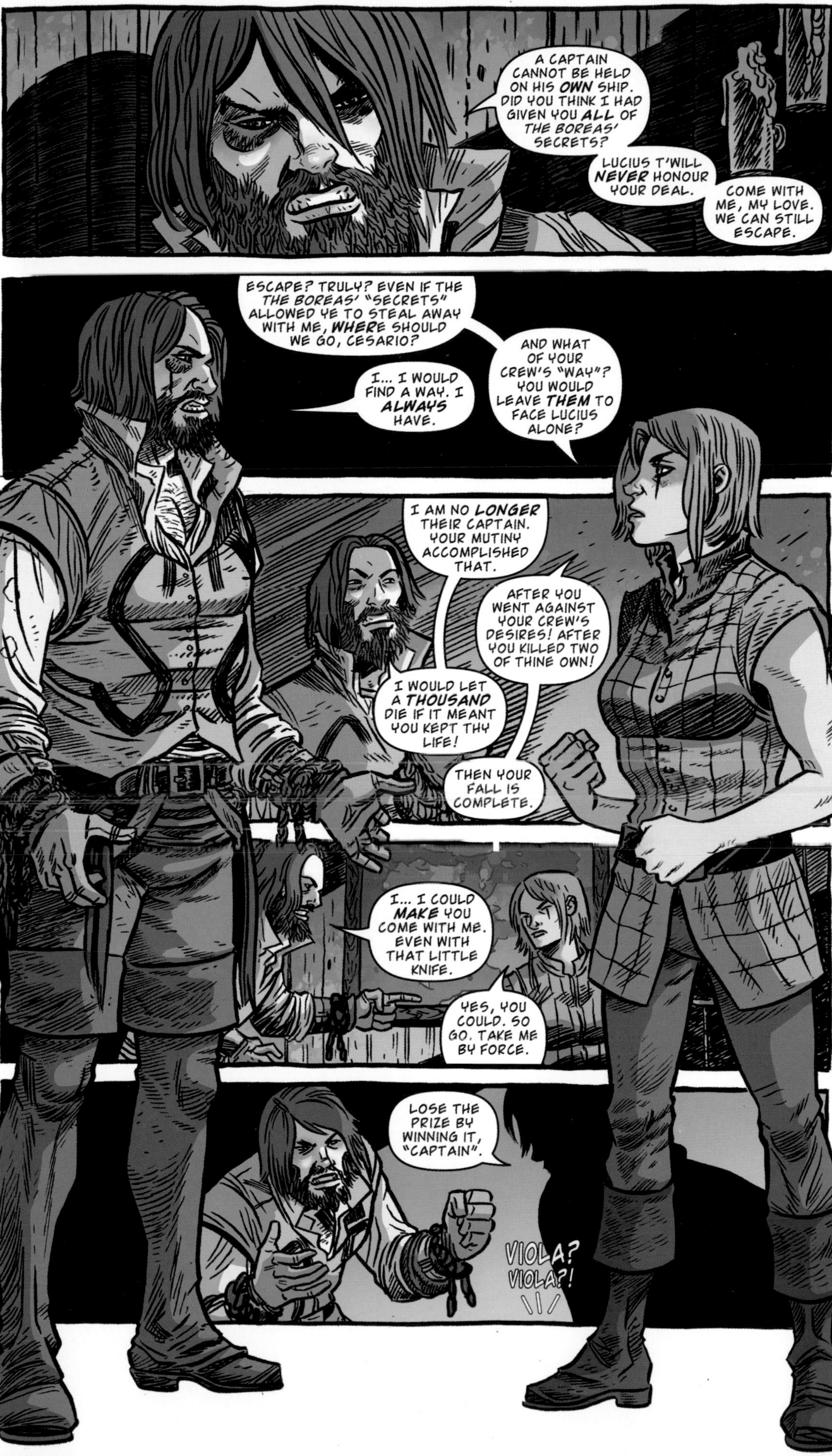
A CAPTAIN CANNOT BE HELD ON HIS OWN SHIP. DID YOU THINK I HAD GIVEN YOU ALL OF THE BOREAS' SECRETS?
LUCIUS T'WILL NEVER HONOUR YOUR DEAL.
COME WITH ME, MY LOVE. WE CAN STILL ESCAPE.
ESCAPE? TRULY? EVEN IF THE THE BOREAS' "SECRETS" ALLOWED YE TO STEAL AWAY WITH ME, WHERE SHOULD WE GO, CESARIO?
I... I WOULD FIND A WAY. I ALWAYS HAVE.
AND WHAT OF YOUR CREW'S "WAY"? YOU WOULD LEAVE THEM TO FACE LUCIUS ALONE?
I AM NO LONGER THEIR CAPTAIN. YOUR MUTINY ACCOMPLISHED THAT.
AFTER YOU WENT AGAINST YOUR CREW'S DESIRES! AFTER YOU KILLED TWO OF THINE OWN!
I WOULD LET A THOUSAND DIE IF IT MEANT YOU KEPT THY LIFE!
THEN YOUR FALL IS COMPLETE.
I... I COULD MAKE YOU COME WITH ME. EVEN WITH THAT LITTLE KNIFE.
YES, YOU COULD. SO GO. TAKE ME BY FORCE.
LOSE THE PRIZE BY WINNING IT, "CAPTAIN".
VIOLA? VIOLA?!

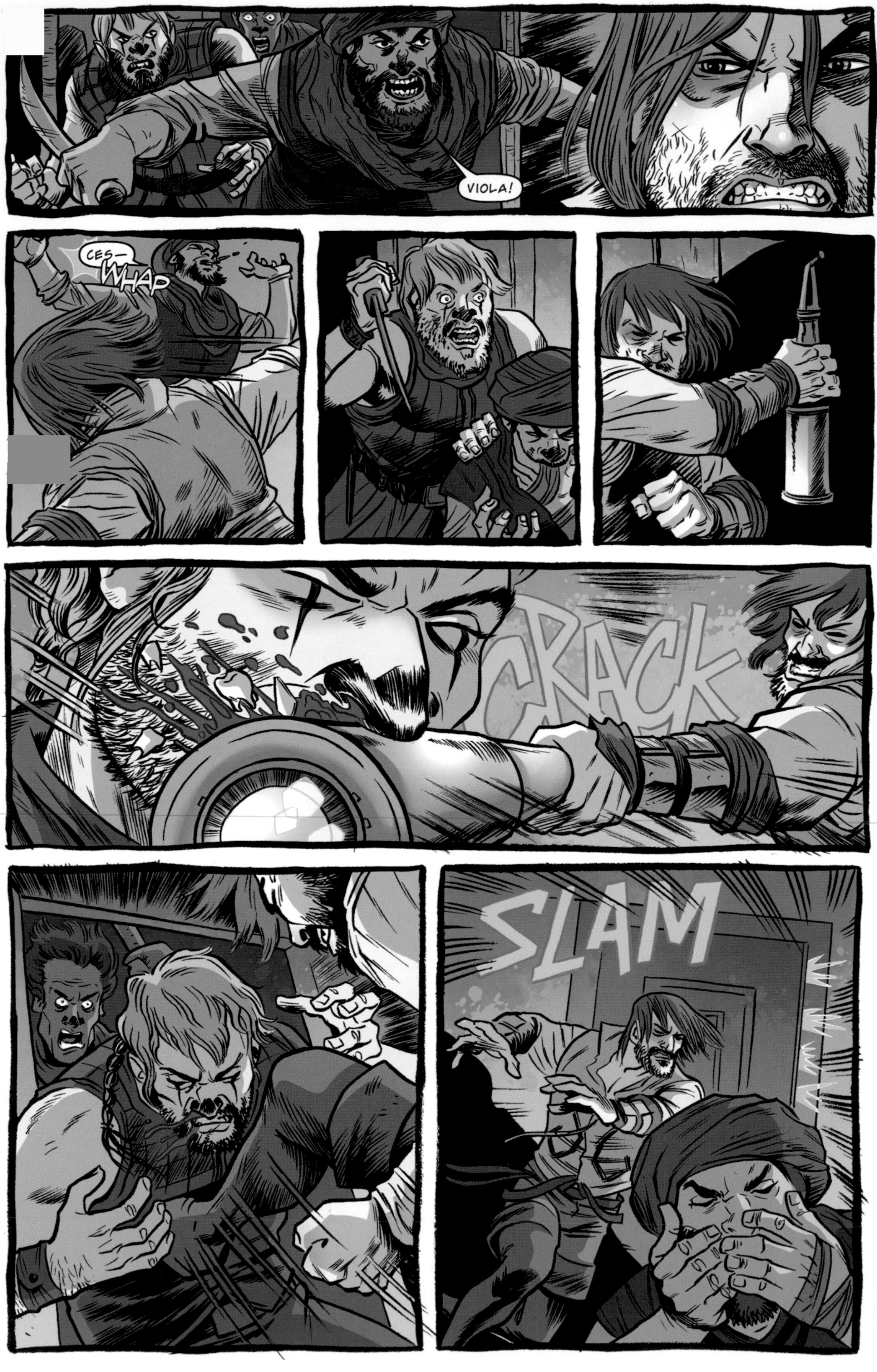
VIOLA!
CES—
WHAP
CRACK
SLAM

SLAM SLAM SLAM SLAM

VIOLA! VIOLA!

COME WITH ME OR WHITMORE SHALL MEET HIS *END!*

NO. I KNOW YOU ARE A NOTORIOUS LIAR.

YOU DOUBT THAT I WILL KILL HIM? YOU DOUBT MY *WORDS?!*

CCCCKK. CCCCK.

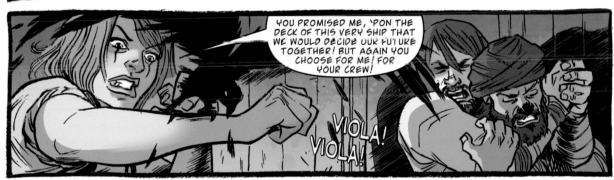

YOU PROMISED ME, 'PON THE DECK OF THIS VERY SHIP THAT WE WOULD DECIDE OUR FUTURE TOGETHER! BUT AGAIN YOU CHOOSE FOR ME! FOR YOUR CREW!

VIOLA! VIOLA!

I WILL DO A CAPTAIN'S DUTY AND FACE THE CANNIBAL MYSELF.

THAT LETTER SHALL BE YOUR *DEATH WARRANT!*

THUD THUD

IF LUCIUS BETRAYS US THEN I WILL DIE WITH BLOOD IN MY MOUTH AND STEEL IN MY HAND. AS A *TRUE PIRATE CAPTAIN* WOULD.

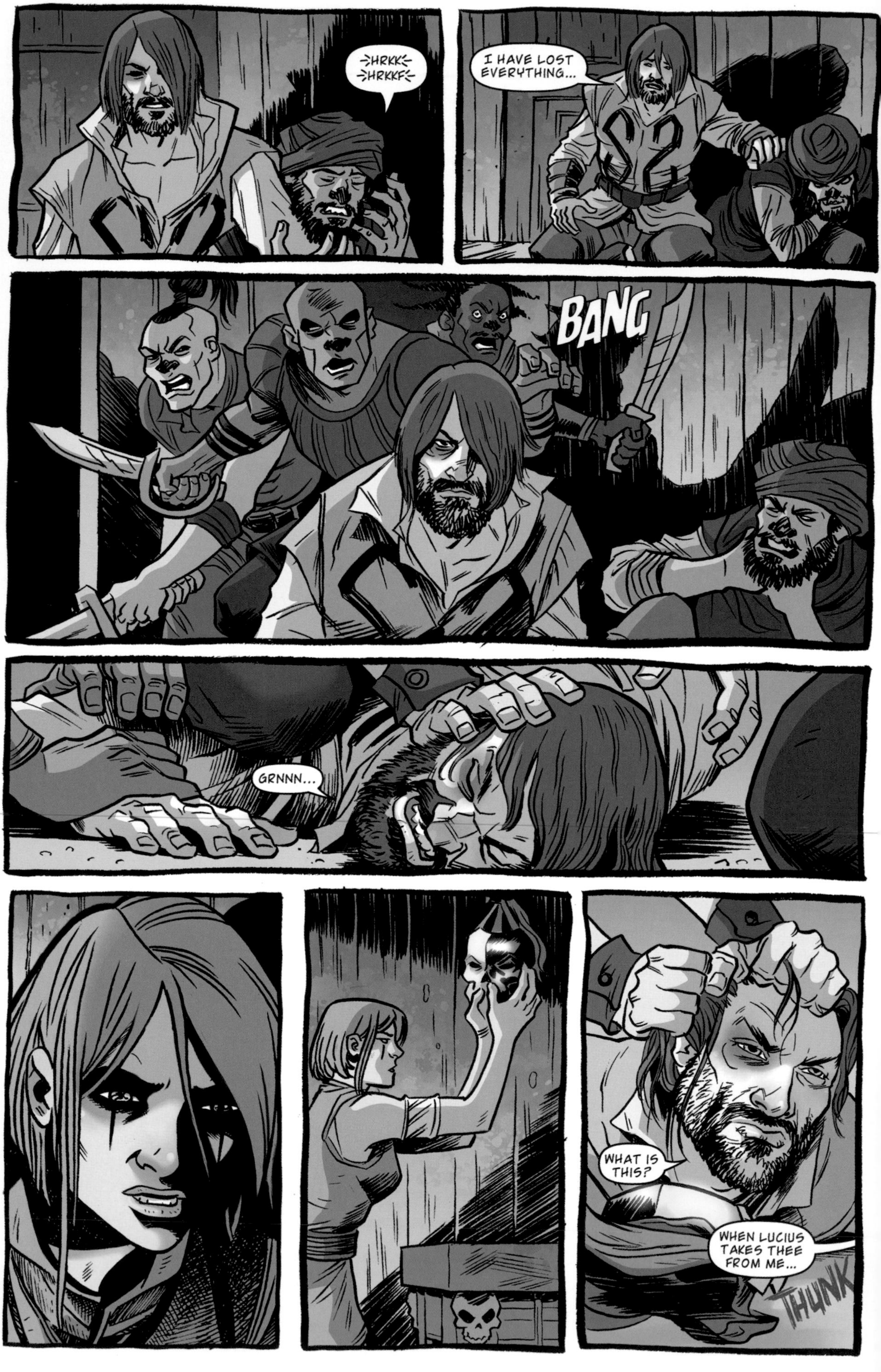

HRKK
HRKKF
I HAVE LOST EVERYTHING...
BANG
GRNNN...
WHAT IS THIS?
WHEN LUCIUS TAKES THEE FROM ME...
THUNK

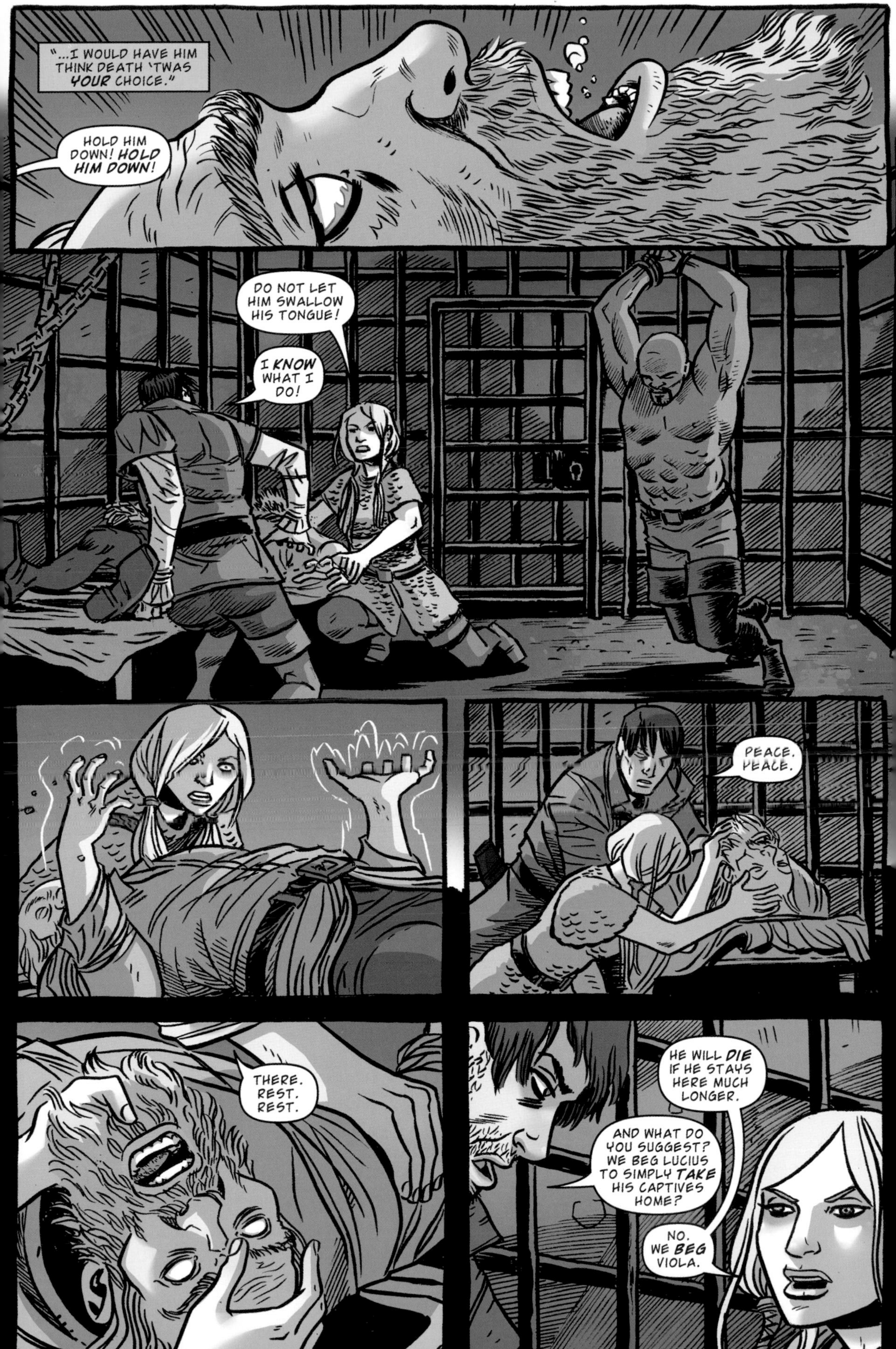
"...I WOULD HAVE HIM THINK DEATH 'TWAS YOUR CHOICE."
HOLD HIM DOWN! HOLD HIM DOWN!
DO NOT LET HIM SWALLOW HIS TONGUE!
I KNOW WHAT I DO!
PEACE. PEACE.
THERE. REST. REST.
HE WILL DIE IF HE STAYS HERE MUCH LONGER.
AND WHAT DO YOU SUGGEST? WE BEG LUCIUS TO SIMPLY TAKE HIS CAPTIVES HOME?
NO. WE BEG VIOLA.

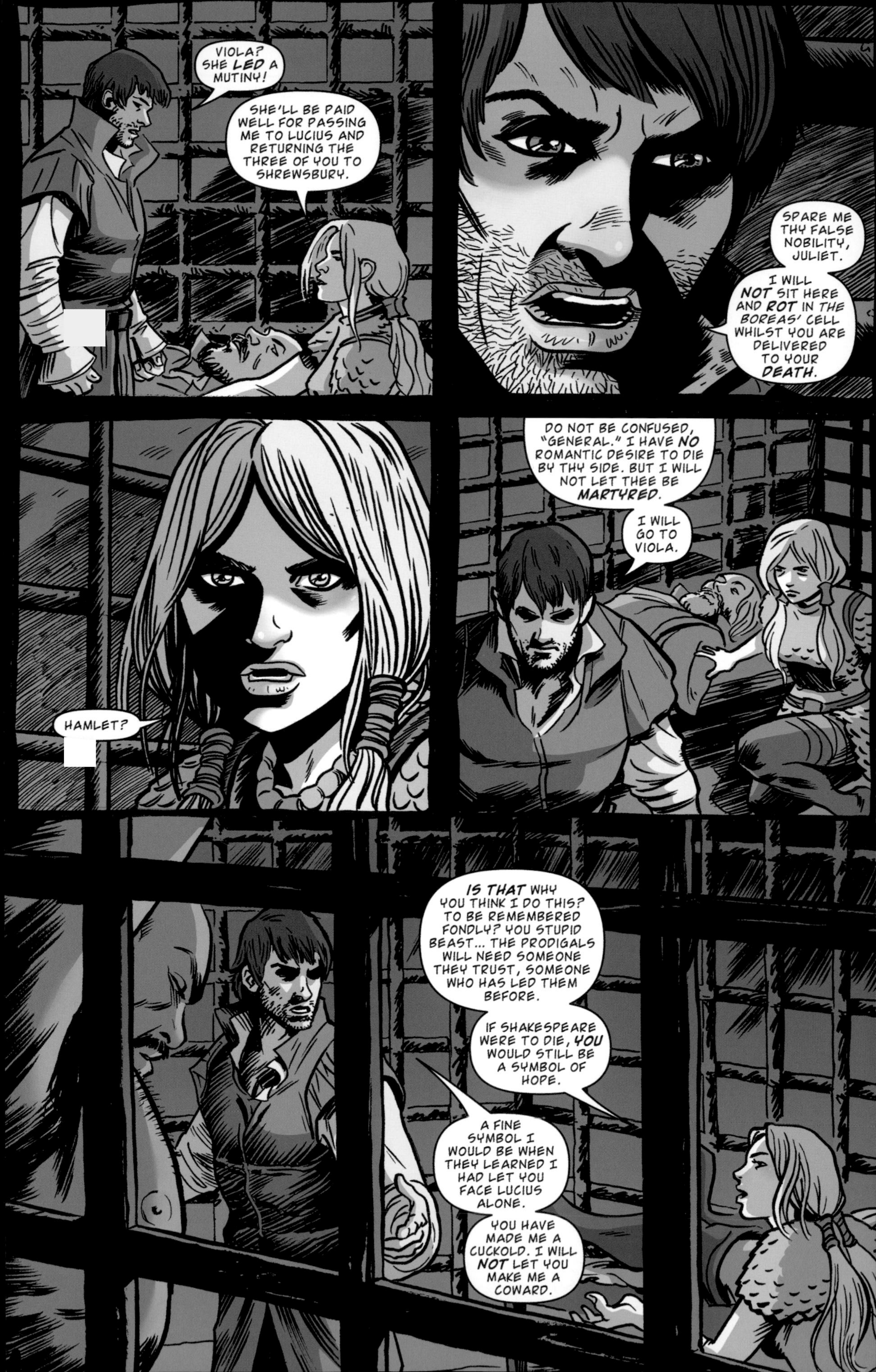
VIOLA? SHE LED A MUTINY!
SHE'LL BE PAID WELL FOR PASSING ME TO LUCIUS AND RETURNING THE THREE OF YOU TO SHREWSBURY.
SPARE ME THY FALSE NOBILITY, JULIET.
I WILL NOT SIT HERE AND ROT IN THE BOREAS' CELL WHILST YOU ARE DELIVERED TO YOUR DEATH.
HAMLET?
DO NOT BE CONFUSED, "GENERAL." I HAVE NO ROMANTIC DESIRE TO DIE BY THY SIDE. BUT I WILL NOT LET THEE BE MARTYRED.
I WILL GO TO VIOLA.
IS THAT WHY YOU THINK I DO THIS? TO BE REMEMBERED FONDLY? YOU STUPID BEAST... THE PRODIGALS WILL NEED SOMEONE THEY TRUST, SOMEONE WHO HAS LED THEM BEFORE.
IF SHAKESPEARE WERE TO DIE, YOU WOULD STILL BE A SYMBOL OF HOPE.
A FINE SYMBOL I WOULD BE WHEN THEY LEARNED I HAD LET YOU FACE LUCIUS ALONE.
YOU HAVE MADE ME A CUCKOLD. I WILL NOT LET YOU MAKE ME A COWARD.

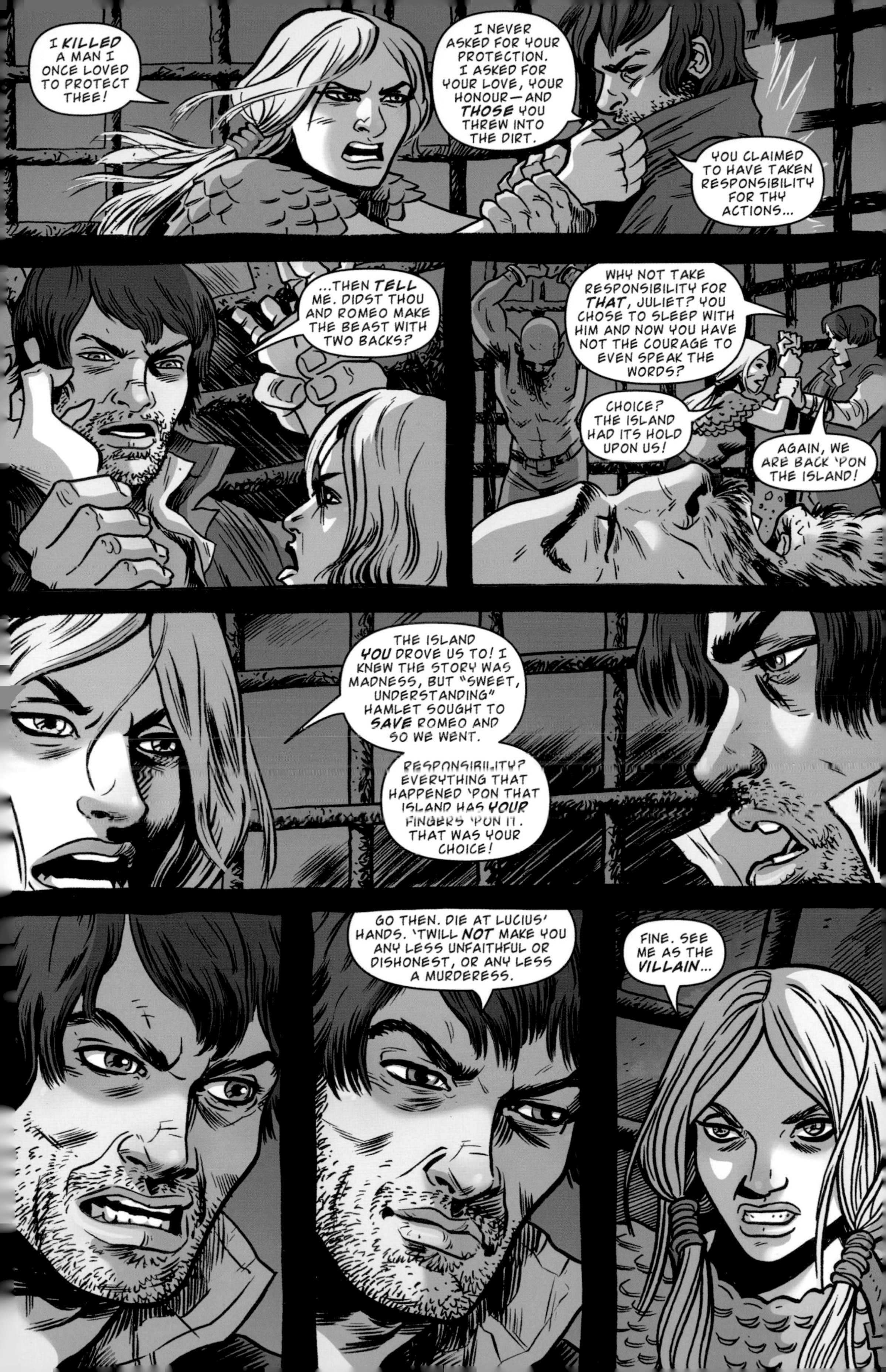

I KILLED A MAN I ONCE LOVED TO PROTECT THEE!
I NEVER ASKED FOR YOUR PROTECTION. I ASKED FOR YOUR LOVE, YOUR HONOUR—AND THOSE YOU THREW INTO THE DIRT.
YOU CLAIMED TO HAVE TAKEN RESPONSIBILITY FOR THY ACTIONS...
...THEN TELL ME. DIDST THOU AND ROMEO MAKE THE BEAST WITH TWO BACKS?
WHY NOT TAKE RESPONSIBILITY FOR THAT, JULIET? YOU CHOSE TO SLEEP WITH HIM AND NOW YOU HAVE NOT THE COURAGE TO EVEN SPEAK THE WORDS?
CHOICE? THE ISLAND HAD ITS HOLD UPON US!
AGAIN, WE ARE BACK 'PON THE ISLAND!
THE ISLAND YOU DROVE US TO! I KNEW THE STORY WAS MADNESS, BUT "SWEET, UNDERSTANDING" HAMLET SOUGHT TO SAVE ROMEO AND SO WE WENT.
RESPONSIBILITY? EVERYTHING THAT HAPPENED 'PON THAT ISLAND HAS YOUR FINGERS 'PON IT. THAT WAS YOUR CHOICE!
GO THEN. DIE AT LUCIUS' HANDS. 'TWILL NOT MAKE YOU ANY LESS UNFAITHFUL OR DISHONEST, OR ANY LESS A MURDERESS.
FINE. SEE ME AS THE VILLAIN...

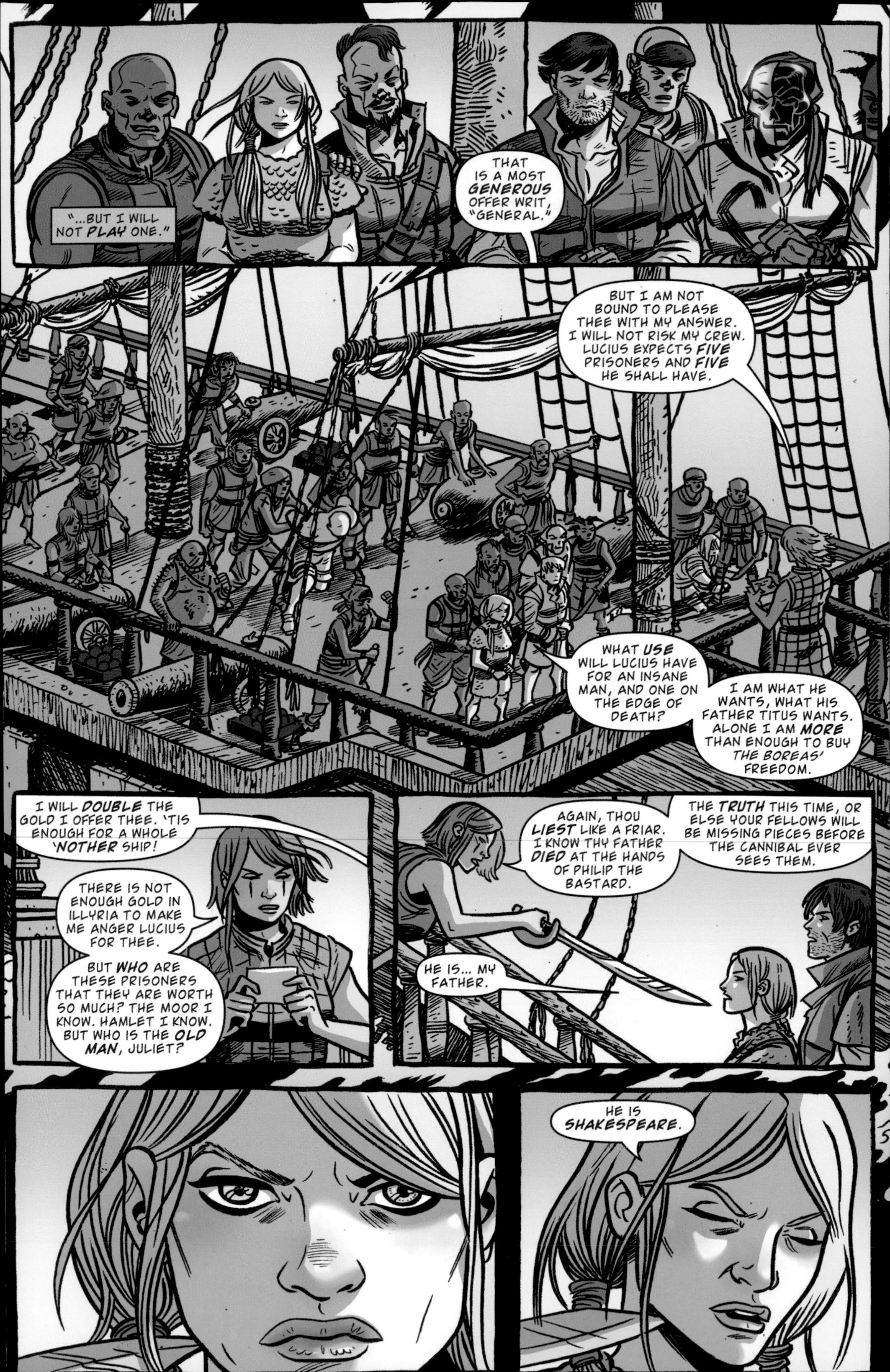

"...BUT I WILL NOT PLAY ONE."
THAT IS A MOST GENEROUS OFFER WRIT, "GENERAL."
BUT I AM NOT BOUND TO PLEASE THEE WITH MY ANSWER. I WILL NOT RISK MY CREW. LUCIUS EXPECTS FIVE PRISONERS AND FIVE HE SHALL HAVE.
WHAT USE WILL LUCIUS HAVE FOR AN INSANE MAN, AND ONE ON THE EDGE OF DEATH?
I AM WHAT HE WANTS, WHAT HIS FATHER TITUS WANTS. ALONE I AM MORE THAN ENOUGH TO BUY THE BOREAS' FREEDOM.
I WILL DOUBLE THE GOLD I OFFER THEE. 'TIS ENOUGH FOR A WHOLE 'NOTHER SHIP!
THERE IS NOT ENOUGH GOLD IN ILLYRIA TO MAKE ME ANGER LUCIUS FOR THEE.
BUT WHO ARE THESE PRISONERS THAT THEY ARE WORTH SO MUCH? THE MOOR I KNOW. HAMLET I KNOW. BUT WHO IS THE OLD MAN, JULIET?
AGAIN, THOU LIEST LIKE A FRIAR. I KNOW THY FATHER DIED AT THE HANDS OF PHILIP THE BASTARD.
THE TRUTH THIS TIME, OR ELSE YOUR FELLOWS WILL BE MISSING PIECES BEFORE THE CANNIBAL EVER SEES THEM.
HE IS... MY FATHER.
HE IS SHAKESPEARE.

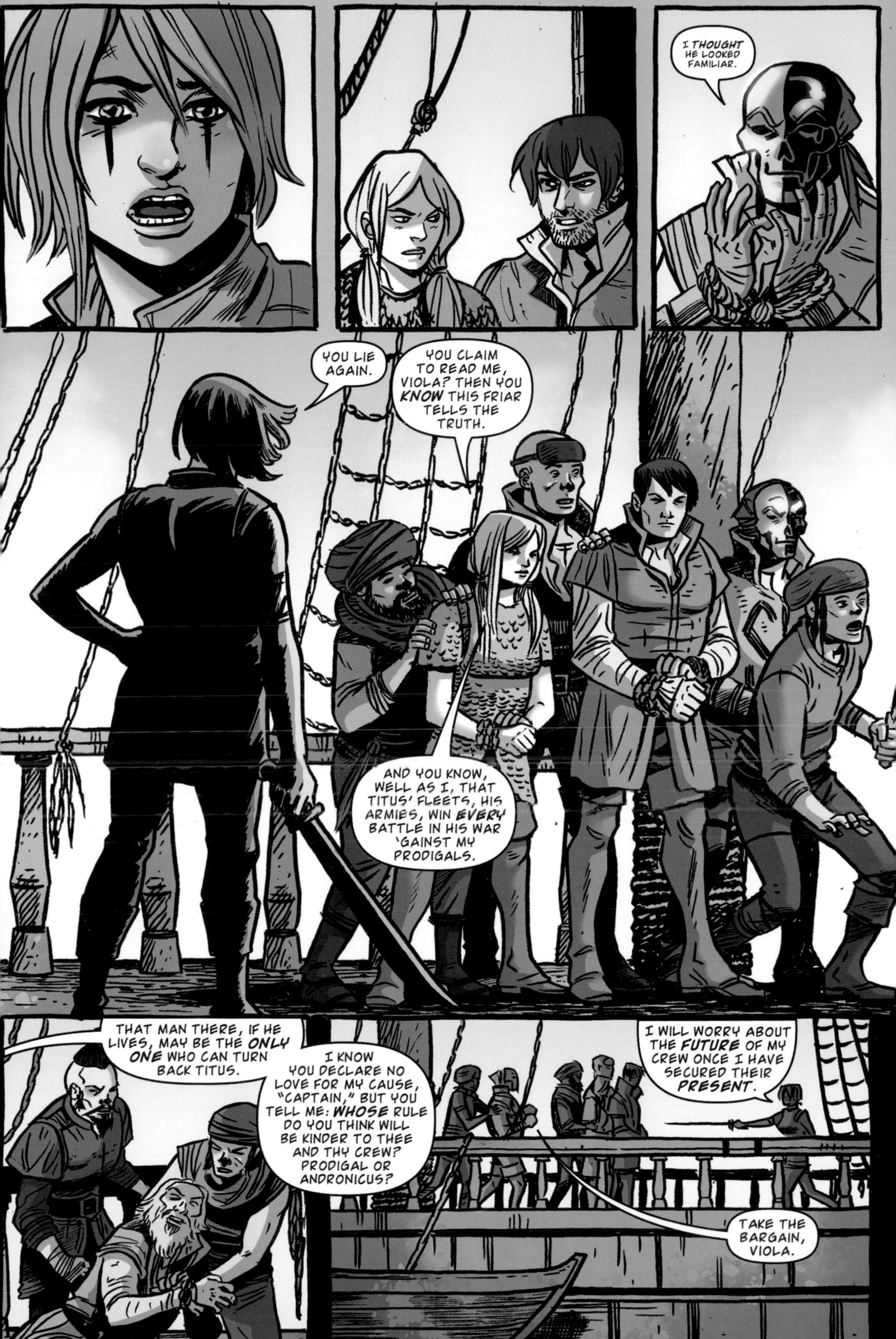
I THOUGHT HE LOOKED FAMILIAR.
YOU LIE AGAIN.
YOU CLAIM TO READ ME, VIOLA? THEN YOU KNOW THIS FRIAR TELLS THE TRUTH.
AND YOU KNOW, WELL AS I, THAT TITUS' FLEETS, HIS ARMIES, WIN EVERY BATTLE IN HIS WAR 'GAINST MY PRODIGALS.
THAT MAN THERE, IF HE LIVES, MAY BE THE ONLY ONE WHO CAN TURN BACK TITUS.
I KNOW YOU DECLARE NO LOVE FOR MY CAUSE, "CAPTAIN," BUT YOU TELL ME: WHOSE RULE DO YOU THINK WILL BE KINDER TO THEE AND THY CREW? PRODIGAL OR ANDRONICUS?
I WILL WORRY ABOUT THE FUTURE OF MY CREW ONCE I HAVE SECURED THEIR PRESENT.
TAKE THE BARGAIN, VIOLA.

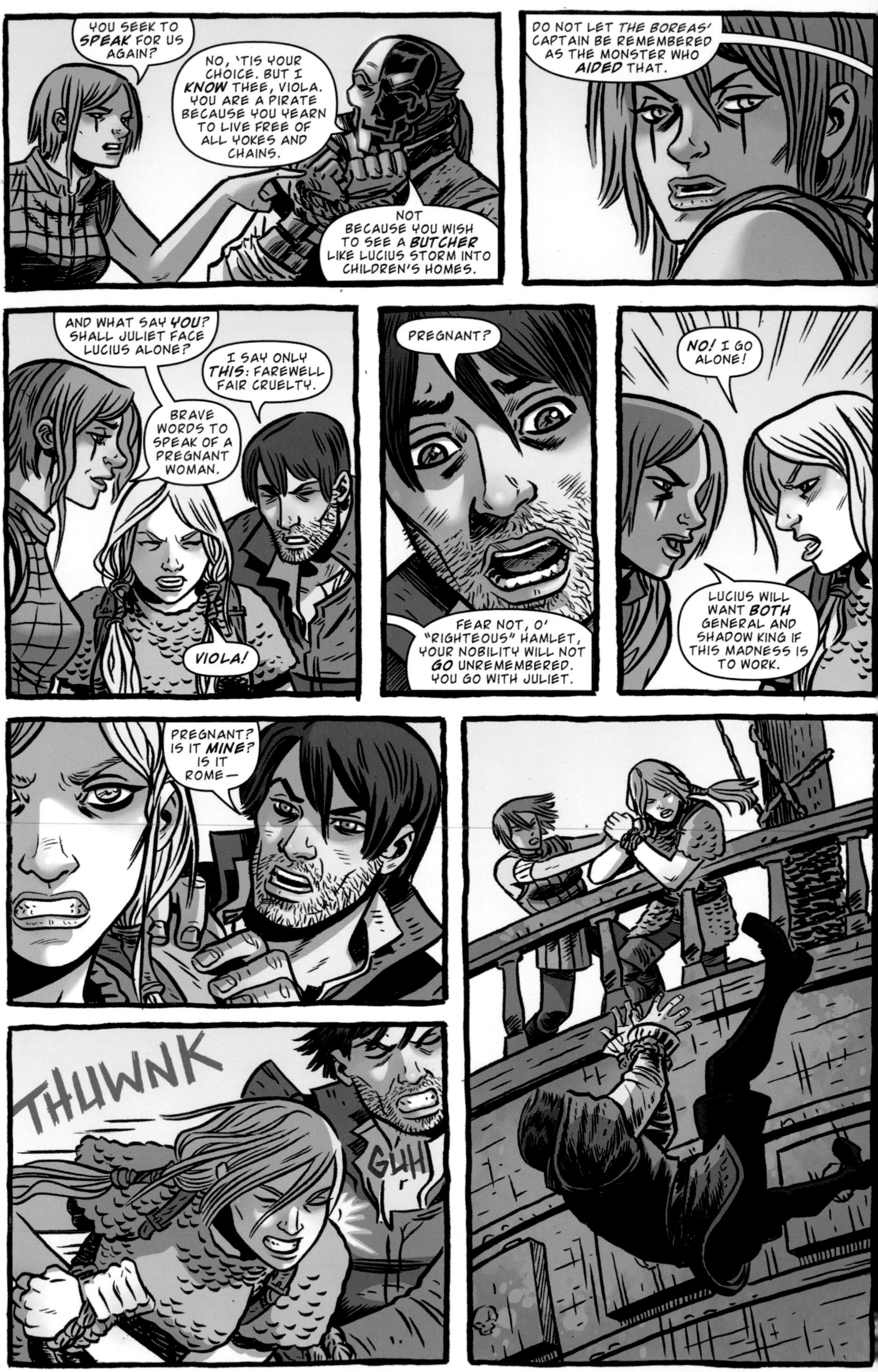
YOU SEEK TO SPEAK FOR US AGAIN?
NO, 'TIS YOUR CHOICE. BUT I KNOW THEE, VIOLA. YOU ARE A PIRATE BECAUSE YOU YEARN TO LIVE FREE OF ALL YOKES AND CHAINS.
NOT BECAUSE YOU WISH TO SEE A BUTCHER LIKE LUCIUS STORM INTO CHILDREN'S HOMES.
DO NOT LET THE BOREAS' CAPTAIN BE REMEMBERED AS THE MONSTER WHO AIDED THAT.
AND WHAT SAY YOU? SHALL JULIET FACE LUCIUS ALONE?
I SAY ONLY THIS: FAREWELL FAIR CRUELTY.
BRAVE WORDS TO SPEAK OF A PREGNANT WOMAN.
VIOLA!
PREGNANT?
FEAR NOT, O' "RIGHTEOUS" HAMLET, YOUR NOBILITY WILL NOT GO UNREMEMBERED. YOU GO WITH JULIET.
NO! I GO ALONE!
LUCIUS WILL WANT BOTH GENERAL AND SHADOW KING IF THIS MADNESS IS TO WORK.
PREGNANT? IS IT MINE? IS IT ROME—
THWNK
GUH

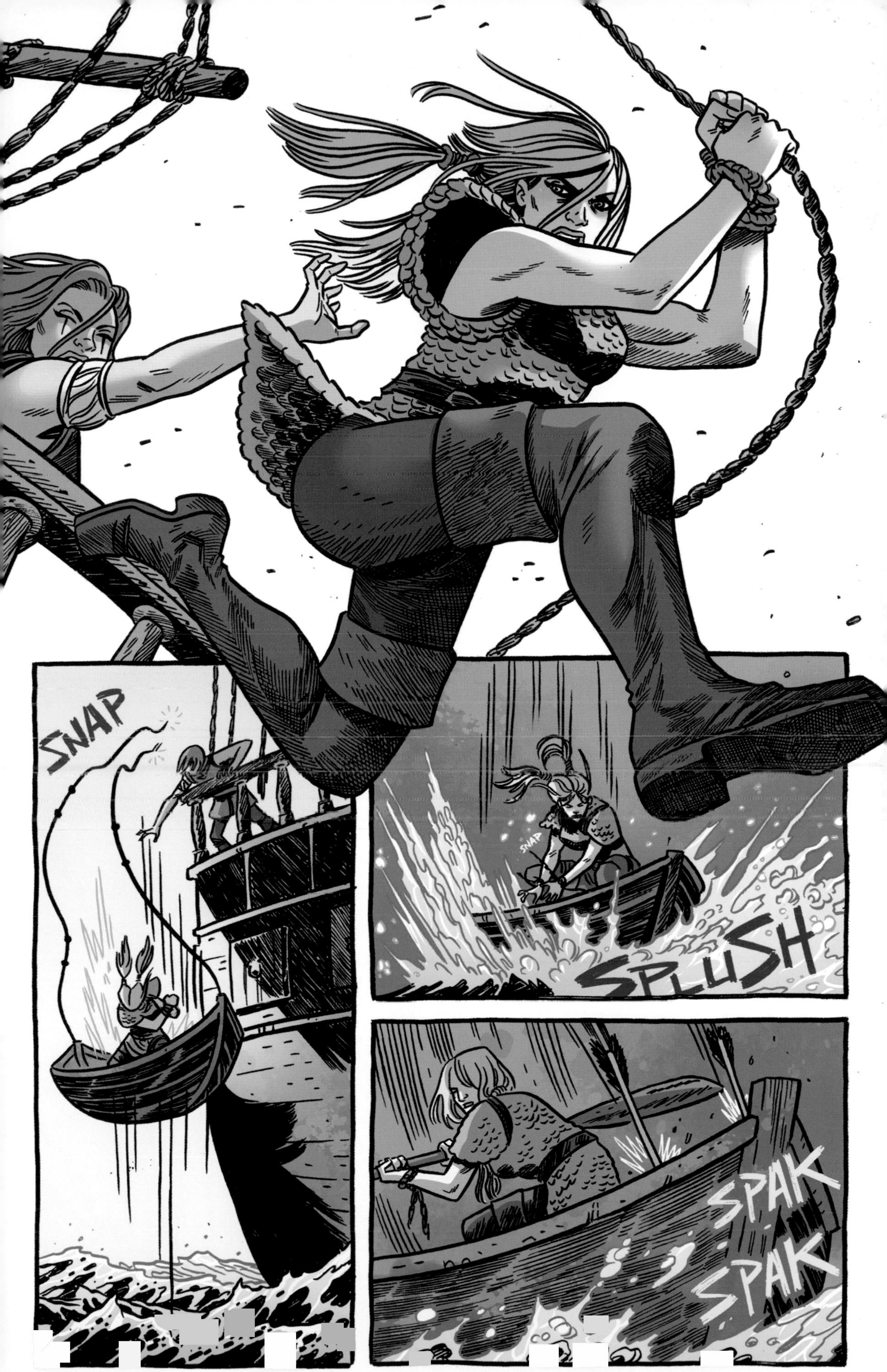
SNAP
SNAP
SPLUSH
SPAK
SPAK

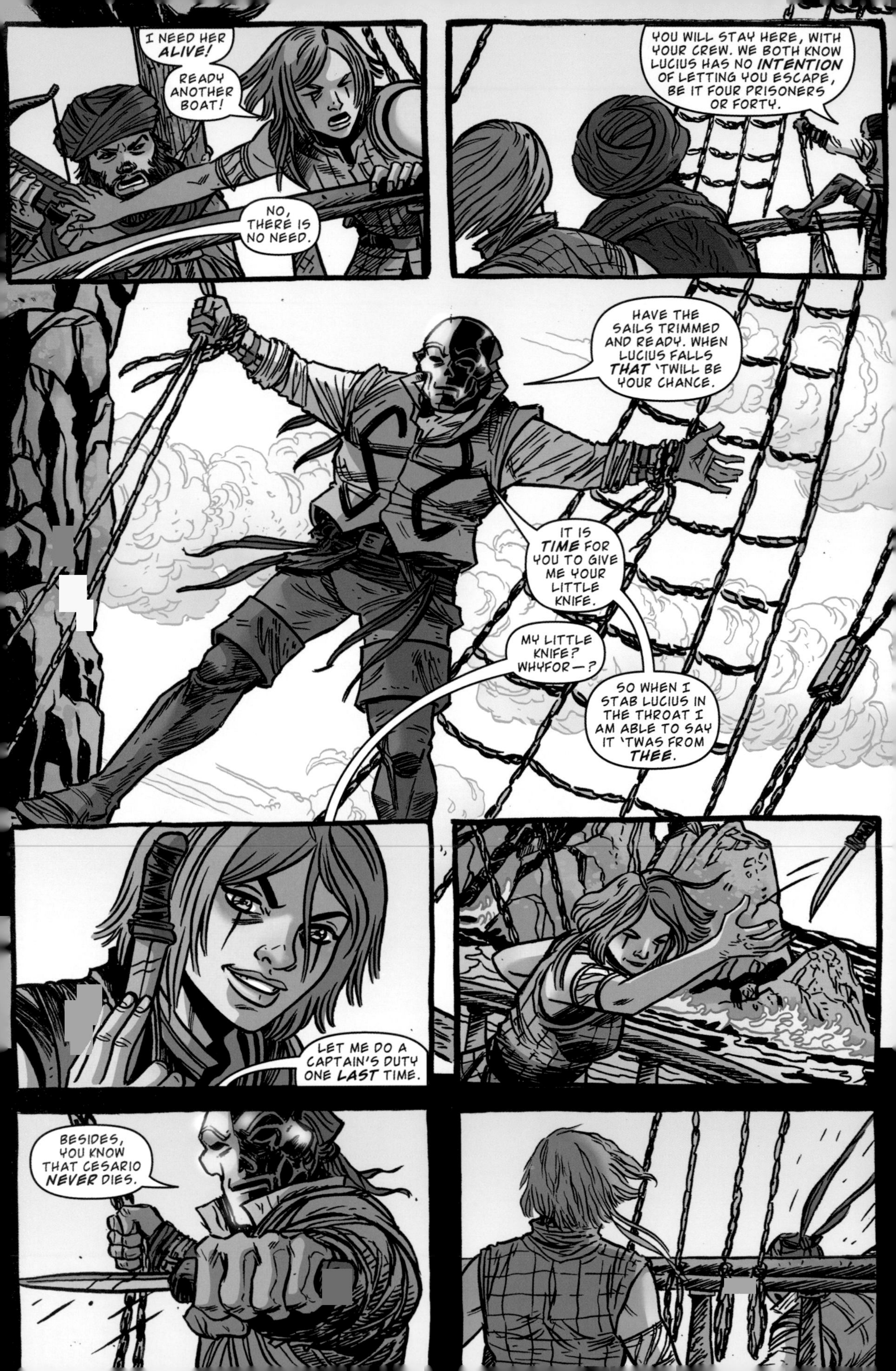
I NEED HER *ALIVE!*
READY ANOTHER BOAT!
NO, THERE IS NO NEED.
YOU WILL STAY HERE, WITH YOUR CREW. WE BOTH KNOW LUCIUS HAS NO *INTENTION* OF LETTING YOU ESCAPE, BE IT FOUR PRISONERS OR FORTY.
HAVE THE SAILS TRIMMED AND READY. WHEN LUCIUS FALLS *THAT* 'TWILL BE YOUR CHANCE.
IT IS *TIME* FOR YOU TO GIVE ME YOUR LITTLE KNIFE.
MY LITTLE KNIFE? WHYFOR—?
SO WHEN I STAB LUCIUS IN THE THROAT I AM ABLE TO SAY IT 'TWAS FROM *THEE*.
LET ME DO A CAPTAIN'S DUTY ONE *LAST* TIME.
BESIDES, YOU KNOW THAT CESARIO *NEVER* DIES.

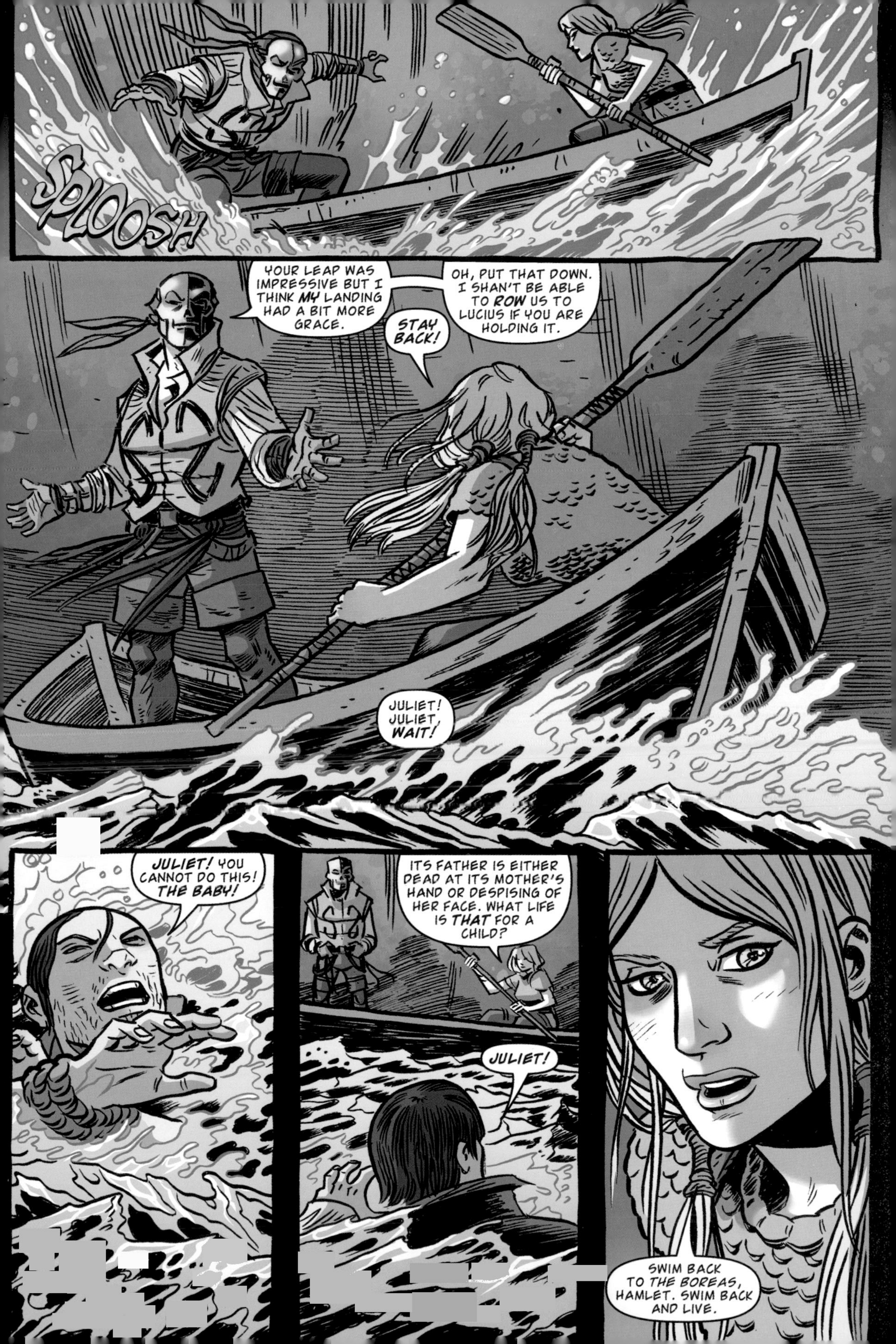
SPLOOSH
YOUR LEAP WAS IMPRESSIVE BUT I THINK MY LANDING HAD A BIT MORE GRACE.
STAY BACK!
OH, PUT THAT DOWN. I SHAN'T BE ABLE TO ROW US TO LUCIUS IF YOU ARE HOLDING IT.
JULIET! JULIET, WAIT!
JULIET! YOU CANNOT DO THIS! THE BABY!
ITS FATHER IS EITHER DEAD AT ITS MOTHER'S HAND OR DESPISING OF HER FACE. WHAT LIFE IS THAT FOR A CHILD?
JULIET!
SWIM BACK TO THE BOREAS, HAMLET. SWIM BACK AND LIVE.

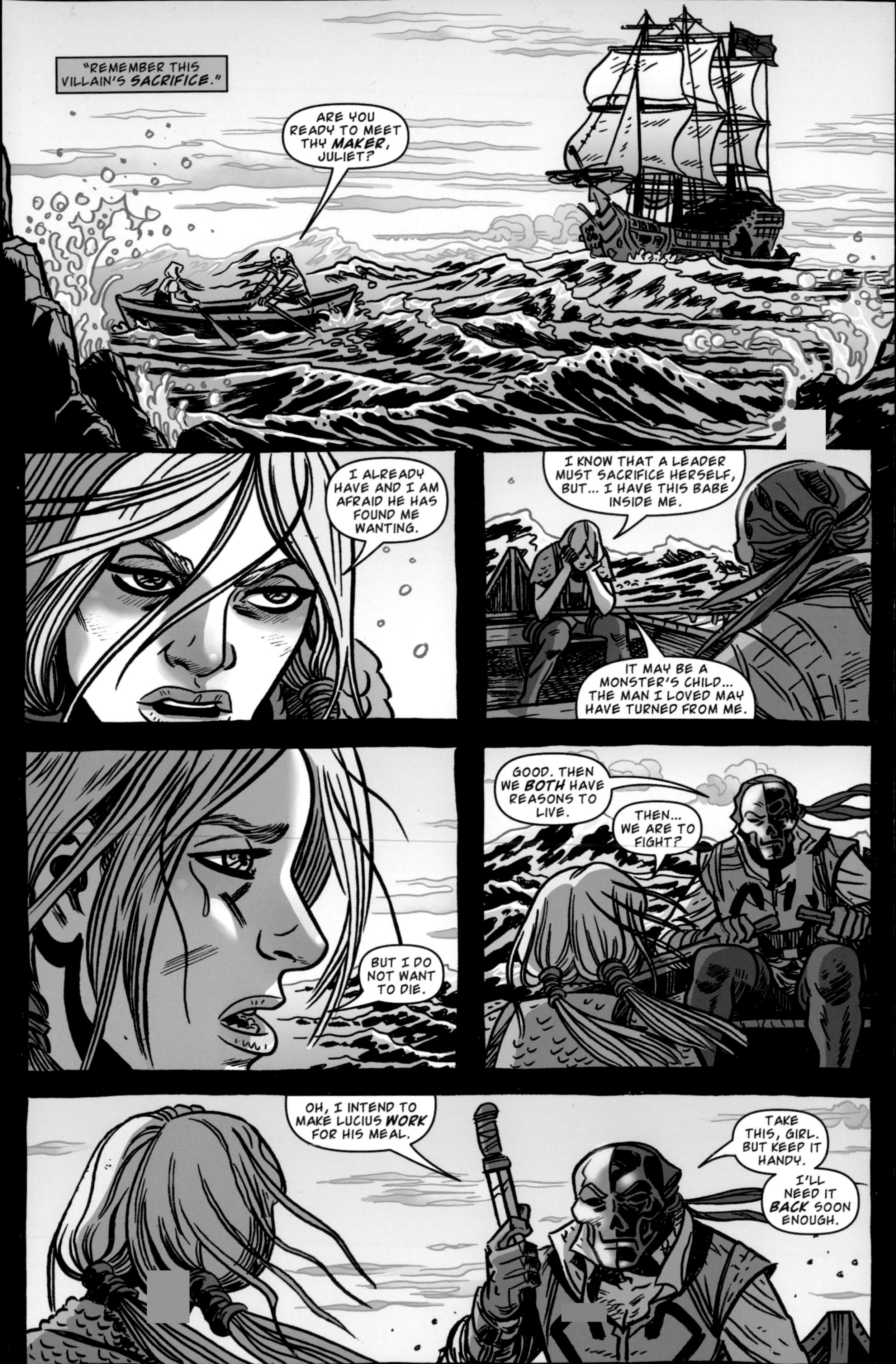

"REMEMBER THIS VILLAIN'S SACRIFICE."
ARE YOU READY TO MEET THY MAKER, JULIET?
I ALREADY HAVE AND I AM AFRAID HE HAS FOUND ME WANTING.
I KNOW THAT A LEADER MUST SACRIFICE HERSELF, BUT... I HAVE THIS BABE INSIDE ME.
IT MAY BE A MONSTER'S CHILD... THE MAN I LOVED MAY HAVE TURNED FROM ME.
BUT I DO NOT WANT TO DIE.
GOOD. THEN WE BOTH HAVE REASONS TO LIVE.
THEN... WE ARE TO FIGHT?
OH, I INTEND TO MAKE LUCIUS WORK FOR HIS MEAL.
TAKE THIS, GIRL. BUT KEEP IT HANDY.
I'LL NEED IT BACK SOON ENOUGH.

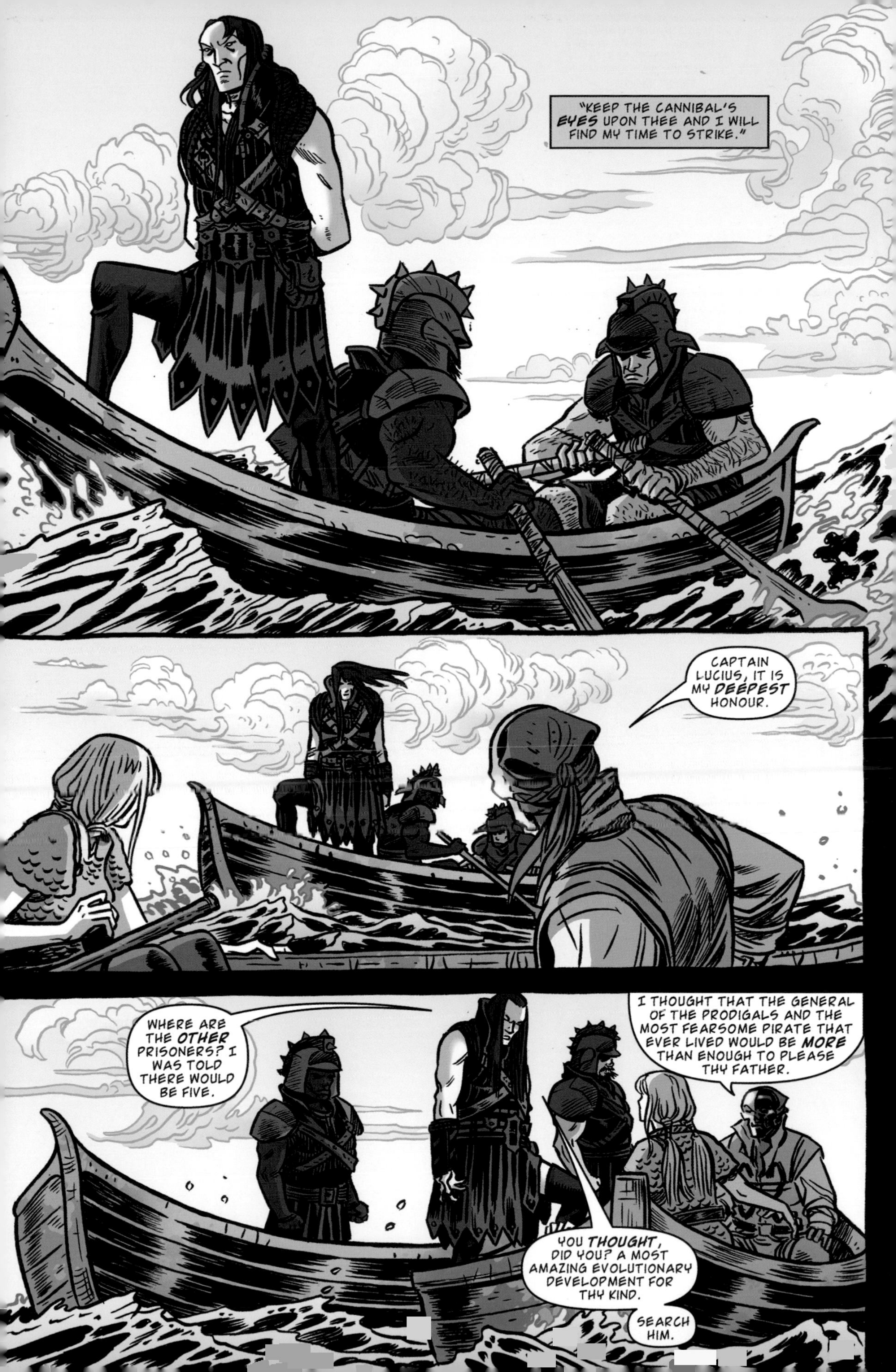

"KEEP THE CANNIBAL'S EYES UPON THEE AND I WILL FIND MY TIME TO STRIKE."
CAPTAIN LUCIUS, IT IS MY DEEPEST HONOUR.
WHERE ARE THE OTHER PRISONERS? I WAS TOLD THERE WOULD BE FIVE.
I THOUGHT THAT THE GENERAL OF THE PRODIGALS AND THE MOST FEARSOME PIRATE THAT EVER LIVED WOULD BE MORE THAN ENOUGH TO PLEASE THY FATHER.
YOU THOUGHT, DID YOU? A MOST AMAZING EVOLUTIONARY DEVELOPMENT FOR THY KIND.
SEARCH HIM.

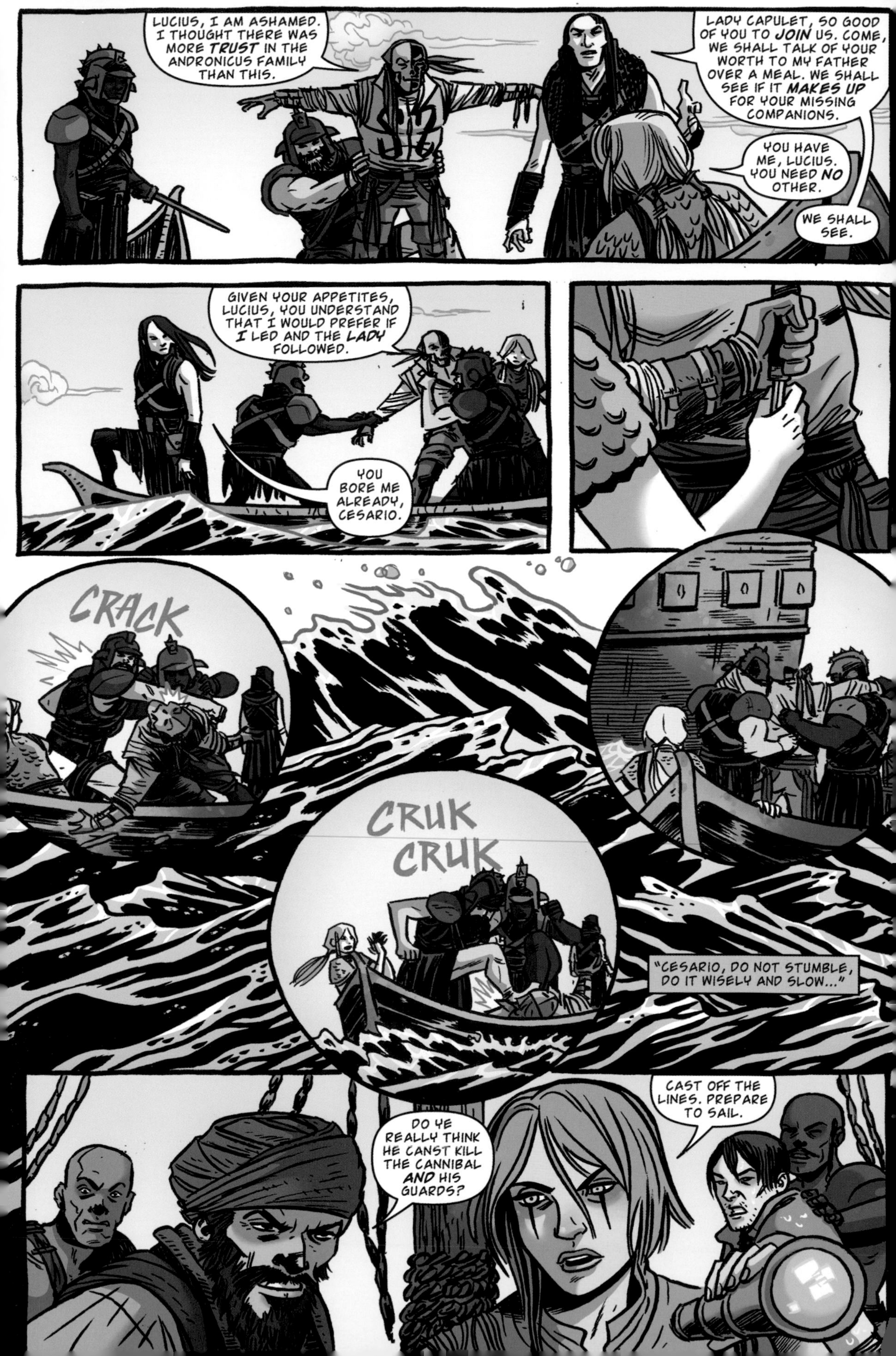

LUCIUS, I AM ASHAMED. I THOUGHT THERE WAS MORE TRUST IN THE ANDRONICUS FAMILY THAN THIS.
LADY CAPULET, SO GOOD OF YOU TO JOIN US. COME, WE SHALL TALK OF YOUR WORTH TO MY FATHER OVER A MEAL. WE SHALL SEE IF IT MAKES UP FOR YOUR MISSING COMPANIONS.
YOU HAVE ME, LUCIUS. YOU NEED NO OTHER.
WE SHALL SEE.
GIVEN YOUR APPETITES, LUCIUS, YOU UNDERSTAND THAT I WOULD PREFER IF I LED AND THE LADY FOLLOWED.
YOU BORE ME ALREADY, CESARIO.
CRACK
CRUK CRUK
"CESARIO, DO NOT STUMBLE, DO IT WISELY AND SLOW..."
CAST OFF THE LINES. PREPARE TO SAIL.
DO YE REALLY THINK HE CANST KILL THE CANNIBAL AND HIS GUARDS?

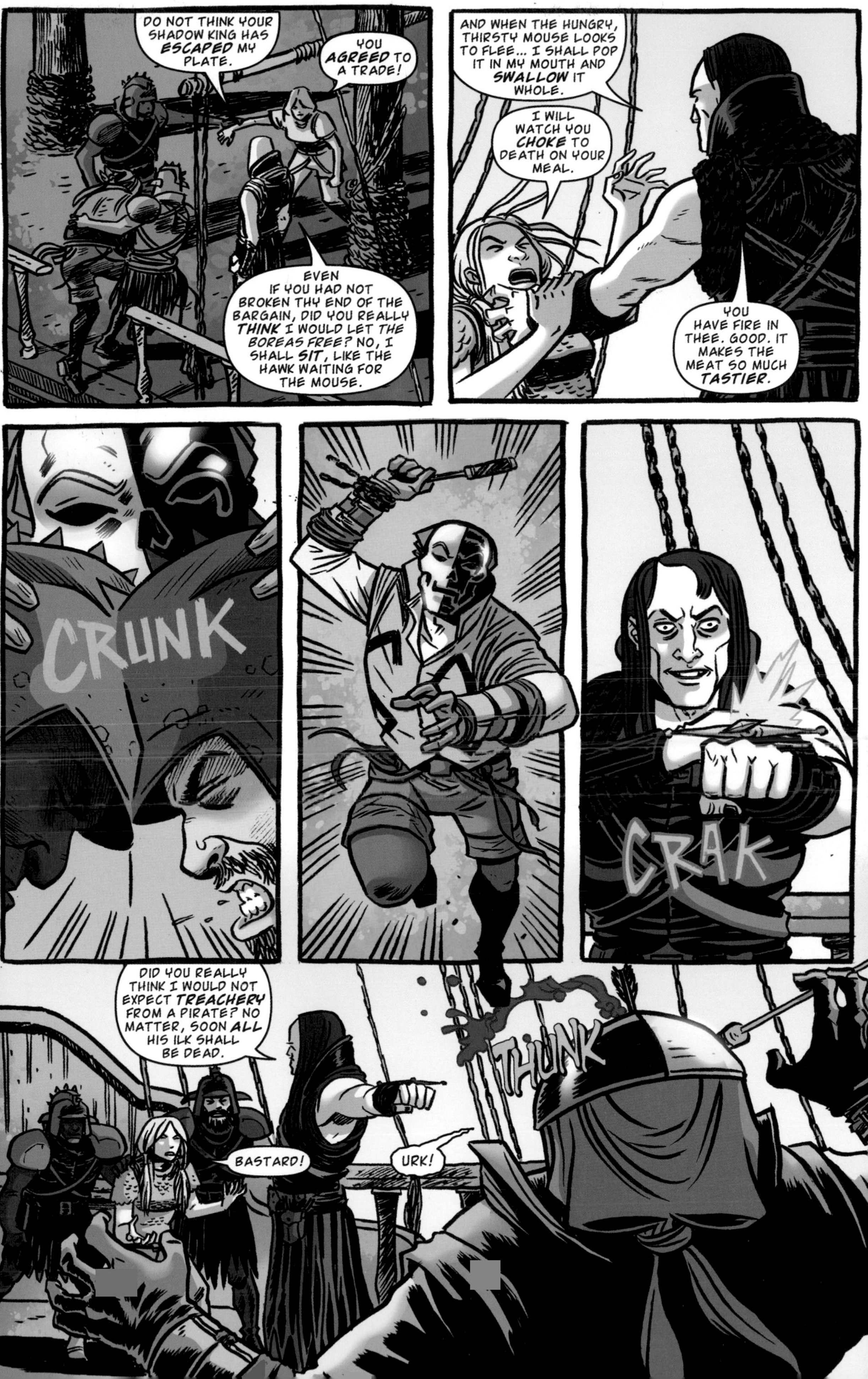
DO NOT THINK YOUR SHADOW KING HAS ESCAPED MY PLATE.
YOU AGREED TO A TRADE!
EVEN IF YOU HAD NOT BROKEN THY END OF THE BARGAIN, DID YOU REALLY THINK I WOULD LET THE BOREAS FREE? NO, I SHALL SIT, LIKE THE HAWK WAITING FOR THE MOUSE.
AND WHEN THE HUNGRY, THIRSTY MOUSE LOOKS TO FLEE... I SHALL POP IT IN MY MOUTH AND SWALLOW IT WHOLE.
I WILL WATCH YOU CHOKE TO DEATH ON YOUR MEAL.
YOU HAVE FIRE IN THEE. GOOD. IT MAKES THE MEAT SO MUCH TASTIER.
CRUNK
CRAK
DID YOU REALLY THINK I WOULD NOT EXPECT TREACHERY FROM A PIRATE? NO MATTER, SOON ALL HIS ILK SHALL BE DEAD.
THUNK
BASTARD!
URK!

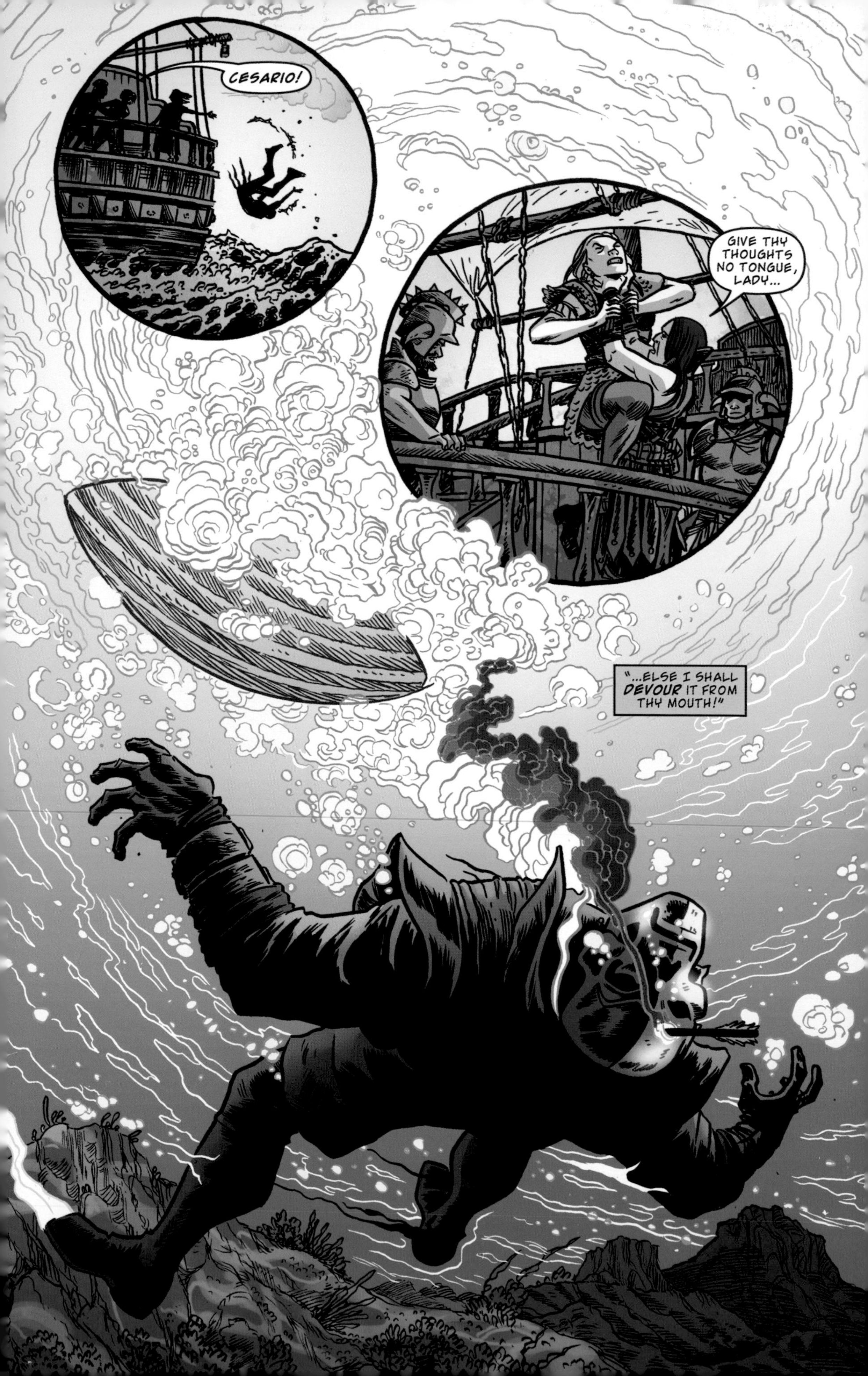
CESARIO!
GIVE THY THOUGHTS NO TONGUE, LADY...
"...ELSE I SHALL DEVOUR IT FROM THY MOUTH!"

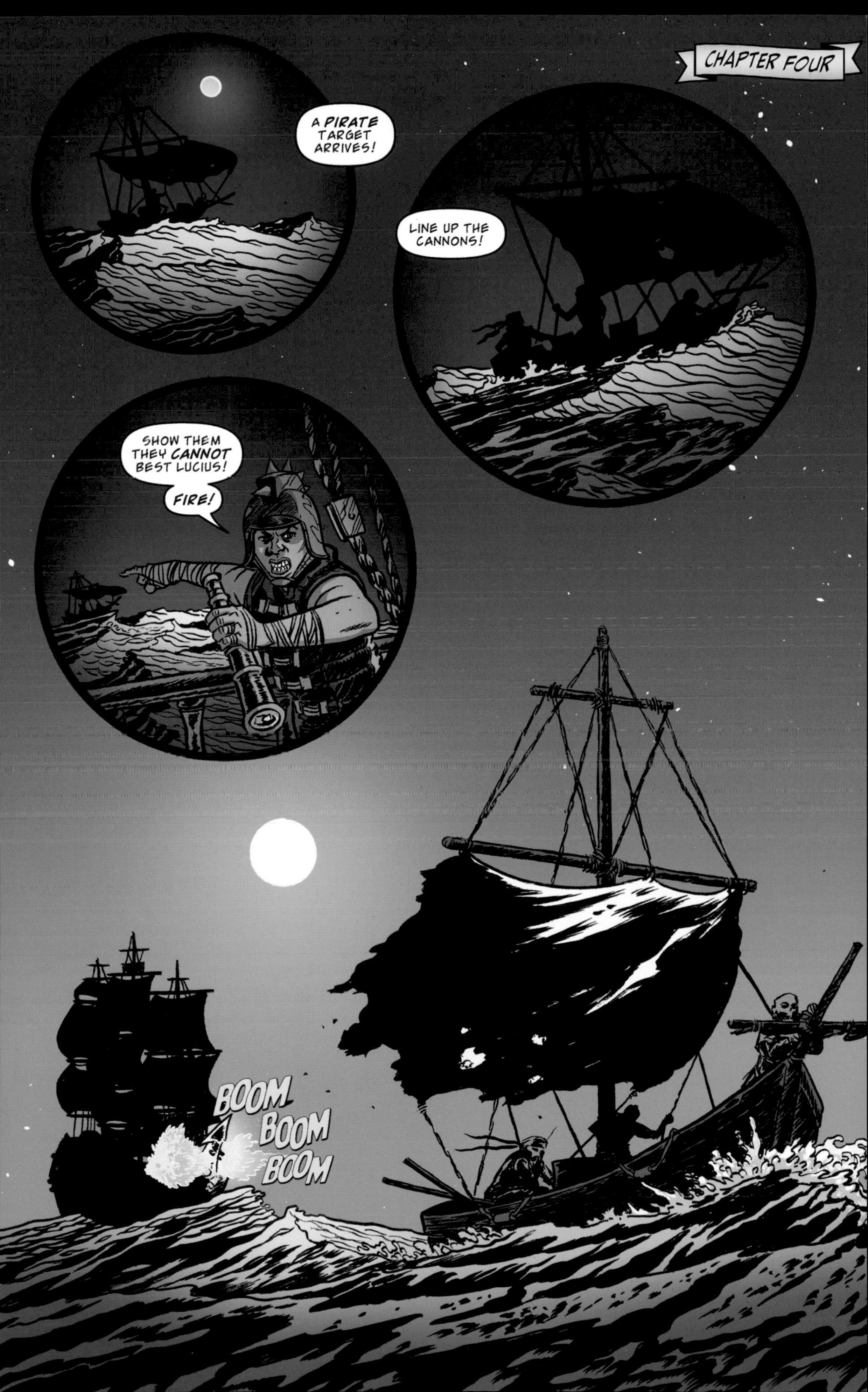
CHAPTER FOUR
A PIRATE TARGET ARRIVES!
LINE UP THE CANNONS!
SHOW THEM THEY CANNOT BEST LUCIUS!
FIRE!
BOOM
BOOM
BOOM

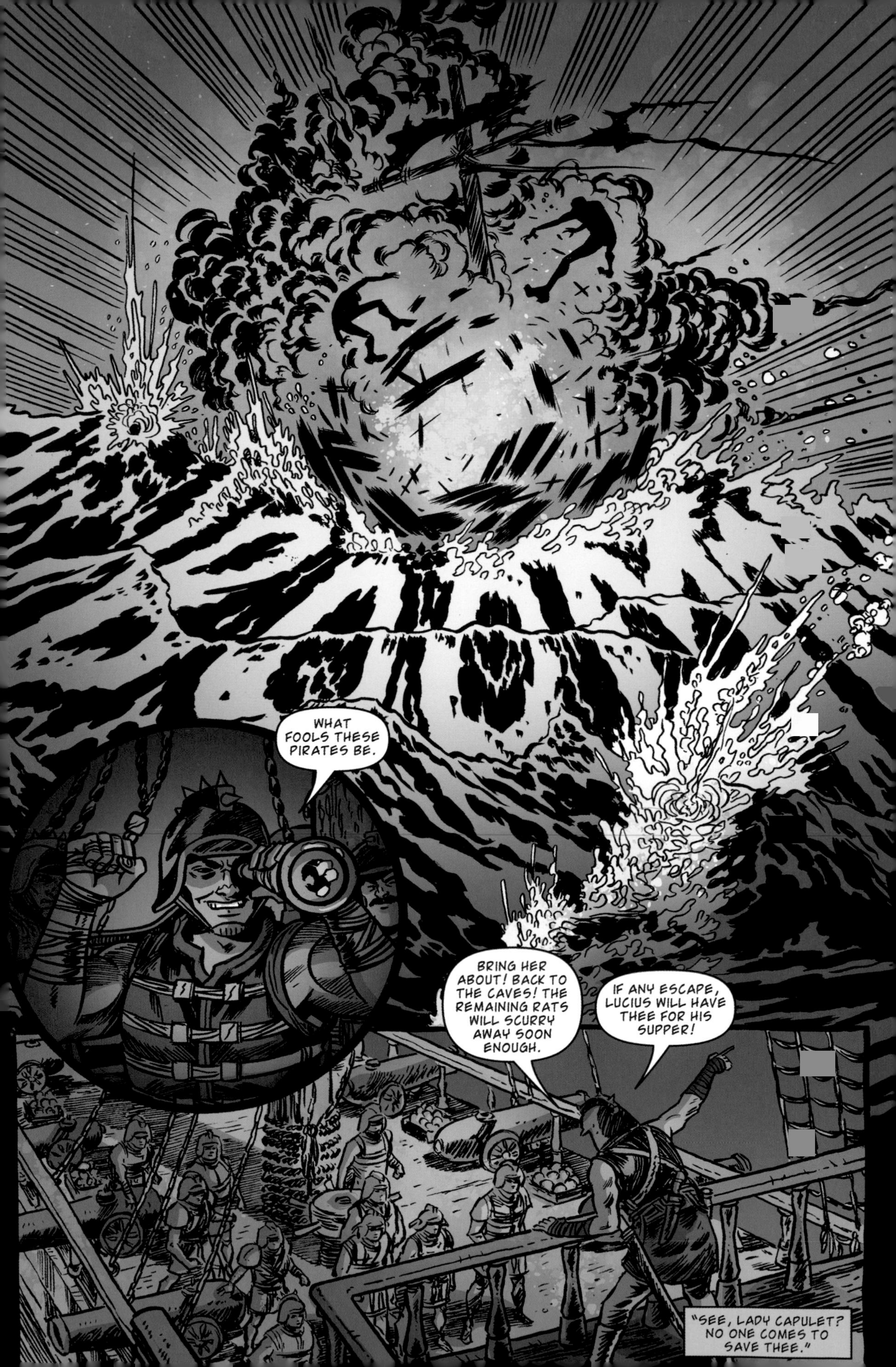
WHAT FOOLS THESE PIRATES BE.
BRING HER ABOUT! BACK TO THE CAVES! THE REMAINING RATS WILL SCURRY AWAY SOON ENOUGH.
IF ANY ESCAPE, LUCIUS WILL HAVE THEE FOR HIS SUPPER!
"SEE, LADY CAPULET? NO ONE COMES TO SAVE THEE."

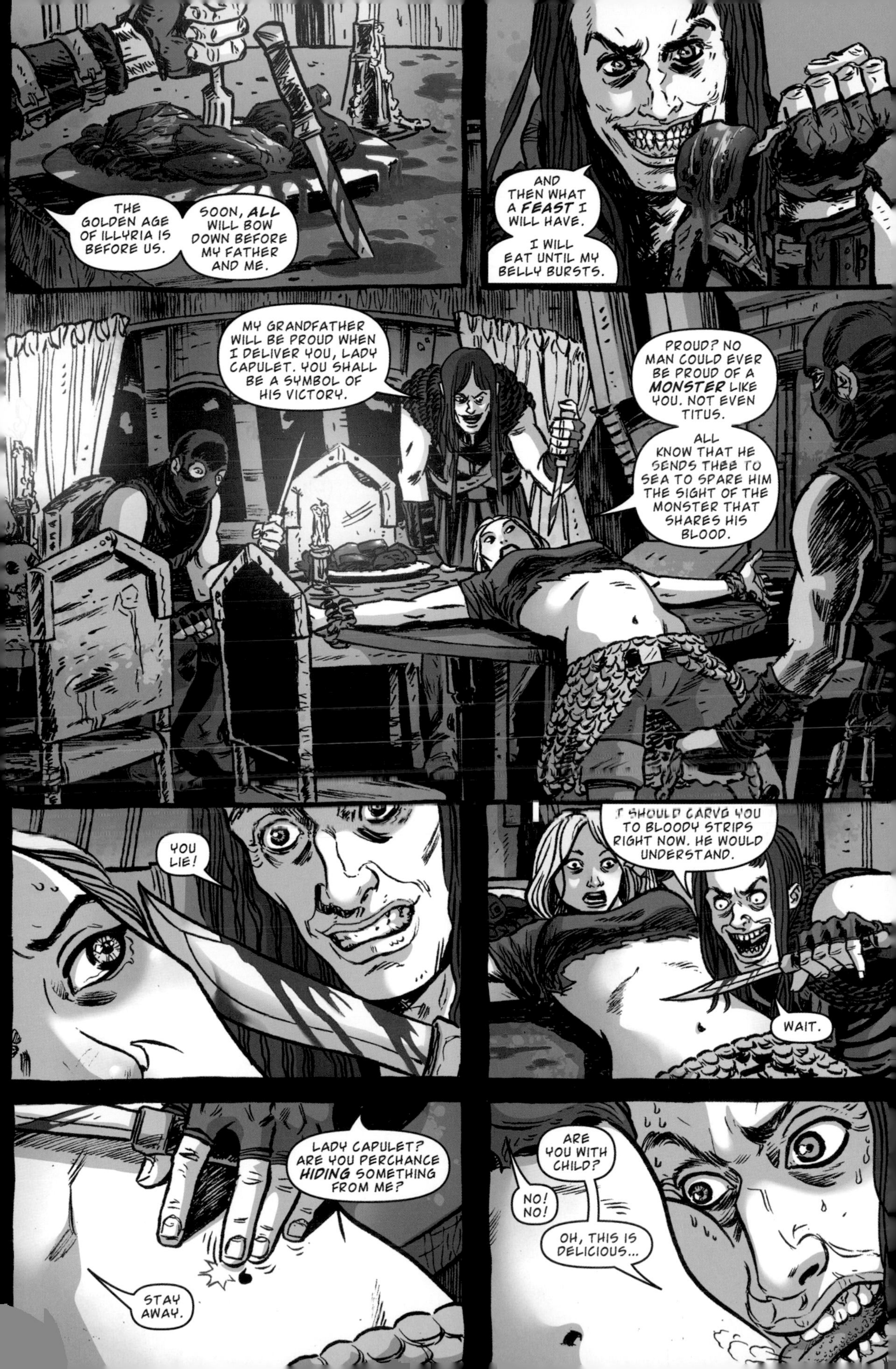
THE GOLDEN AGE OF ILLYRIA IS BEFORE US.
SOON, ALL WILL BOW DOWN BEFORE MY FATHER AND ME.
AND THEN WHAT A FEAST I WILL HAVE.
I WILL EAT UNTIL MY BELLY BURSTS.
MY GRANDFATHER WILL BE PROUD WHEN I DELIVER YOU, LADY CAPULET. YOU SHALL BE A SYMBOL OF HIS VICTORY.
PROUD? NO MAN COULD EVER BE PROUD OF A MONSTER LIKE YOU. NOT EVEN TITUS.
ALL KNOW THAT HE SENDS THEE TO SEA TO SPARE HIM THE SIGHT OF THE MONSTER THAT SHARES HIS BLOOD.
YOU LIE!
I SHOULD CARVE YOU TO BLOODY STRIPS RIGHT NOW. HE WOULD UNDERSTAND.
WAIT.
LADY CAPULET? ARE YOU PERCHANCE HIDING SOMETHING FROM ME?
STAY AWAY.
ARE YOU WITH CHILD?
NO! NO!
OH, THIS IS DELICIOUS...

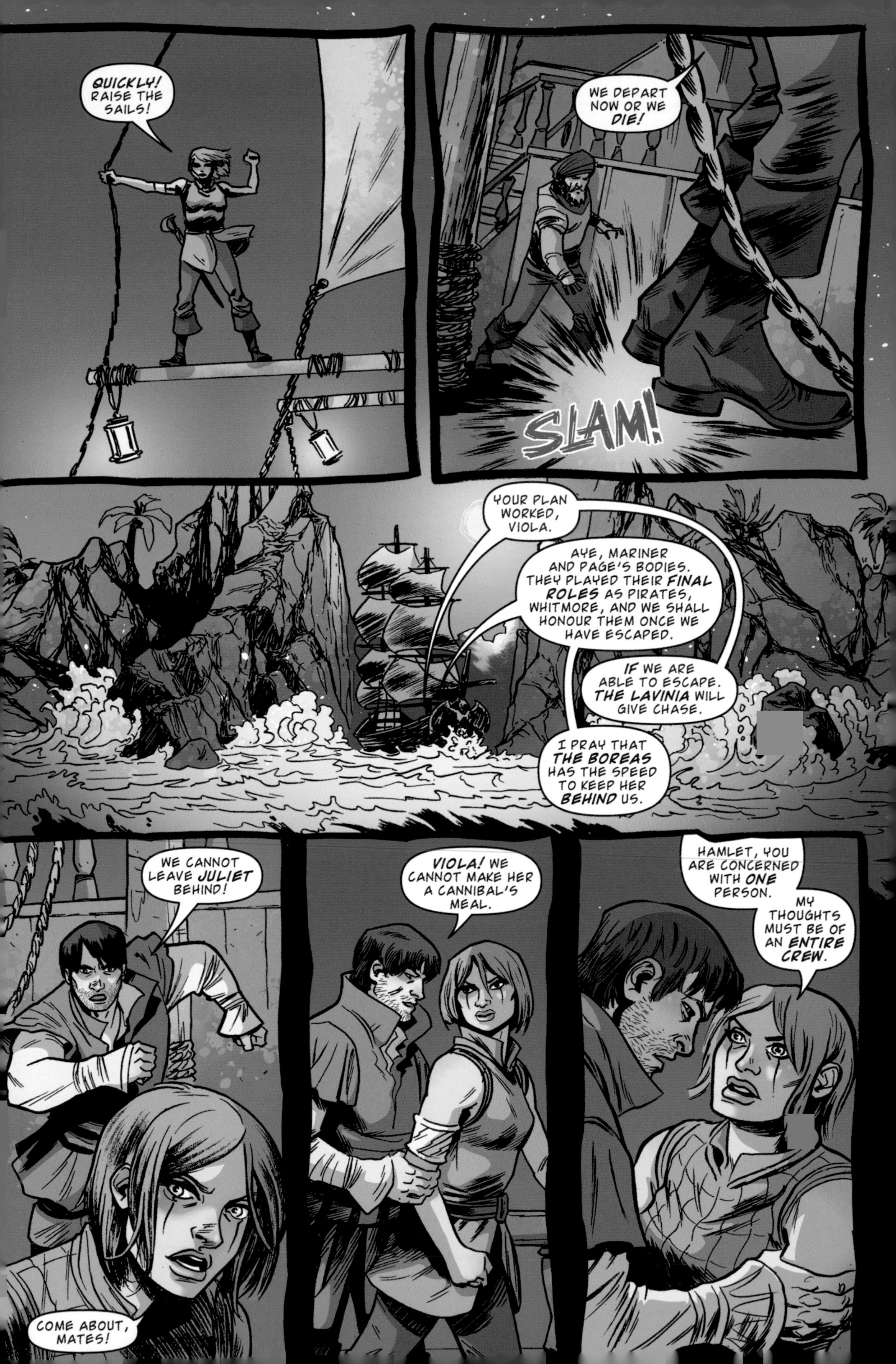
QUICKLY! RAISE THE SAILS!
WE DEPART NOW OR WE DIE!
SLAM!
YOUR PLAN WORKED, VIOLA.
AYE, MARINER AND PAGE'S BODIES. THEY PLAYED THEIR FINAL ROLES AS PIRATES, WHITMORE, AND WE SHALL HONOUR THEM ONCE WE HAVE ESCAPED.
IF WE ARE ABLE TO ESCAPE. THE LAVINIA WILL GIVE CHASE.
I PRAY THAT THE BOREAS HAS THE SPEED TO KEEP HER BEHIND US.
WE CANNOT LEAVE JULIET BEHIND!
COME ABOUT, MATES!
VIOLA! WE CANNOT MAKE HER A CANNIBAL'S MEAL.
HAMLET, YOU ARE CONCERNED WITH ONE PERSON.
MY THOUGHTS MUST BE OF AN ENTIRE CREW.

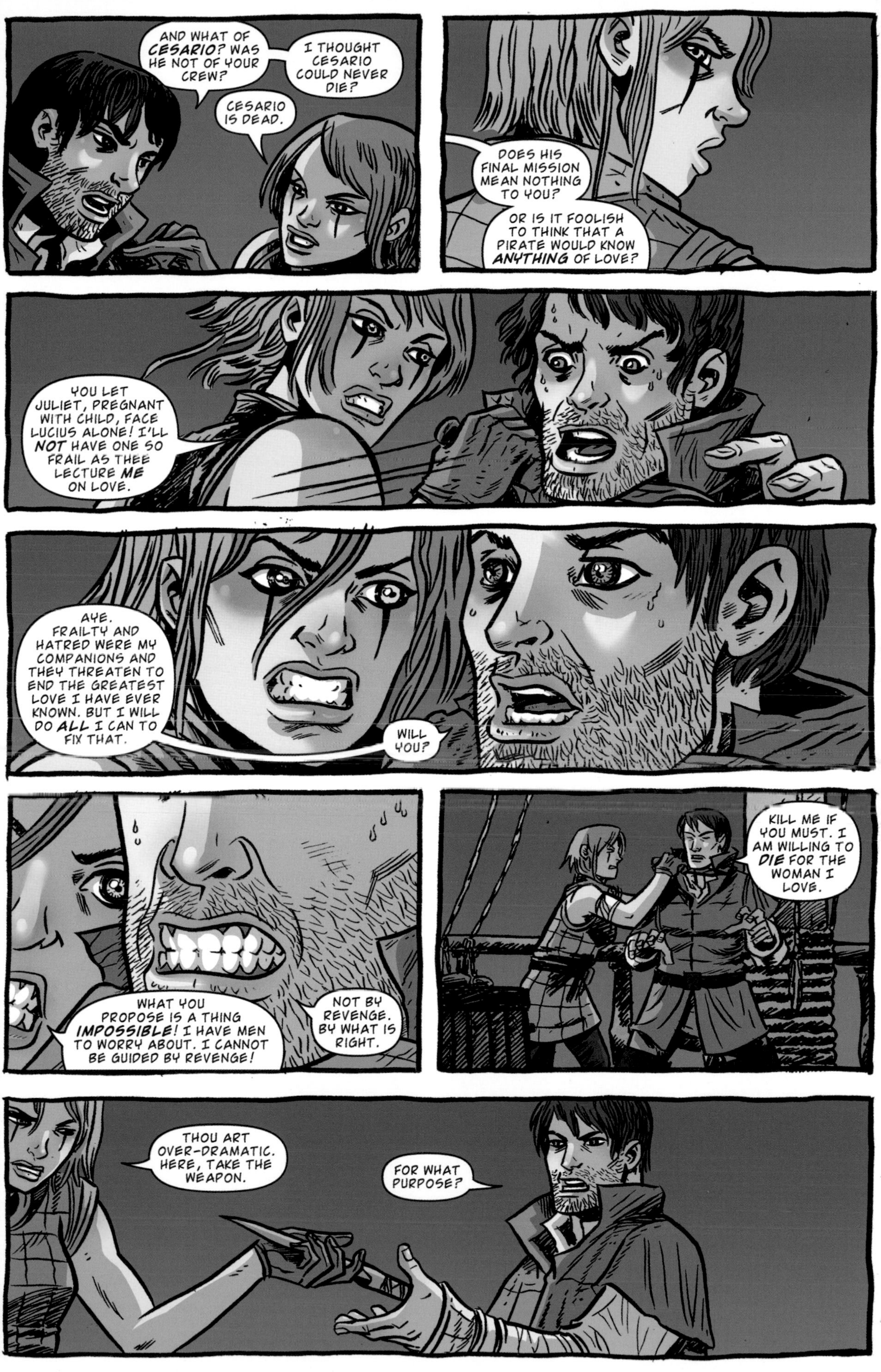
AND WHAT OF CESARIO? WAS HE NOT OF YOUR CREW?
I THOUGHT CESARIO COULD NEVER DIE?
CESARIO IS DEAD.
DOES HIS FINAL MISSION MEAN NOTHING TO YOU?
OR IS IT FOOLISH TO THINK THAT A PIRATE WOULD KNOW ANYTHING OF LOVE?
YOU LET JULIET, PREGNANT WITH CHILD, FACE LUCIUS ALONE! I'LL NOT HAVE ONE SO FRAIL AS THEE LECTURE ME ON LOVE.
AYE. FRAILTY AND HATRED WERE MY COMPANIONS AND THEY THREATEN TO END THE GREATEST LOVE I HAVE EVER KNOWN. BUT I WILL DO ALL I CAN TO FIX THAT.
WILL YOU?
WHAT YOU PROPOSE IS A THING IMPOSSIBLE! I HAVE MEN TO WORRY ABOUT. I CANNOT BE GUIDED BY REVENGE!
NOT BY REVENGE. BY WHAT IS RIGHT.
KILL ME IF YOU MUST. I AM WILLING TO DIE FOR THE WOMAN I LOVE.
THOU ART OVER-DRAMATIC. HERE, TAKE THE WEAPON.
FOR WHAT PURPOSE?

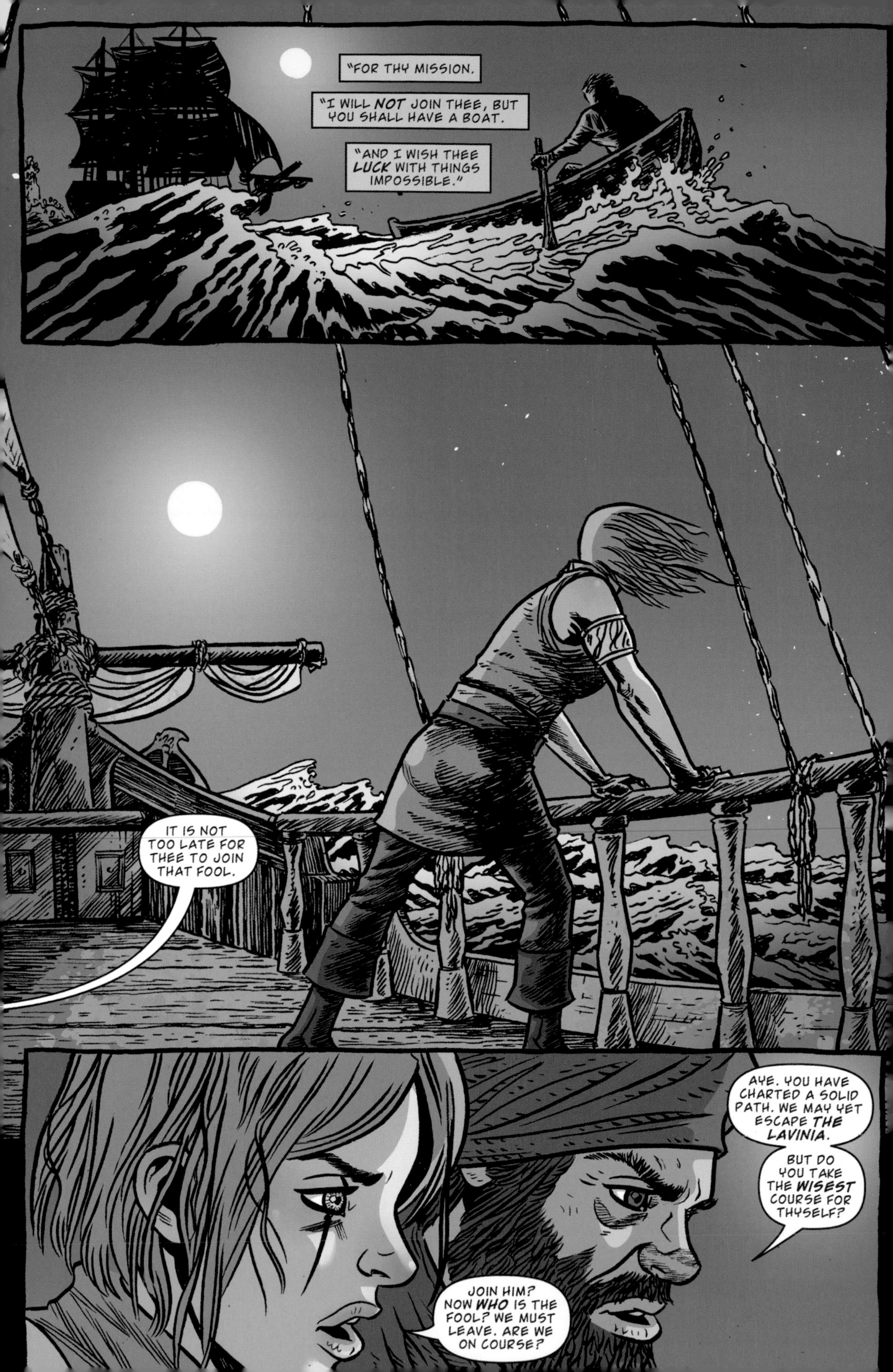
"FOR THY MISSION.
"I WILL NOT JOIN THEE, BUT YOU SHALL HAVE A BOAT.
"AND I WISH THEE LUCK WITH THINGS IMPOSSIBLE."
IT IS NOT TOO LATE FOR THEE TO JOIN THAT FOOL.
JOIN HIM? NOW WHO IS THE FOOL? WE MUST LEAVE. ARE WE ON COURSE?
AYE. YOU HAVE CHARTED A SOLID PATH. WE MAY YET ESCAPE THE LAVINIA.
BUT DO YOU TAKE THE WISEST COURSE FOR THYSELF?

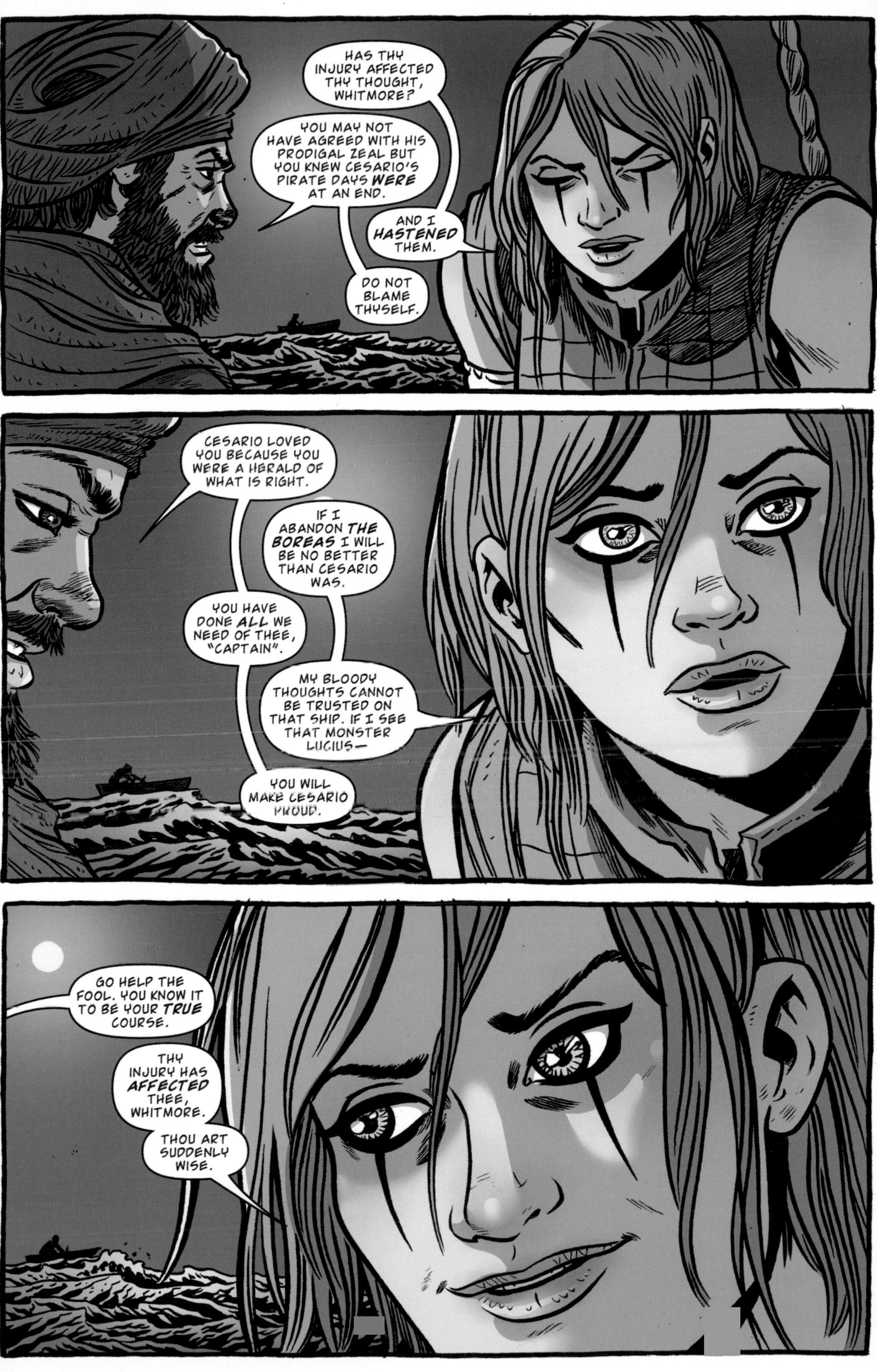
HAS THY INJURY AFFECTED THY THOUGHT, WHITMORE?
YOU MAY NOT HAVE AGREED WITH HIS PRODIGAL ZEAL BUT YOU KNEW CESARIO'S PIRATE DAYS *WERE* AT AN END.
AND I *HASTENED* THEM.
DO NOT BLAME THYSELF.
CESARIO LOVED YOU BECAUSE YOU WERE A HERALD OF WHAT IS RIGHT.
IF I ABANDON *THE BOREAS* I WILL BE NO BETTER THAN CESARIO WAS.
YOU HAVE DONE *ALL* WE NEED OF THEE, "CAPTAIN".
MY BLOODY THOUGHTS CANNOT BE TRUSTED ON THAT SHIP. IF I SEE THAT MONSTER LUCIUS—
YOU WILL MAKE CESARIO PROUD.
GO HELP THE FOOL. YOU KNOW IT TO BE YOUR *TRUE* COURSE.
THY INJURY HAS *AFFECTED* THEE, WHITMORE.
THOU ART SUDDENLY WISE.

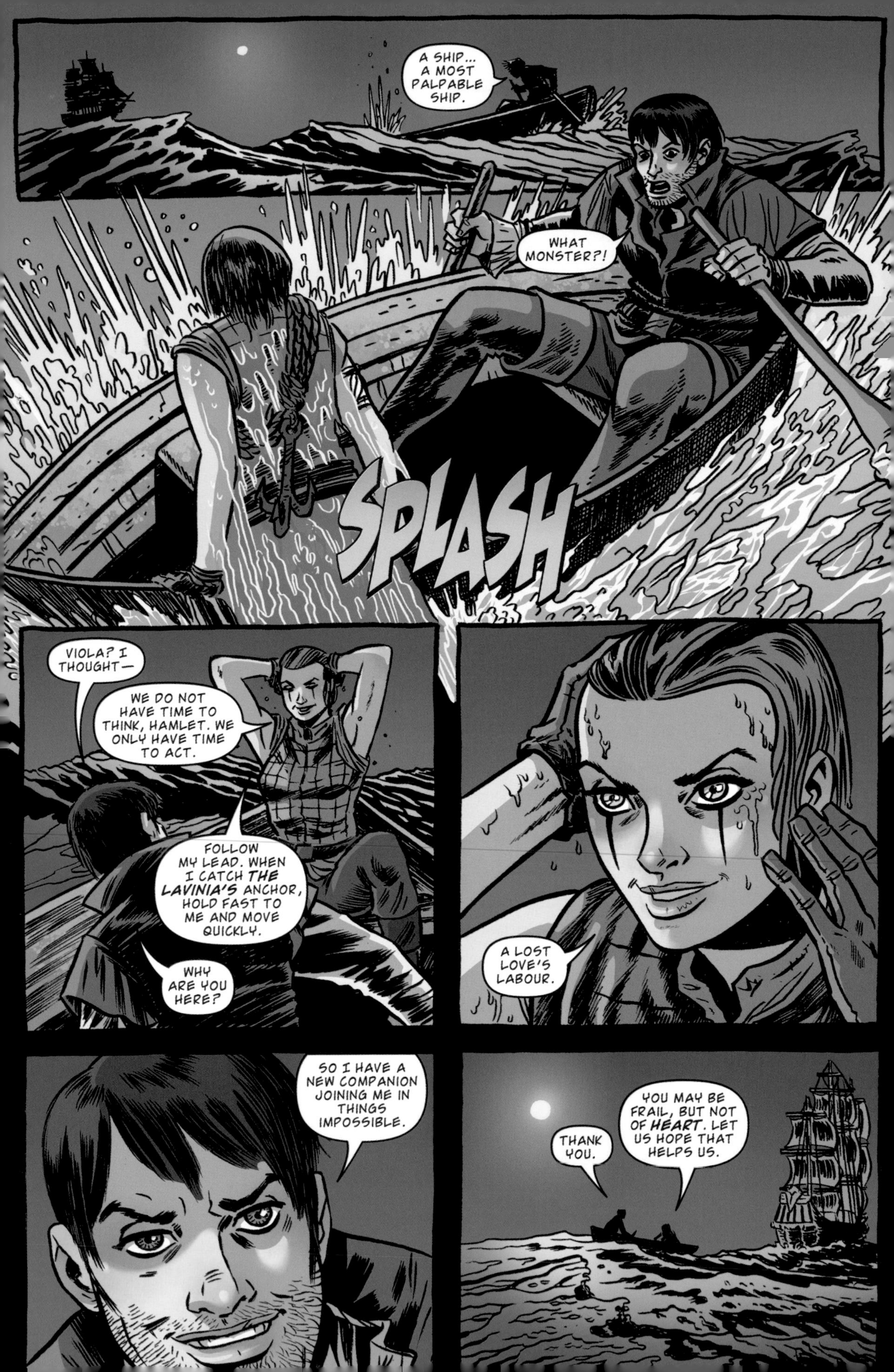
A SHIP... A MOST PALPABLE SHIP.
WHAT MONSTER?!
SPLASH
VIOLA? I THOUGHT—
WE DO NOT HAVE TIME TO THINK, HAMLET. WE ONLY HAVE TIME TO ACT.
FOLLOW MY LEAD. WHEN I CATCH THE LAVINIA'S ANCHOR, HOLD FAST TO ME AND MOVE QUICKLY.
WHY ARE YOU HERE?
A LOST LOVE'S LABOUR.
SO I HAVE A NEW COMPANION JOINING ME IN THINGS IMPOSSIBLE.
THANK YOU.
YOU MAY BE FRAIL, BUT NOT OF HEART. LET US HOPE THAT HELPS US.

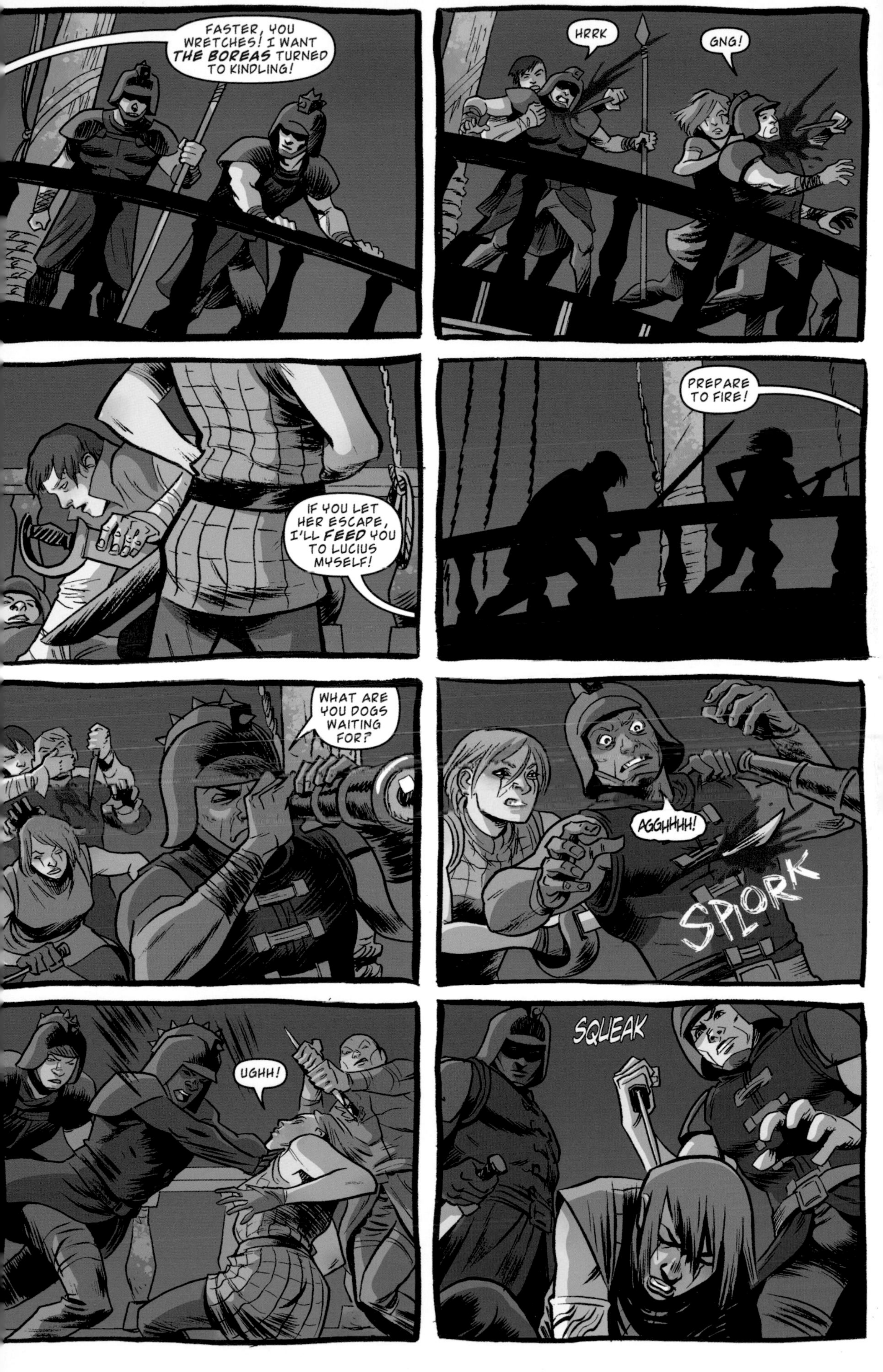
FASTER, YOU WRETCHES! I WANT THE BOREAS TURNED TO KINDLING!
HRRK
GNG!
IF YOU LET HER ESCAPE, I'LL FEED YOU TO LUCIUS MYSELF!
PREPARE TO FIRE!
WHAT ARE YOU DOGS WAITING FOR?
AGGHHHH!
SPLORK
UGHH!
SQUEAK

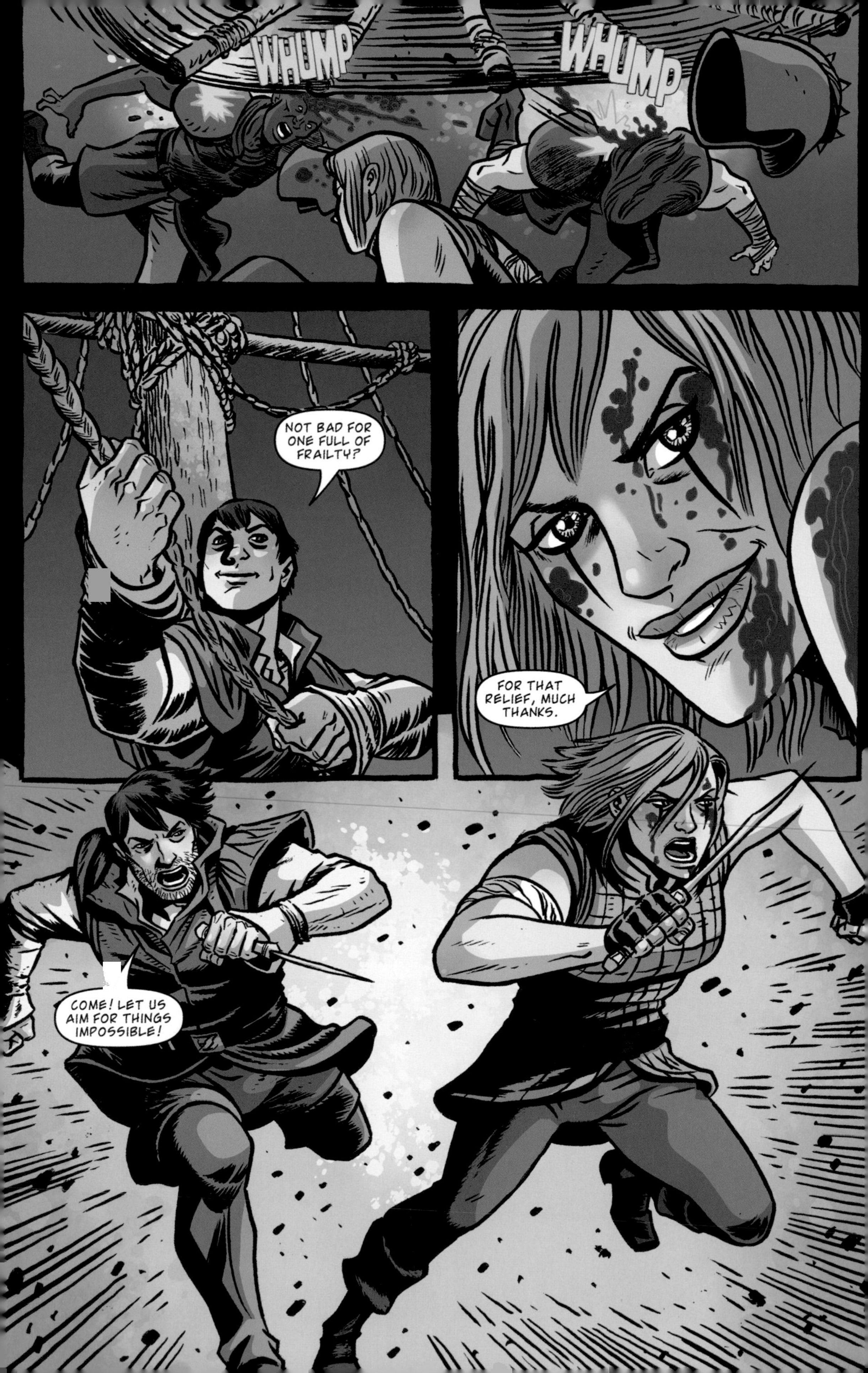
WHUMP
WHUMP
NOT BAD FOR ONE FULL OF FRAILTY?
FOR THAT RELIEF, MUCH THANKS.
COME! LET US AIM FOR THINGS IMPOSSIBLE!

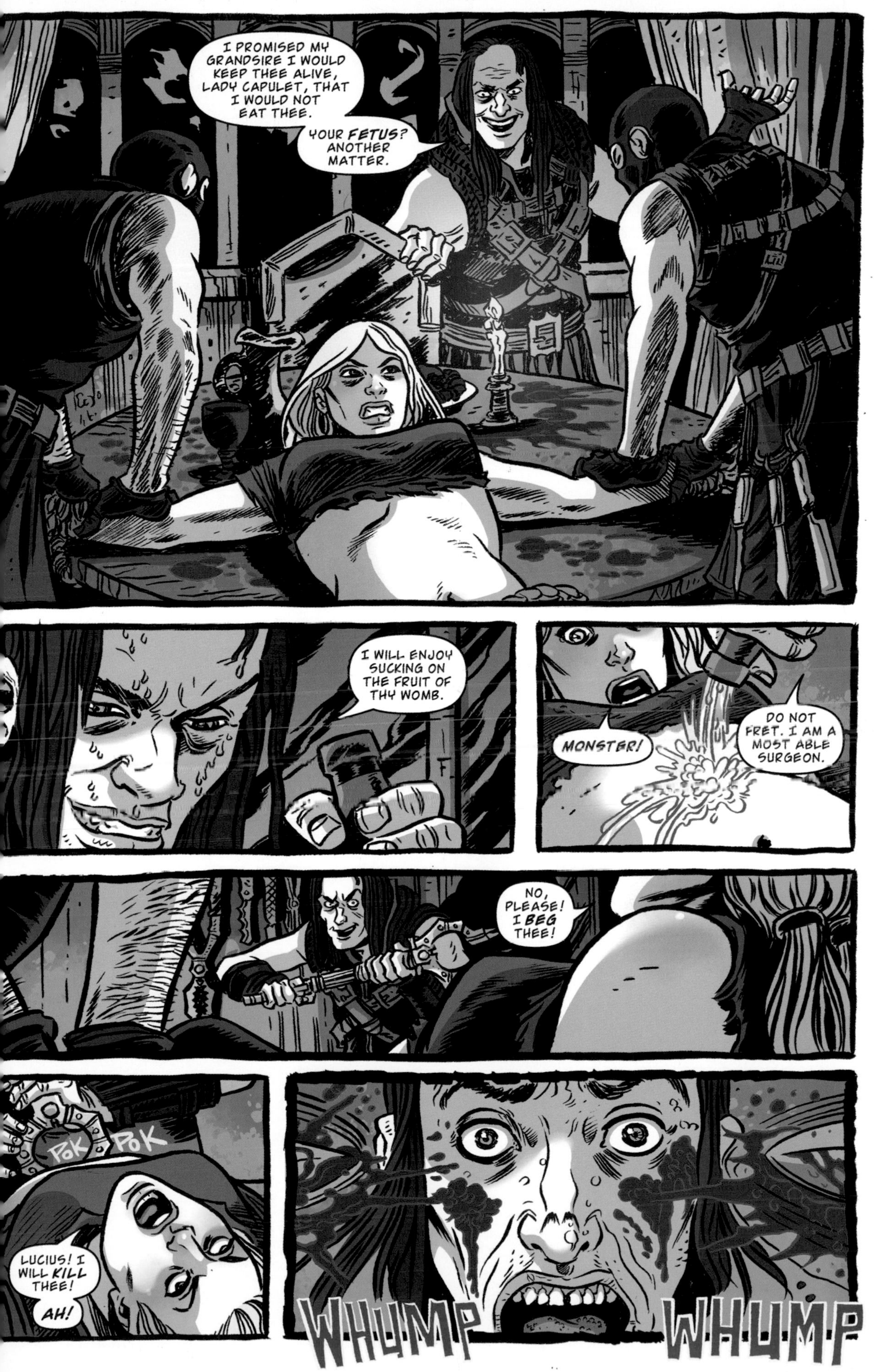
I PROMISED MY GRANDSIRE I WOULD KEEP THEE ALIVE, LADY CAPULET, THAT I WOULD NOT EAT THEE.
YOUR FETUS? ANOTHER MATTER.
I WILL ENJOY SUCKING ON THE FRUIT OF THY WOMB.
MONSTER!
DO NOT FRET. I AM A MOST ABLE SURGEON.
NO, PLEASE! I BEG THEE!
POK POK
LUCIUS! I WILL KILL THEE!
AH!
WHUMP
WHUMP

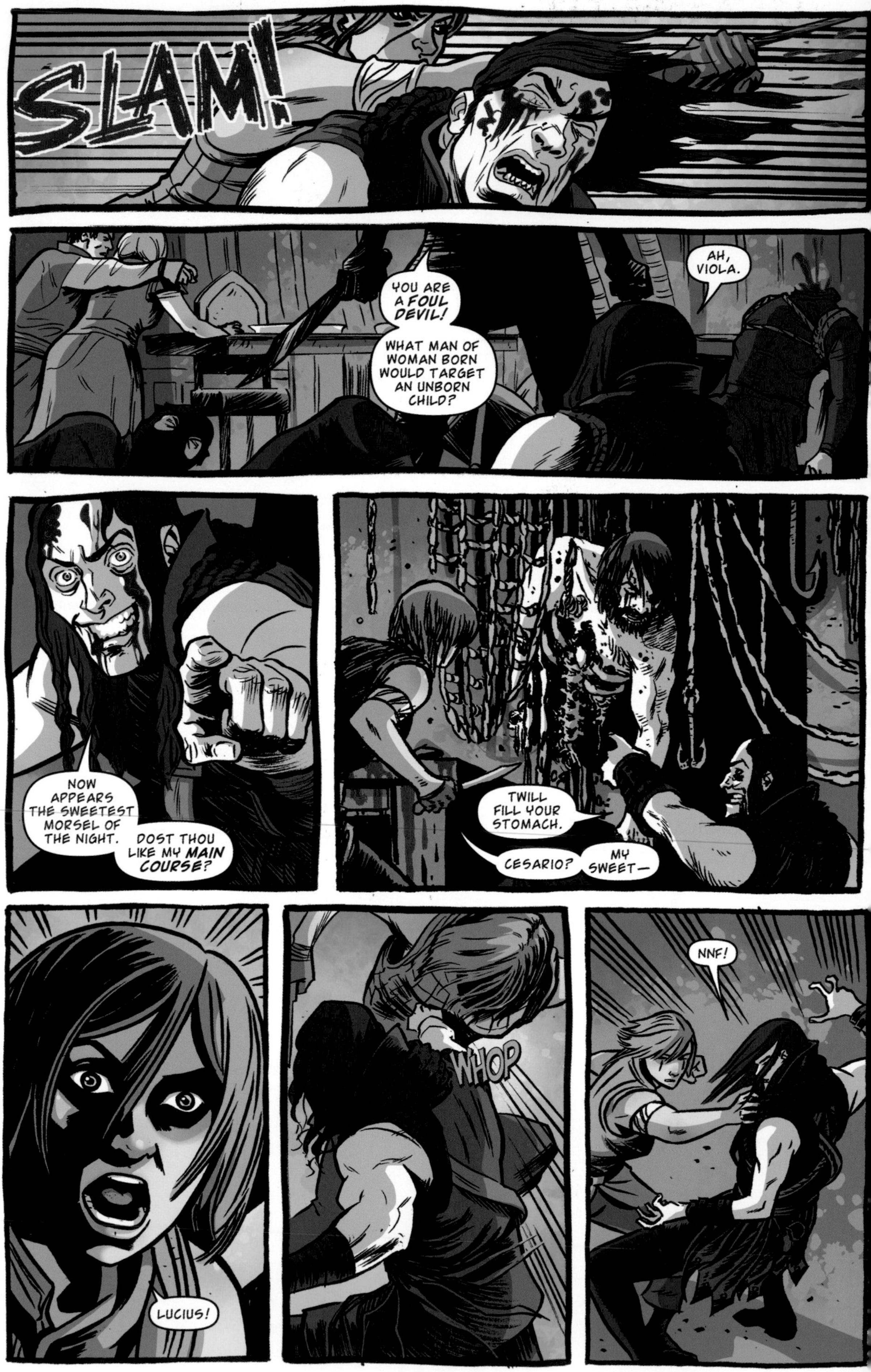
SLAM!
YOU ARE A FOUL DEVIL!
WHAT MAN OF WOMAN BORN WOULD TARGET AN UNBORN CHILD?
AH, VIOLA.
NOW APPEARS THE SWEETEST MORSEL OF THE NIGHT.
DOST THOU LIKE MY MAIN COURSE?
TWILL FILL YOUR STOMACH.
CESARIO?
MY SWEET—
LUCIUS!
WHOP
NNF!

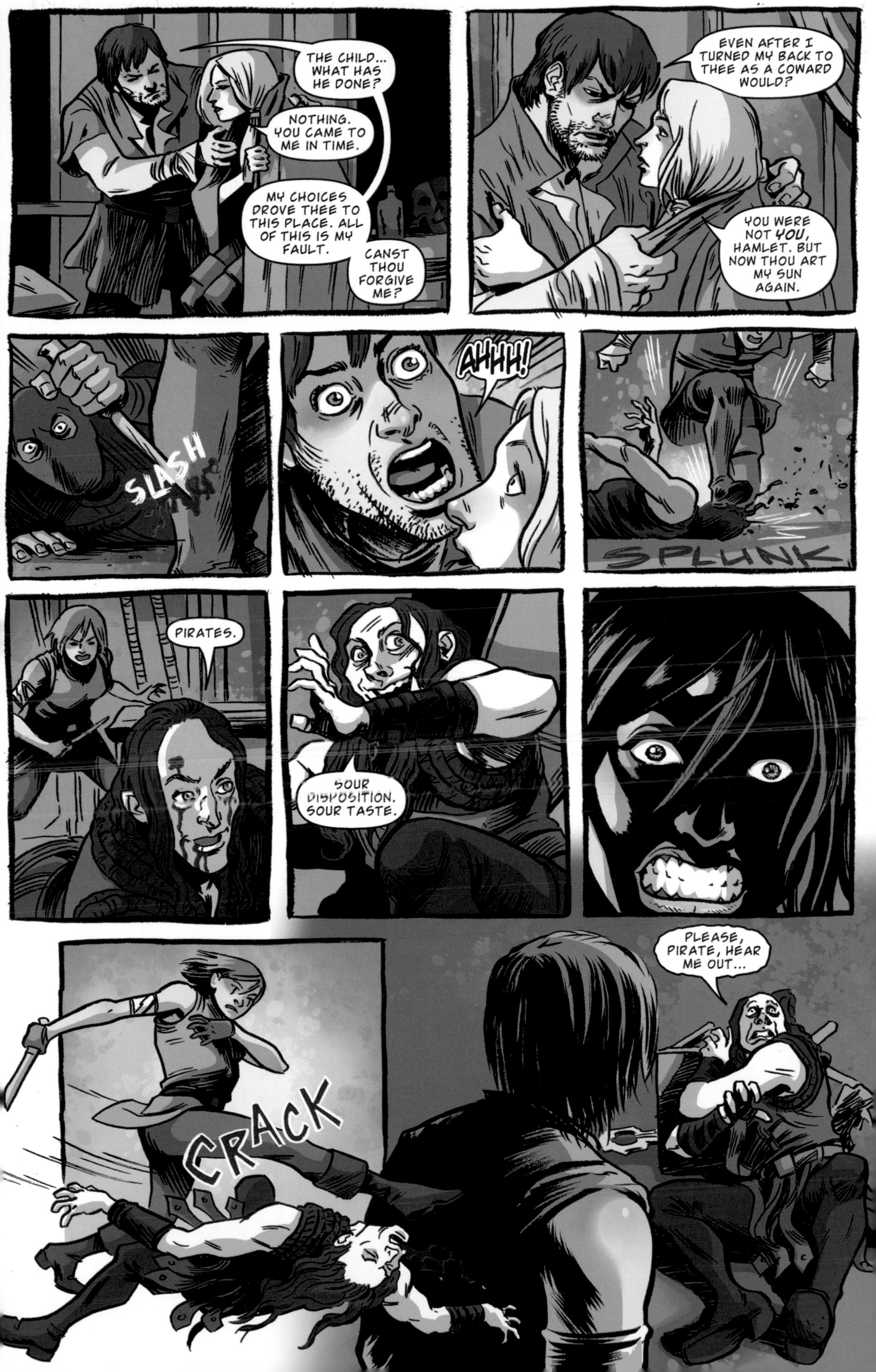
THE CHILD... WHAT HAS HE DONE?
NOTHING. YOU CAME TO ME IN TIME.
MY CHOICES DROVE THEE TO THIS PLACE. ALL OF THIS IS MY FAULT.
CANST THOU FORGIVE ME?
EVEN AFTER I TURNED MY BACK TO THEE AS A COWARD WOULD?
YOU WERE NOT YOU, HAMLET. BUT NOW THOU ART MY SUN AGAIN.
SLASH
AHHH!
SPLUNK
PIRATES.
SOUR DISPOSITION. SOUR TASTE.
CRACK
PLEASE, PIRATE, HEAR ME OUT...

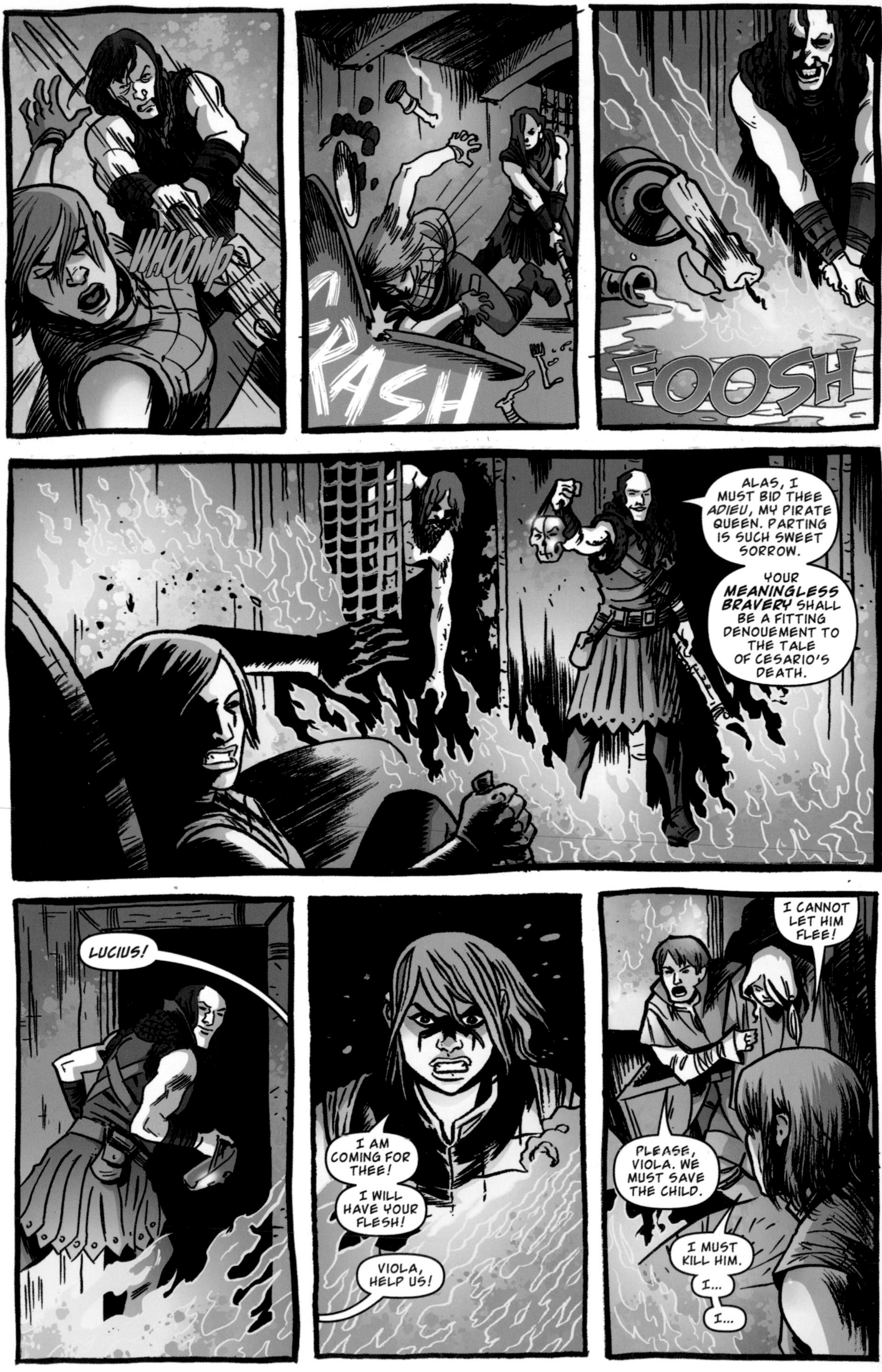
WHOOMP
CRASH
FOOSH
ALAS, I MUST BID THEE ADIEU, MY PIRATE QUEEN. PARTING IS SUCH SWEET SORROW.
YOUR MEANINGLESS BRAVERY SHALL BE A FITTING DENOUEMENT TO THE TALE OF CESARIO'S DEATH.
LUCIUS!
I AM COMING FOR THEE!
I WILL HAVE YOUR FLESH!
VIOLA, HELP US!
I CANNOT LET HIM FLEE!
PLEASE, VIOLA. WE MUST SAVE THE CHILD.
I MUST KILL HIM.
I...
I...

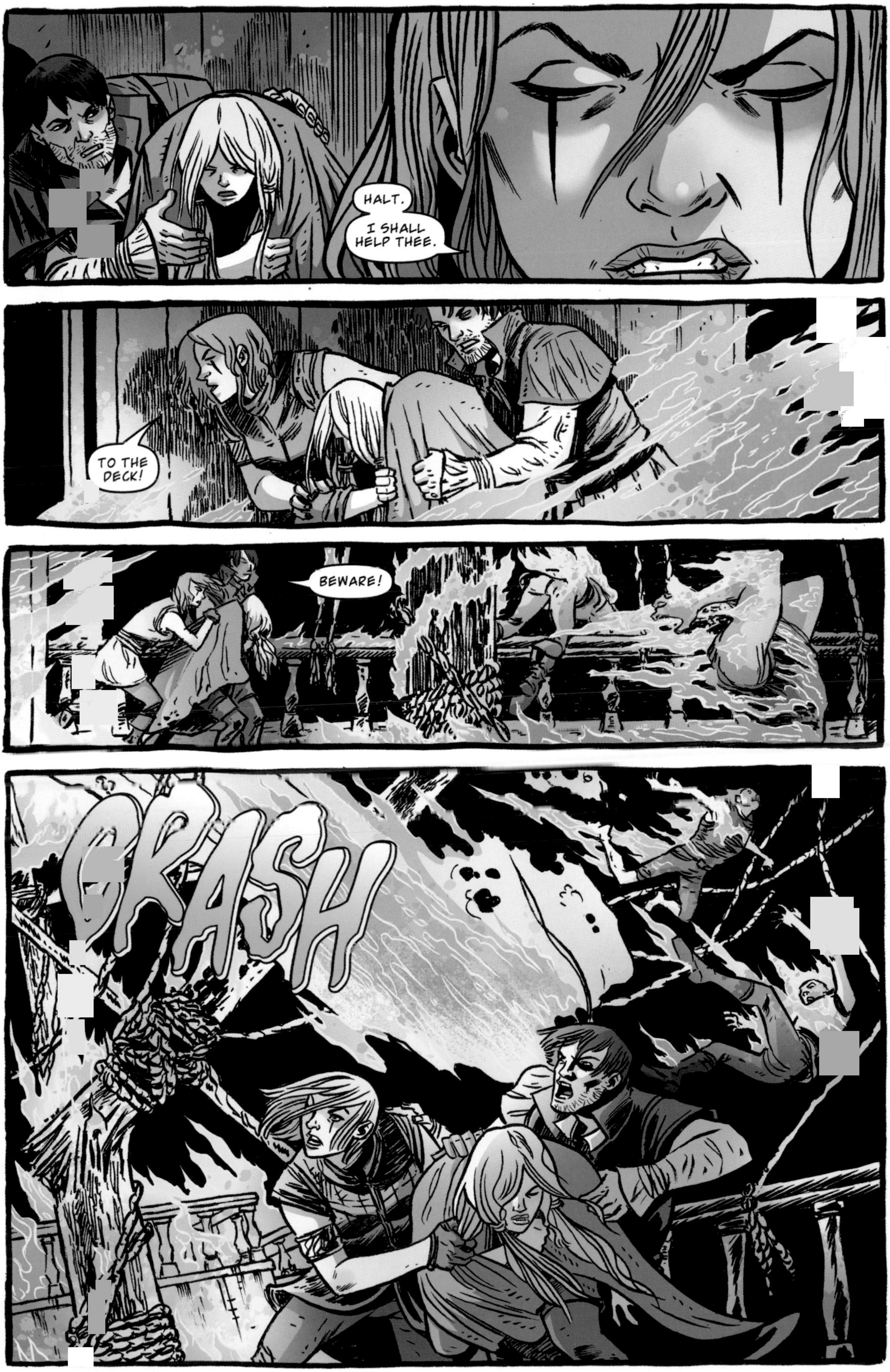
HALT.
I SHALL HELP THEE.
TO THE DECK!
BEWARE!
CRASH

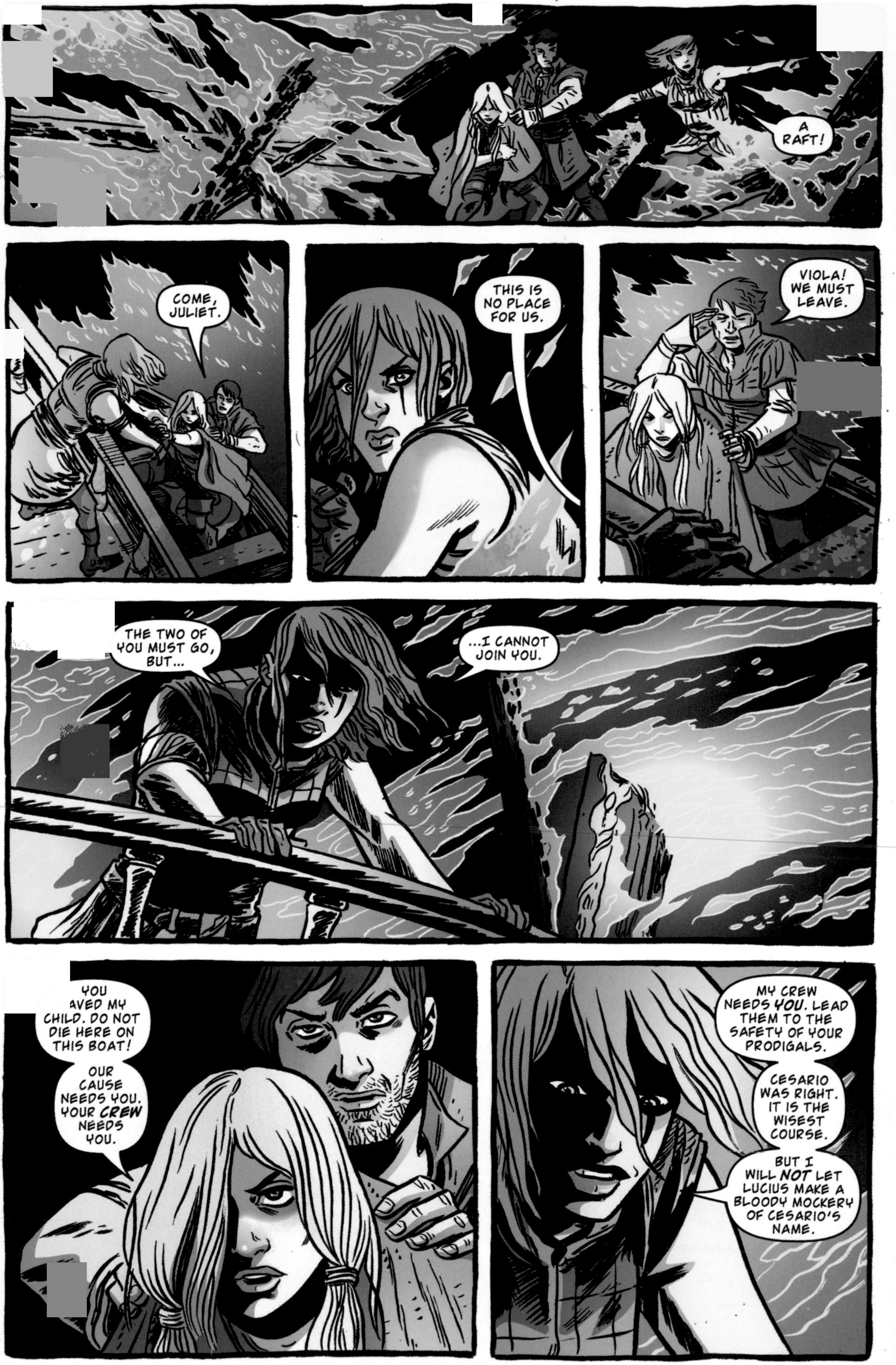
A RAFT!
COME, JULIET.
THIS IS NO PLACE FOR US.
VIOLA! WE MUST LEAVE.
THE TWO OF YOU MUST GO, BUT...
...I CANNOT JOIN YOU.
YOU AVED MY CHILD. DO NOT DIE HERE ON THIS BOAT!
OUR CAUSE NEEDS YOU. YOUR CREW NEEDS YOU.
MY CREW NEEDS YOU. LEAD THEM TO THE SAFETY OF YOUR PRODIGALS.
CESARIO WAS RIGHT. IT IS THE WISEST COURSE.
BUT I WILL NOT LET LUCIUS MAKE A BLOODY MOCKERY OF CESARIO'S NAME.

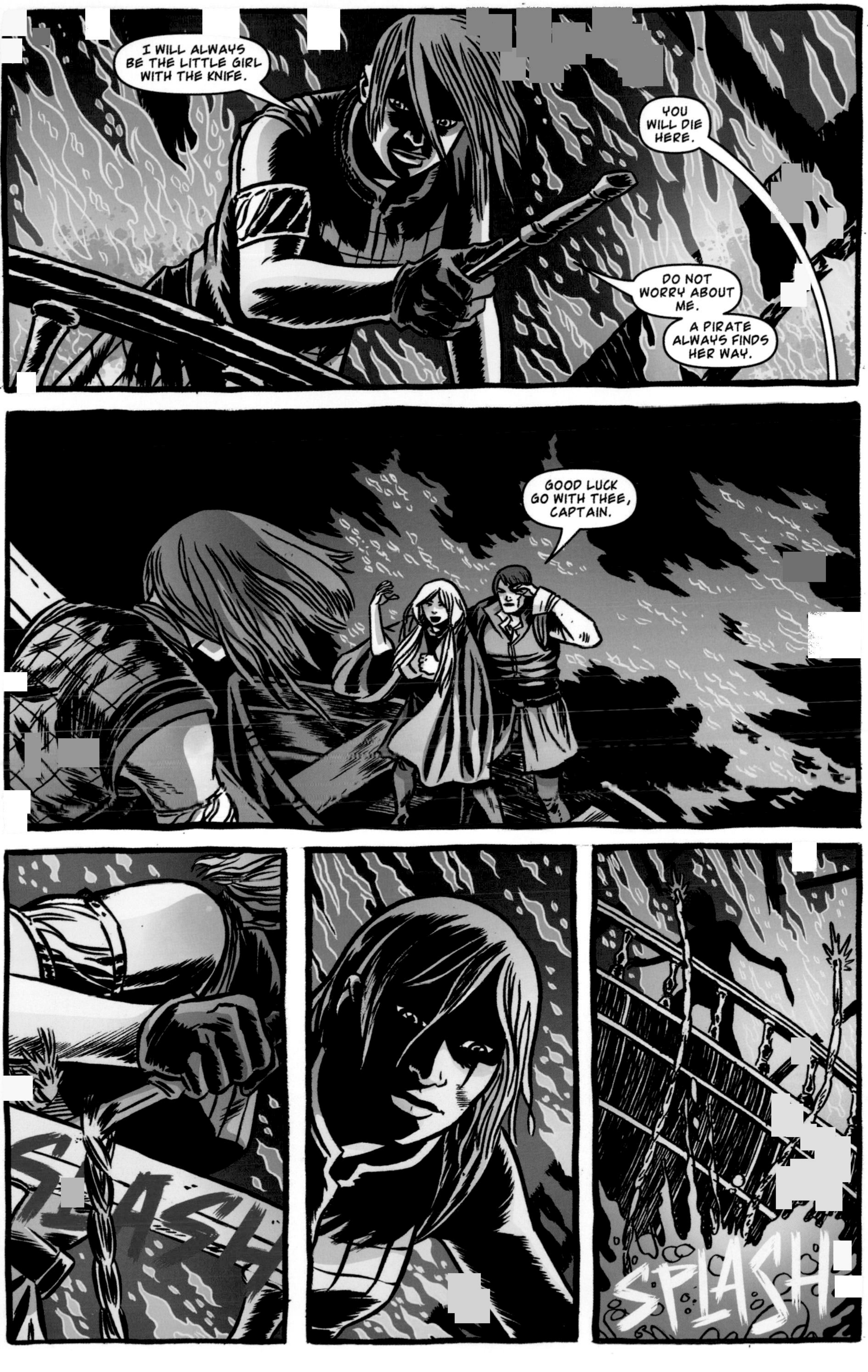
I WILL ALWAYS BE THE LITTLE GIRL WITH THE KNIFE.
YOU WILL DIE HERE.
DO NOT WORRY ABOUT ME.
A PIRATE ALWAYS FINDS HER WAY.
GOOD LUCK GO WITH THEE, CAPTAIN.
SPLASH
SPLASH

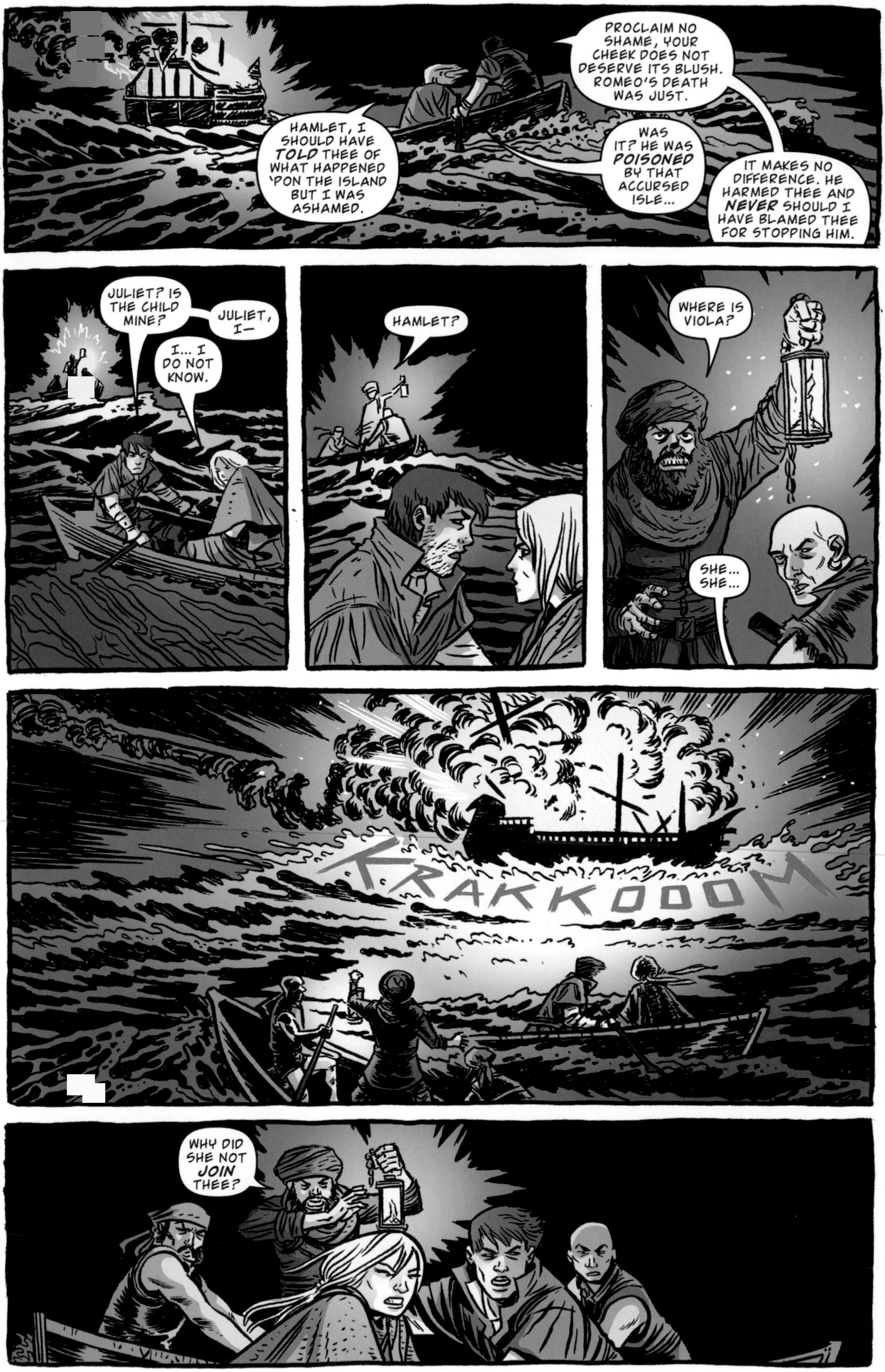

HAMLET, I SHOULD HAVE TOLD THEE OF WHAT HAPPENED 'PON THE ISLAND BUT I WAS ASHAMED.
PROCLAIM NO SHAME, YOUR CHEEK DOES NOT DESERVE ITS BLUSH. ROMEO'S DEATH WAS JUST.
WAS IT? HE WAS POISONED BY THAT ACCURSED ISLE...
IT MAKES NO DIFFERENCE. HE HARMED THEE AND NEVER SHOULD I HAVE BLAMED THEE FOR STOPPING HIM.
JULIET? IS THE CHILD MINE?
JULIET, I—
I... I DO NOT KNOW.
HAMLET?
WHERE IS VIOLA?
SHE... SHE...
KRAKKOOOM
WHY DID SHE NOT JOIN THEE?

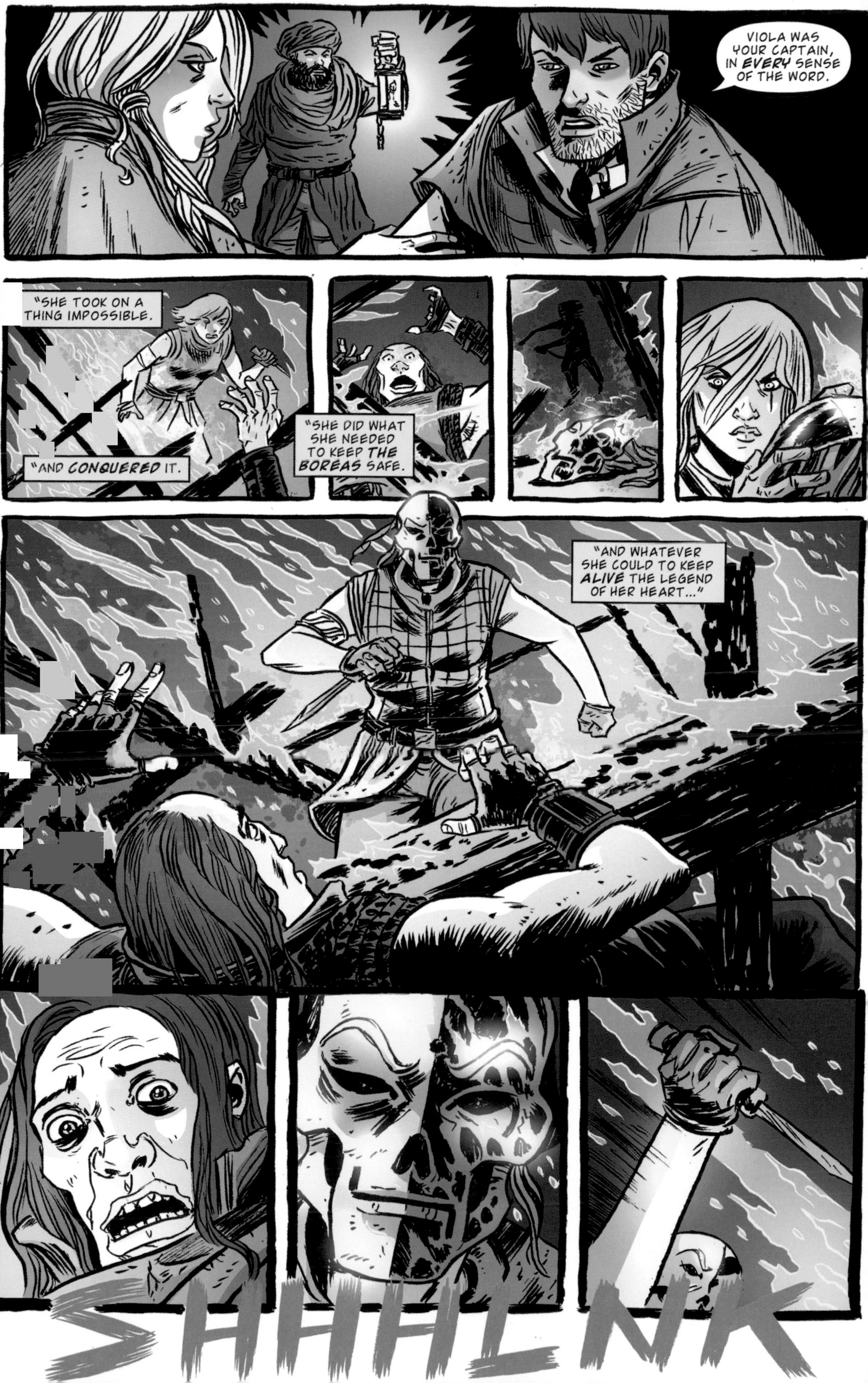
VIOLA WAS YOUR CAPTAIN, IN EVERY SENSE OF THE WORD.
"SHE TOOK ON A THING IMPOSSIBLE.
"AND CONQUERED IT.
"SHE DID WHAT SHE NEEDED TO KEEP THE BOREAS SAFE.
"AND WHATEVER SHE COULD TO KEEP ALIVE THE LEGEND OF HER HEART..."
SHHHLNK

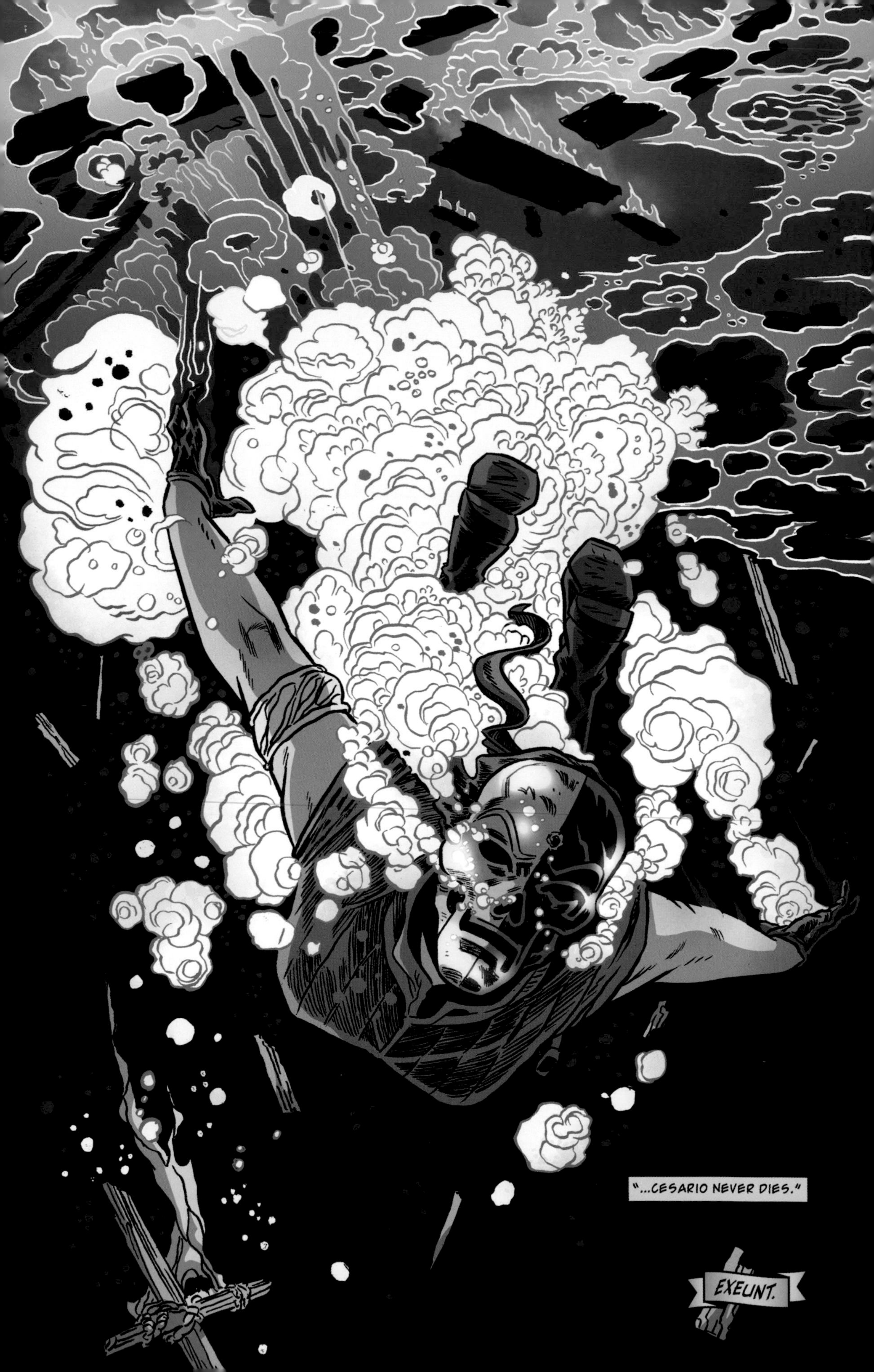
"...CESARIO NEVER DIES."
EXEUNT.

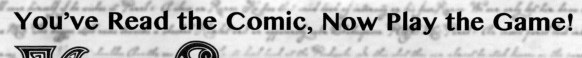

BONUS GALLERY

Featuring artwork from the series as well as the original story:

"Sebastian and the Bear"

WRITTEN BY
Keith WTS Morris

ART & COLORS BY
Vaneda Vireak

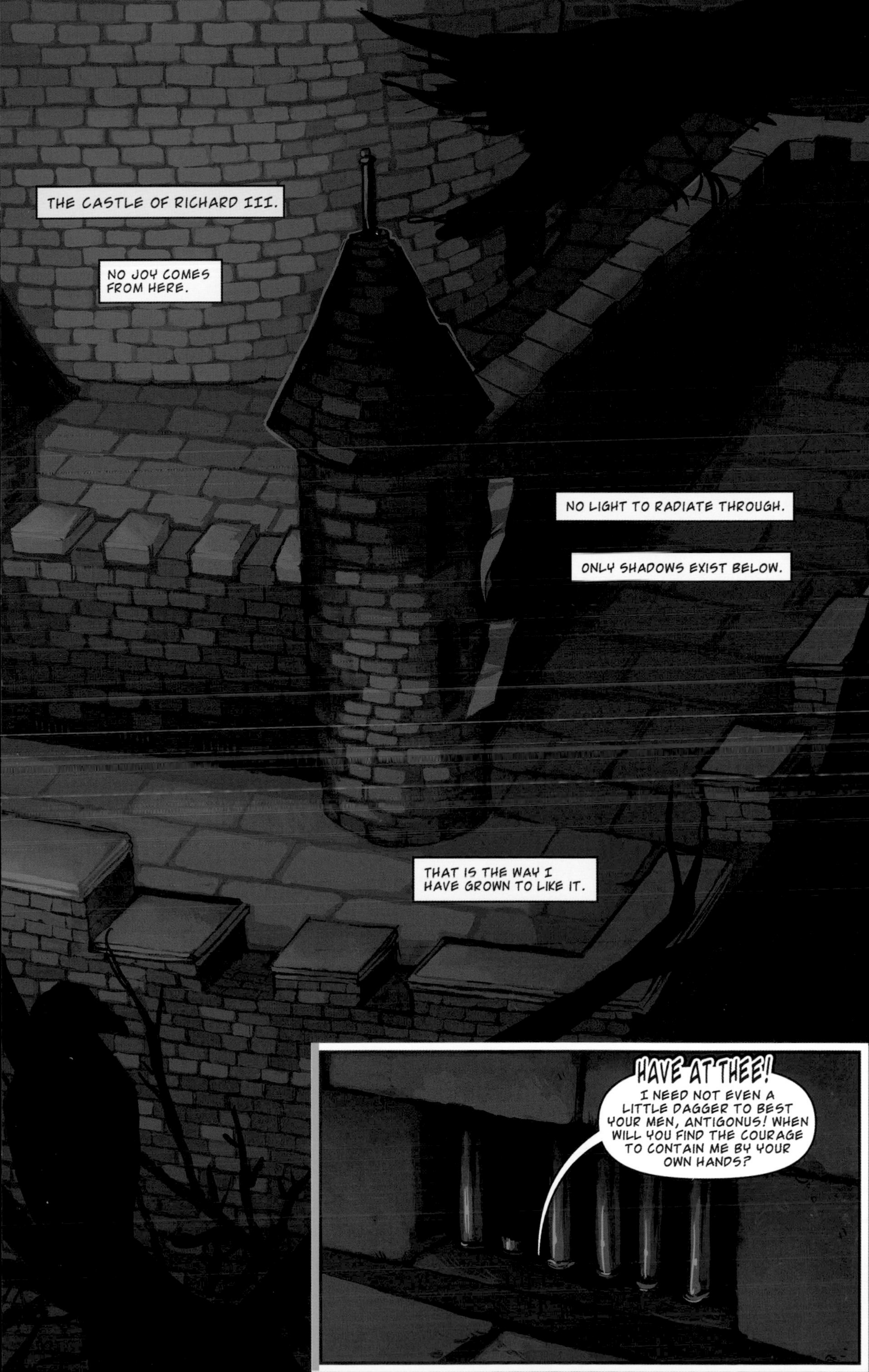
THE CASTLE OF RICHARD III.
NO JOY COMES FROM HERE.
NO LIGHT TO RADIATE THROUGH.
ONLY SHADOWS EXIST BELOW.
THAT IS THE WAY I HAVE GROWN TO LIKE IT.
HAVE AT THEE! I NEED NOT EVEN A LITTLE DAGGER TO BEST YOUR MEN, ANTIGONUS! WHEN WILL YOU FIND THE COURAGE TO CONTAIN ME BY YOUR OWN HANDS?

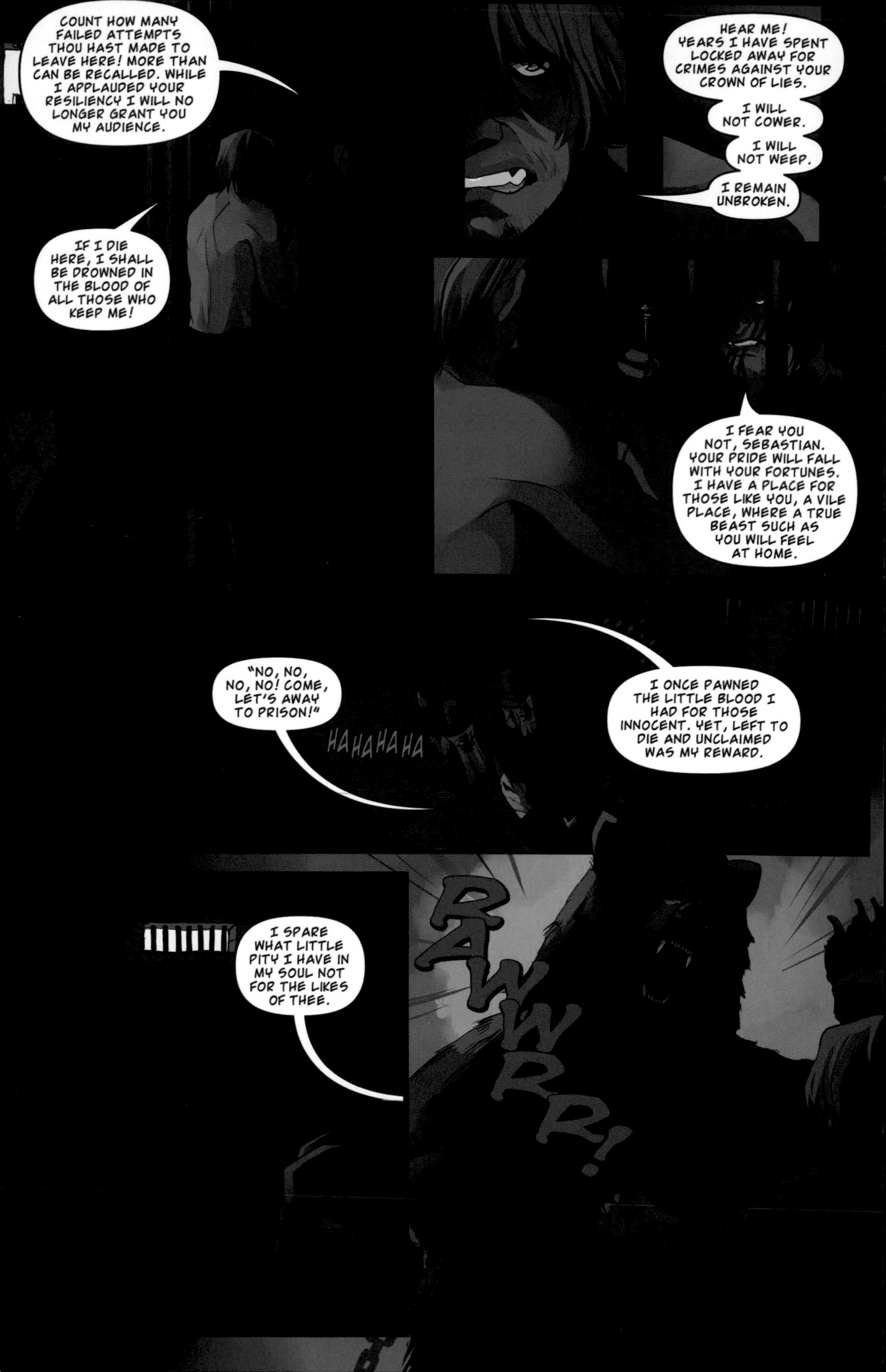
COUNT HOW MANY FAILED ATTEMPTS THOU HAST MADE TO LEAVE HERE! MORE THAN CAN BE RECALLED. WHILE I APPLAUDED YOUR RESILIENCY I WILL NO LONGER GRANT YOU MY AUDIENCE.
IF I DIE HERE, I SHALL BE DROWNED IN THE BLOOD OF ALL THOSE WHO KEEP ME!
HEAR ME! YEARS I HAVE SPENT LOCKED AWAY FOR CRIMES AGAINST YOUR CROWN OF LIES.
I WILL NOT COWER.
I WILL NOT WEEP.
I REMAIN UNBROKEN.
I FEAR YOU NOT, SEBASTIAN. YOUR PRIDE WILL FALL WITH YOUR FORTUNES. I HAVE A PLACE FOR THOSE LIKE YOU, A VILE PLACE, WHERE A TRUE BEAST SUCH AS YOU WILL FEEL AT HOME.
I ONCE PAWNED THE LITTLE BLOOD I HAD FOR THOSE INNOCENT. YET, LEFT TO DIE AND UNCLAIMED WAS MY REWARD.
"NO, NO, NO, NO! COME, LET'S AWAY TO PRISON!"
HAHAHAHA
I SPARE WHAT LITTLE PITY I HAVE IN MY SOUL NOT FOR THE LIKES OF THEE.
RAWWRR!

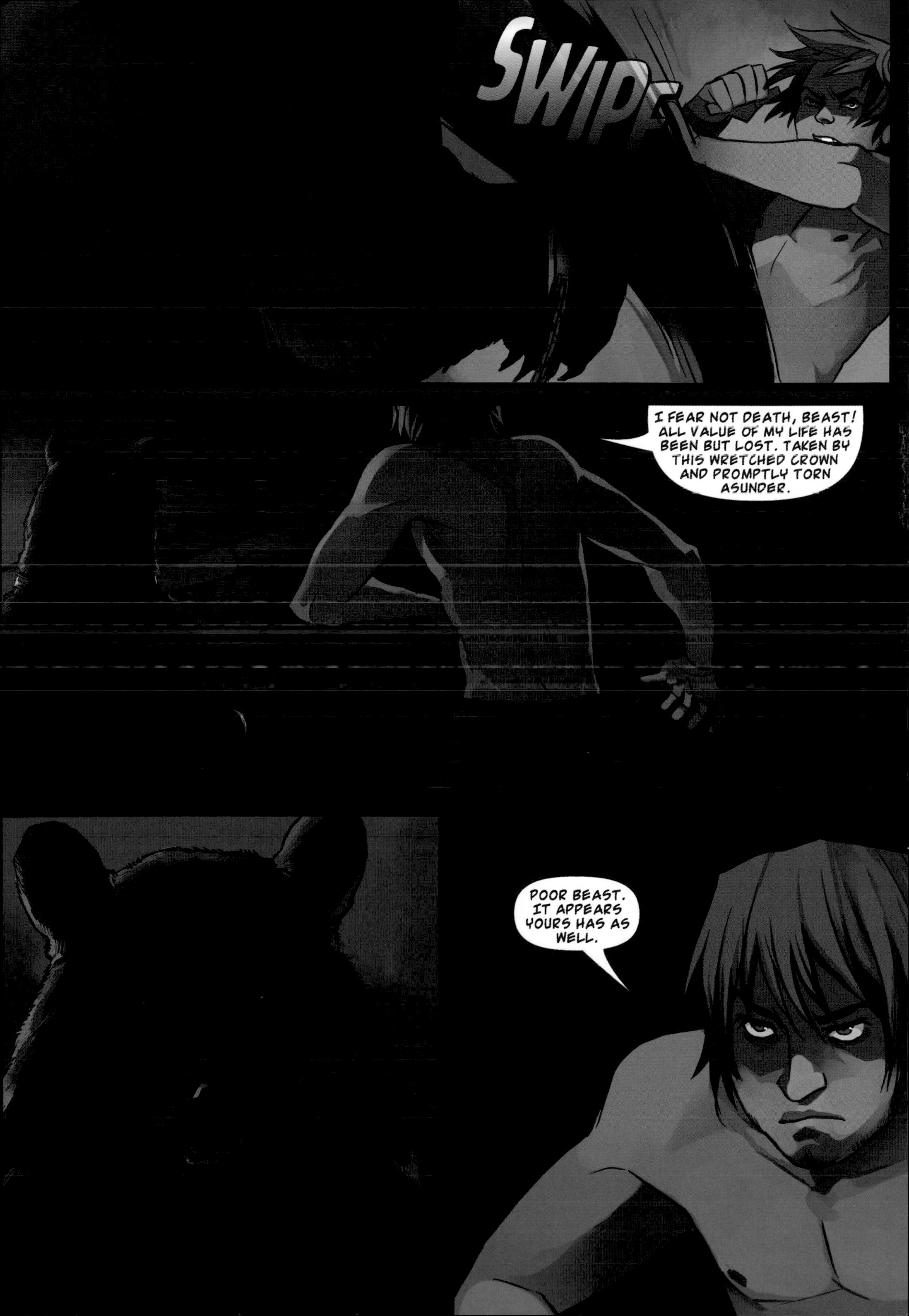
SWIPE
I FEAR NOT DEATH, BEAST! ALL VALUE OF MY LIFE HAS BEEN BUT LOST. TAKEN BY THIS WRETCHED CROWN AND PROMPTLY TORN ASUNDER.
POOR BEAST. IT APPEARS YOURS HAS AS WELL.

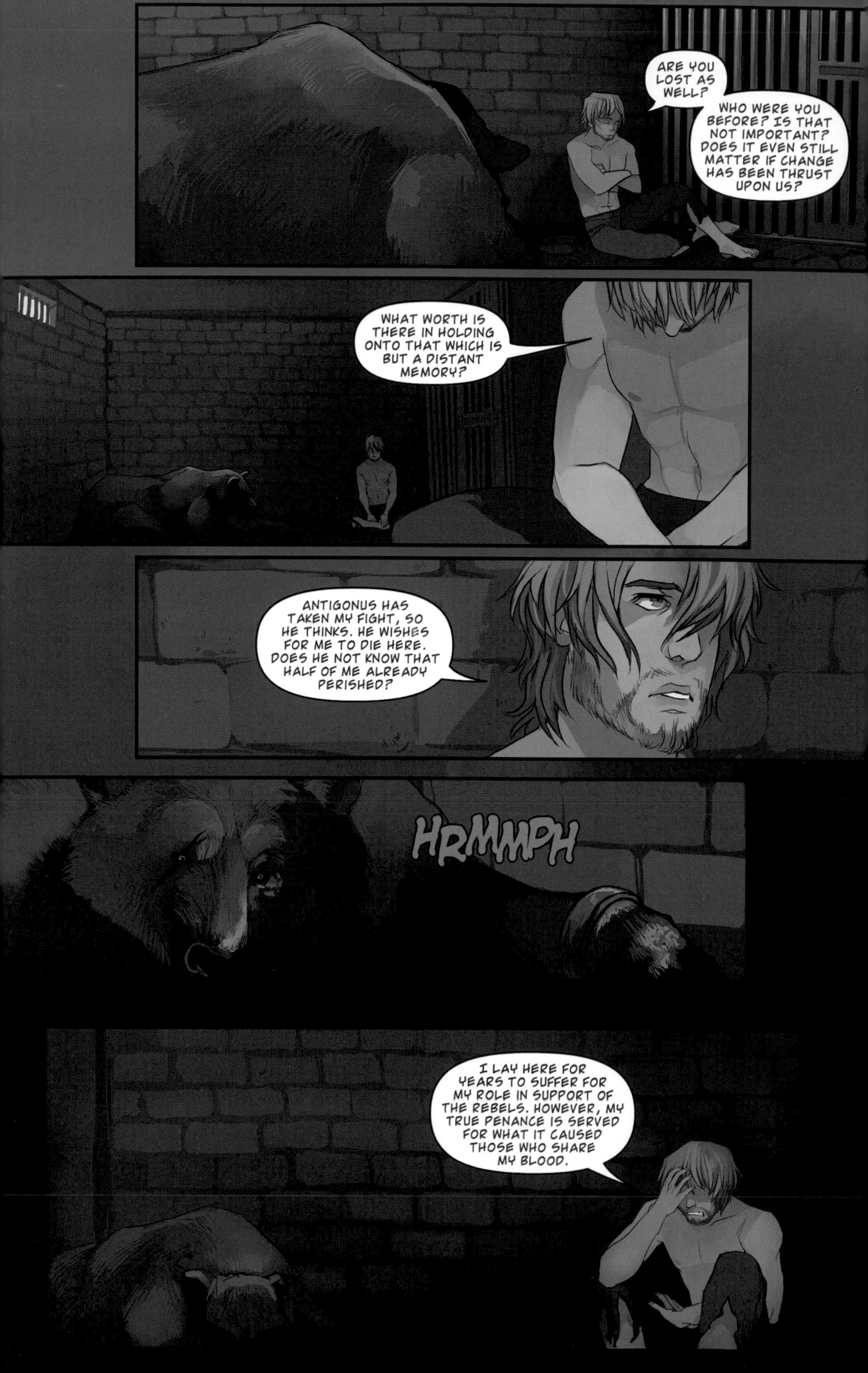

ARE YOU LOST AS WELL?
WHO WERE YOU BEFORE? IS THAT NOT IMPORTANT? DOES IT EVEN STILL MATTER IF CHANGE HAS BEEN THRUST UPON US?
WHAT WORTH IS THERE IN HOLDING ONTO THAT WHICH IS BUT A DISTANT MEMORY?
ANTIGONUS HAS TAKEN MY FIGHT, SO HE THINKS. HE WISHES FOR ME TO DIE HERE. DOES HE NOT KNOW THAT HALF OF ME ALREADY PERISHED?
HRMMPH
I LAY HERE FOR YEARS TO SUFFER FOR MY ROLE IN SUPPORT OF THE REBELS. HOWEVER, MY TRUE PENANCE IS SERVED FOR WHAT IT CAUSED THOSE WHO SHARE MY BLOOD.

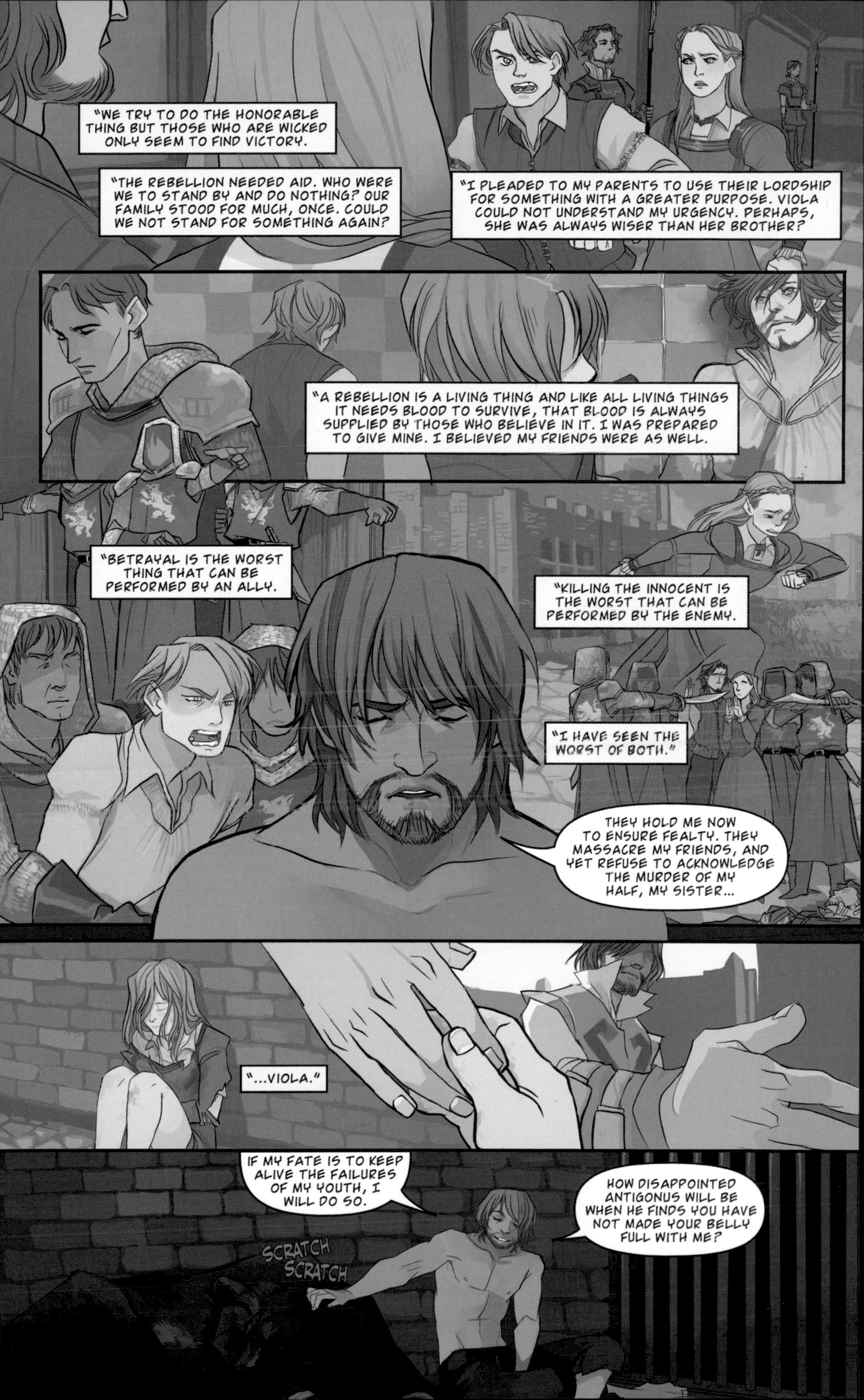
"WE TRY TO DO THE HONORABLE THING BUT THOSE WHO ARE WICKED ONLY SEEM TO FIND VICTORY.
"THE REBELLION NEEDED AID. WHO WERE WE TO STAND BY AND DO NOTHING? OUR FAMILY STOOD FOR MUCH, ONCE. COULD WE NOT STAND FOR SOMETHING AGAIN?
"I PLEADED TO MY PARENTS TO USE THEIR LORDSHIP FOR SOMETHING WITH A GREATER PURPOSE. VIOLA COULD NOT UNDERSTAND MY URGENCY. PERHAPS, SHE WAS ALWAYS WISER THAN HER BROTHER?
"A REBELLION IS A LIVING THING AND LIKE ALL LIVING THINGS IT NEEDS BLOOD TO SURVIVE, THAT BLOOD IS ALWAYS SUPPLIED BY THOSE WHO BELIEVE IN IT. I WAS PREPARED TO GIVE MINE. I BELIEVED MY FRIENDS WERE AS WELL.
"BETRAYAL IS THE WORST THING THAT CAN BE PERFORMED BY AN ALLY.
"KILLING THE INNOCENT IS THE WORST THAT CAN BE PERFORMED BY THE ENEMY.
"I HAVE SEEN THE WORST OF BOTH."
THEY HOLD ME NOW TO ENSURE FEALTY. THEY MASSACRE MY FRIENDS, AND YET REFUSE TO ACKNOWLEDGE THE MURDER OF MY HALF, MY SISTER...
"...VIOLA."
IF MY FATE IS TO KEEP ALIVE THE FAILURES OF MY YOUTH, I WILL DO SO.
HOW DISAPPOINTED ANTIGONUS WILL BE WHEN HE FINDS YOU HAVE NOT MADE YOUR BELLY FULL WITH ME?
SCRATCH
SCRATCH

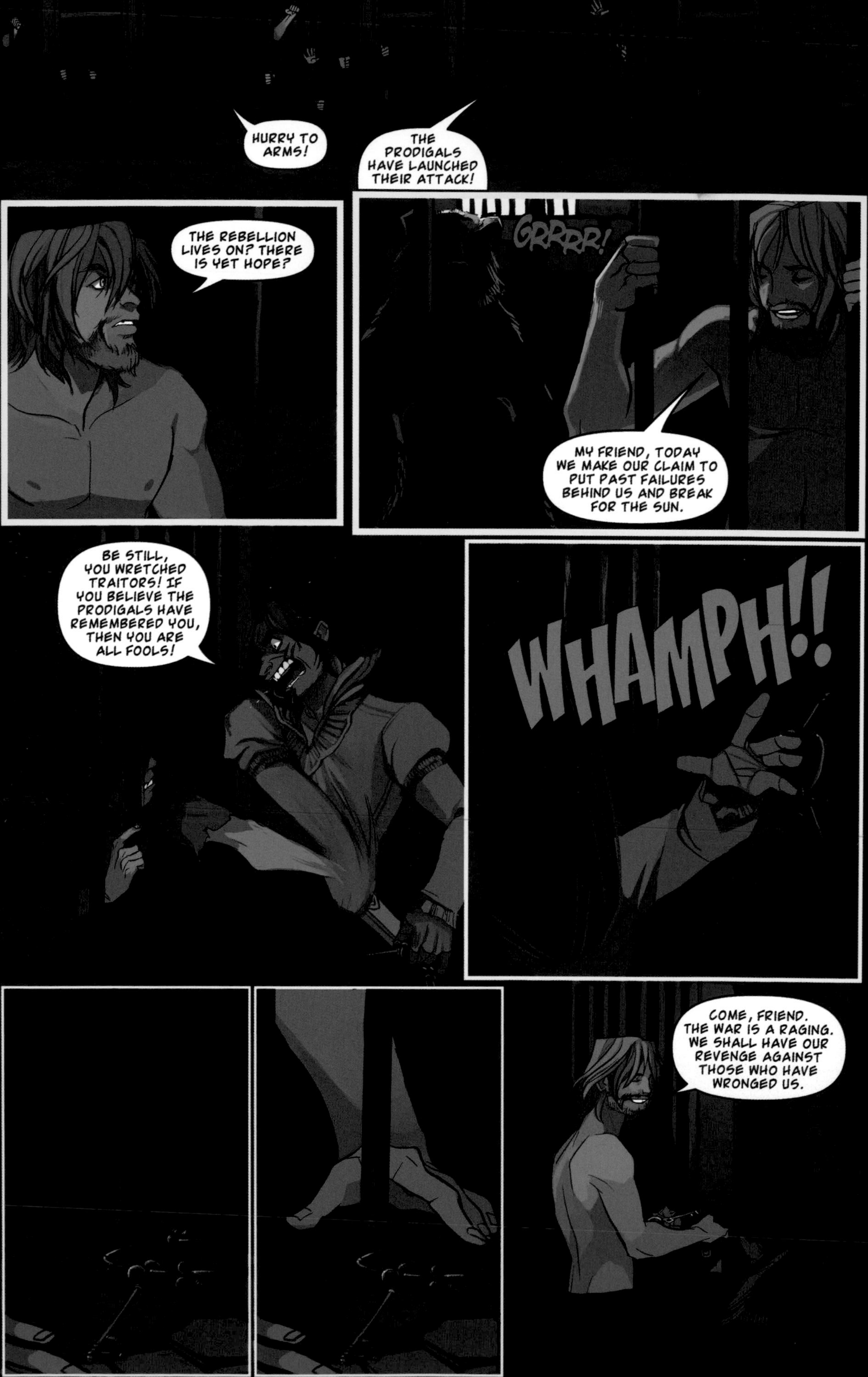
HURRY TO ARMS!
THE PRODIGALS HAVE LAUNCHED THEIR ATTACK!
THE REBELLION LIVES ON? THERE IS YET HOPE?
GRRRR!
MY FRIEND, TODAY WE MAKE OUR CLAIM TO PUT PAST FAILURES BEHIND US AND BREAK FOR THE SUN.
BE STILL, YOU WRETCHED TRAITORS! IF YOU BELIEVE THE PRODIGALS HAVE REMEMBERED YOU, THEN YOU ARE ALL FOOLS!
WHAMPH!!
COME, FRIEND. THE WAR IS A RAGING. WE SHALL HAVE OUR REVENGE AGAINST THOSE WHO HAVE WRONGED US.

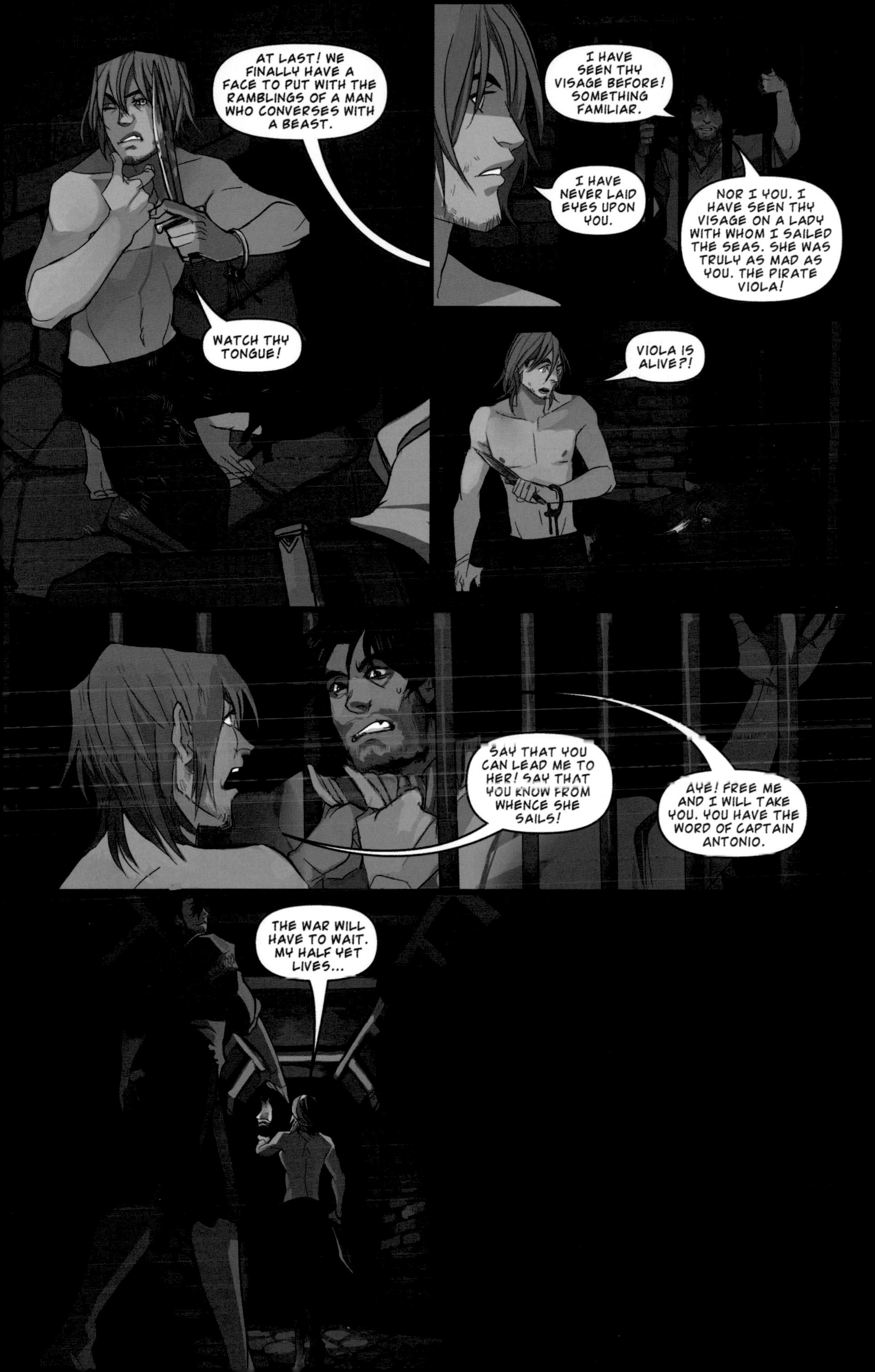
AT LAST! WE FINALLY HAVE A FACE TO PUT WITH THE RAMBLINGS OF A MAN WHO CONVERSES WITH A BEAST.
WATCH THY TONGUE!
I HAVE SEEN THY VISAGE BEFORE! SOMETHING FAMILIAR.
I HAVE NEVER LAID EYES UPON YOU.
NOR I YOU. I HAVE SEEN THY VISAGE ON A LADY WITH WHOM I SAILED THE SEAS. SHE WAS TRULY AS MAD AS YOU. THE PIRATE VIOLA!
VIOLA IS ALIVE?!
SAY THAT YOU CAN LEAD ME TO HER! SAY THAT YOU KNOW FROM WHENCE SHE SAILS!
AYE! FREE ME AND I WILL TAKE YOU. YOU HAVE THE WORD OF CAPTAIN ANTONIO.
THE WAR WILL HAVE TO WAIT. MY HALF YET LIVES...

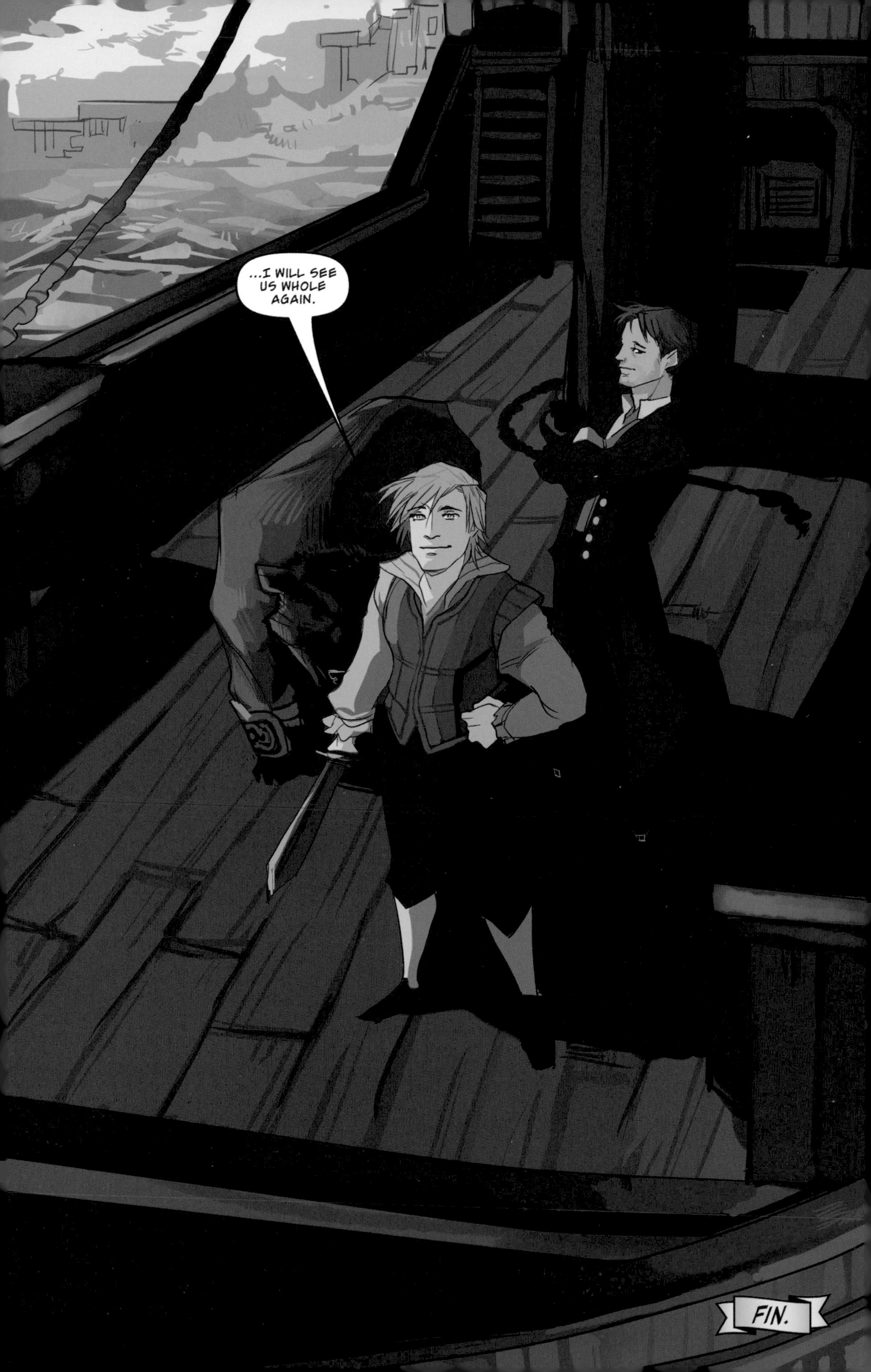
...I WILL SEE US WHOLE AGAIN.
FIN.

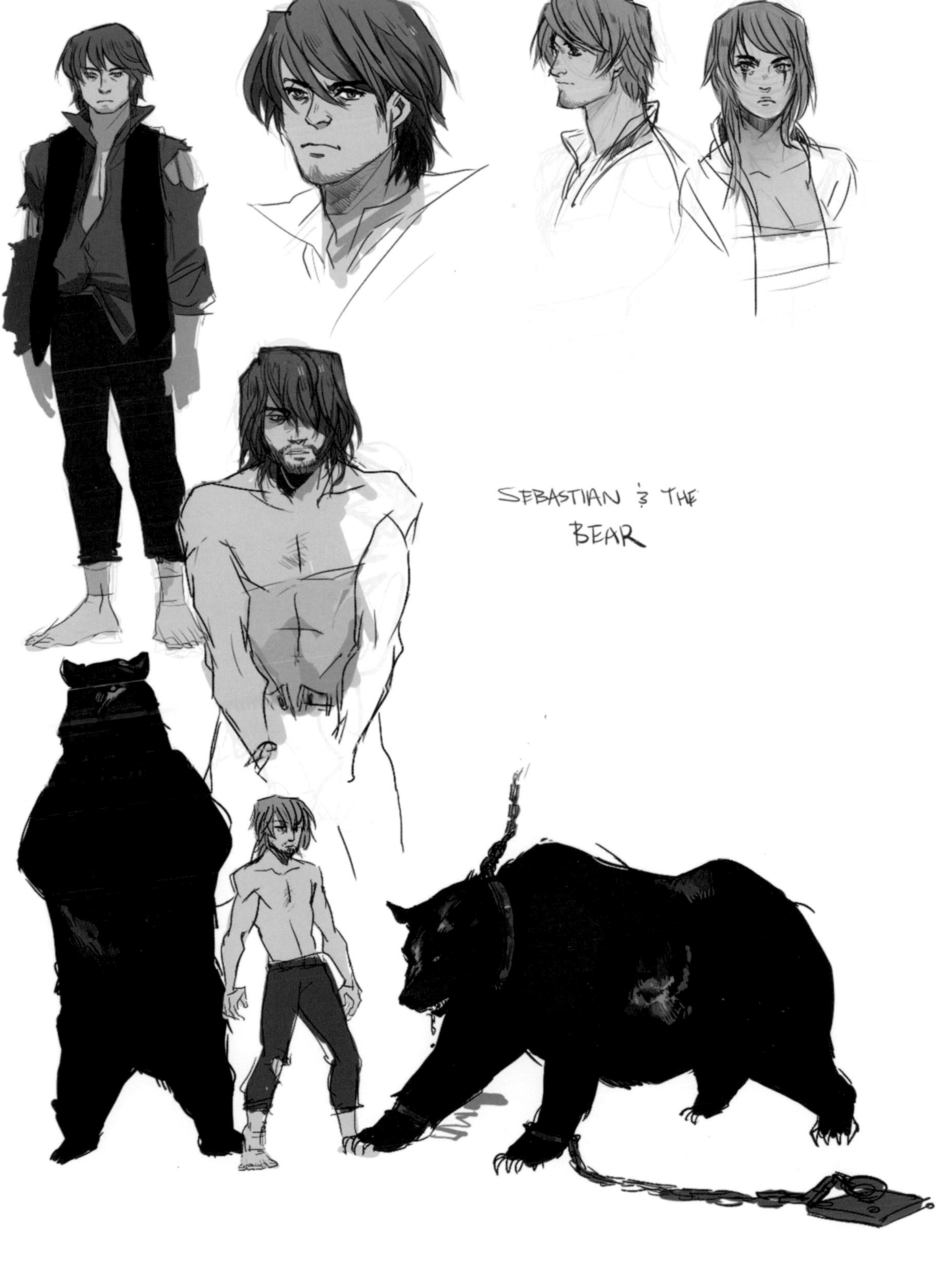
SEBASTIAN & THE
BEAR

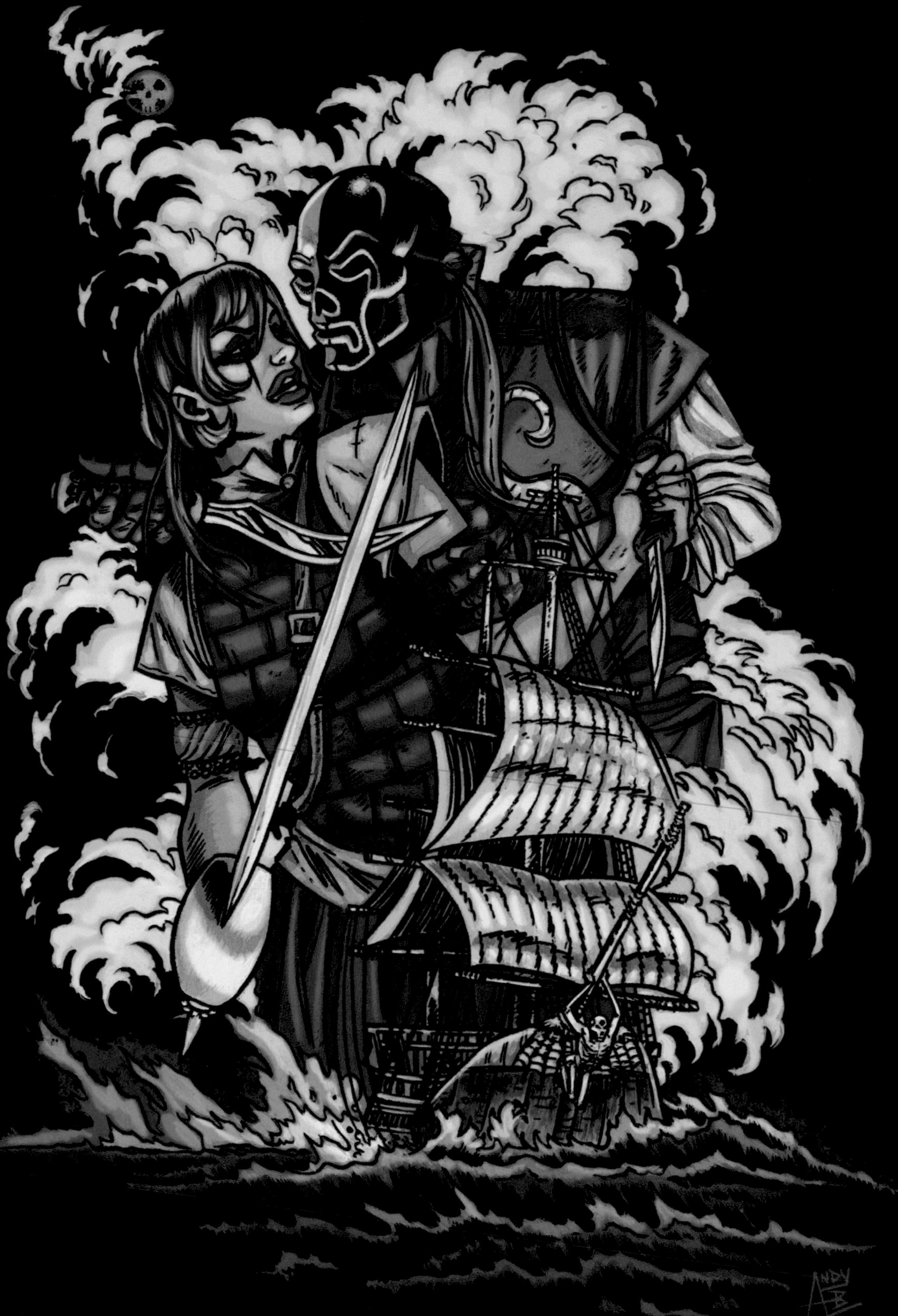

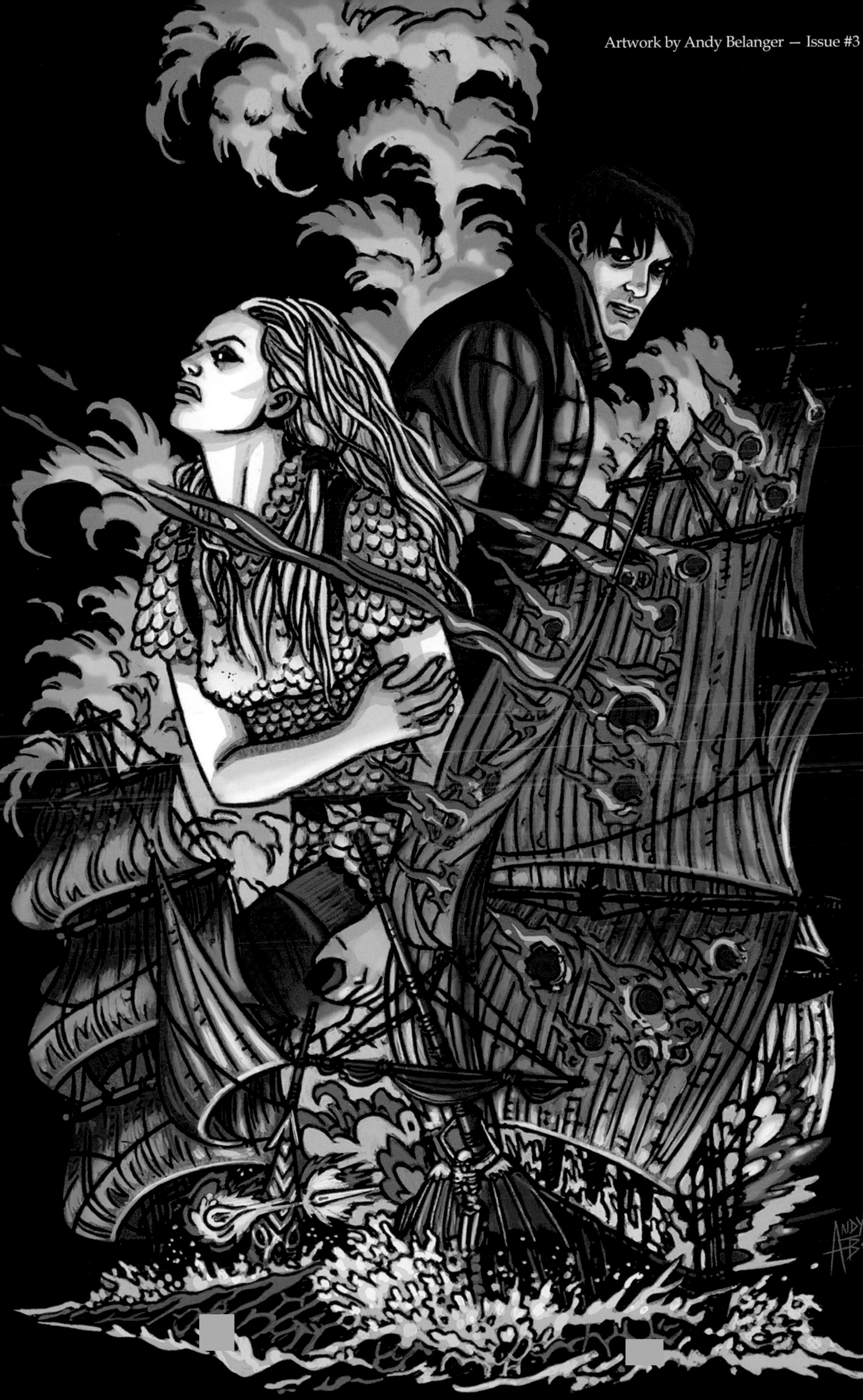

Artwork by Andy Belanger — Issue #3

Artwork by Andy Belanger — Issue #1

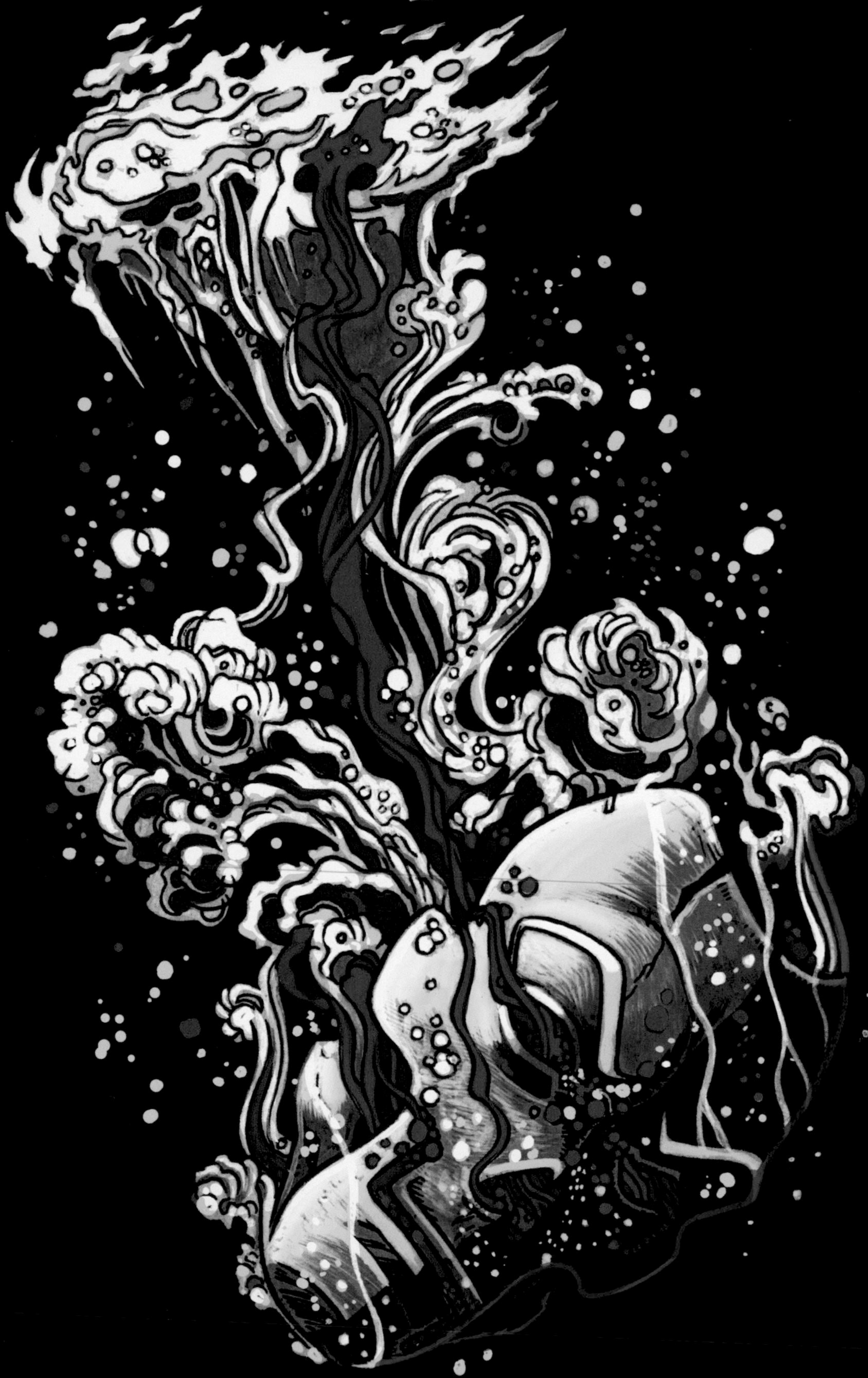

Artwork by JK Woodward — Issue #1

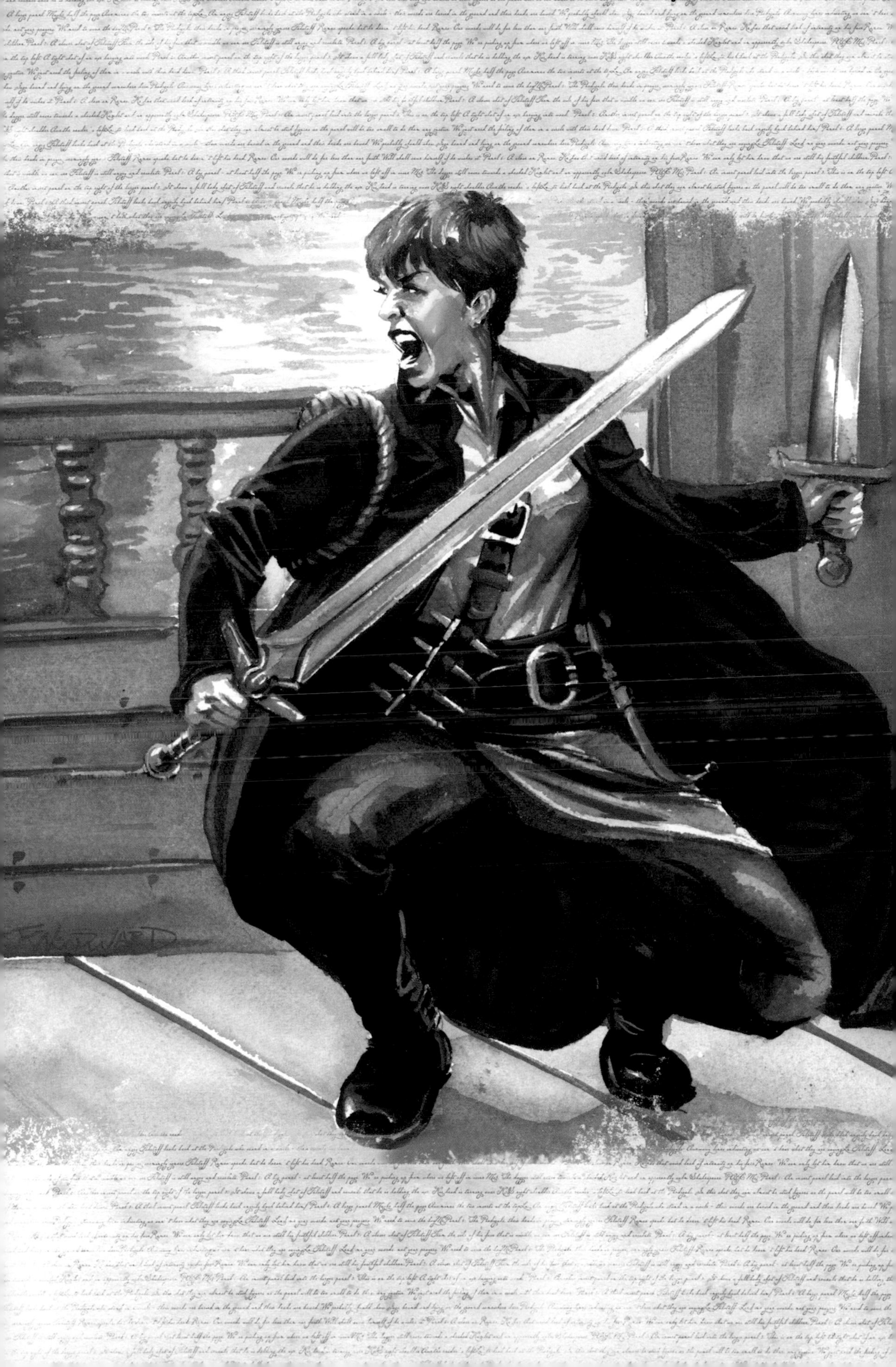

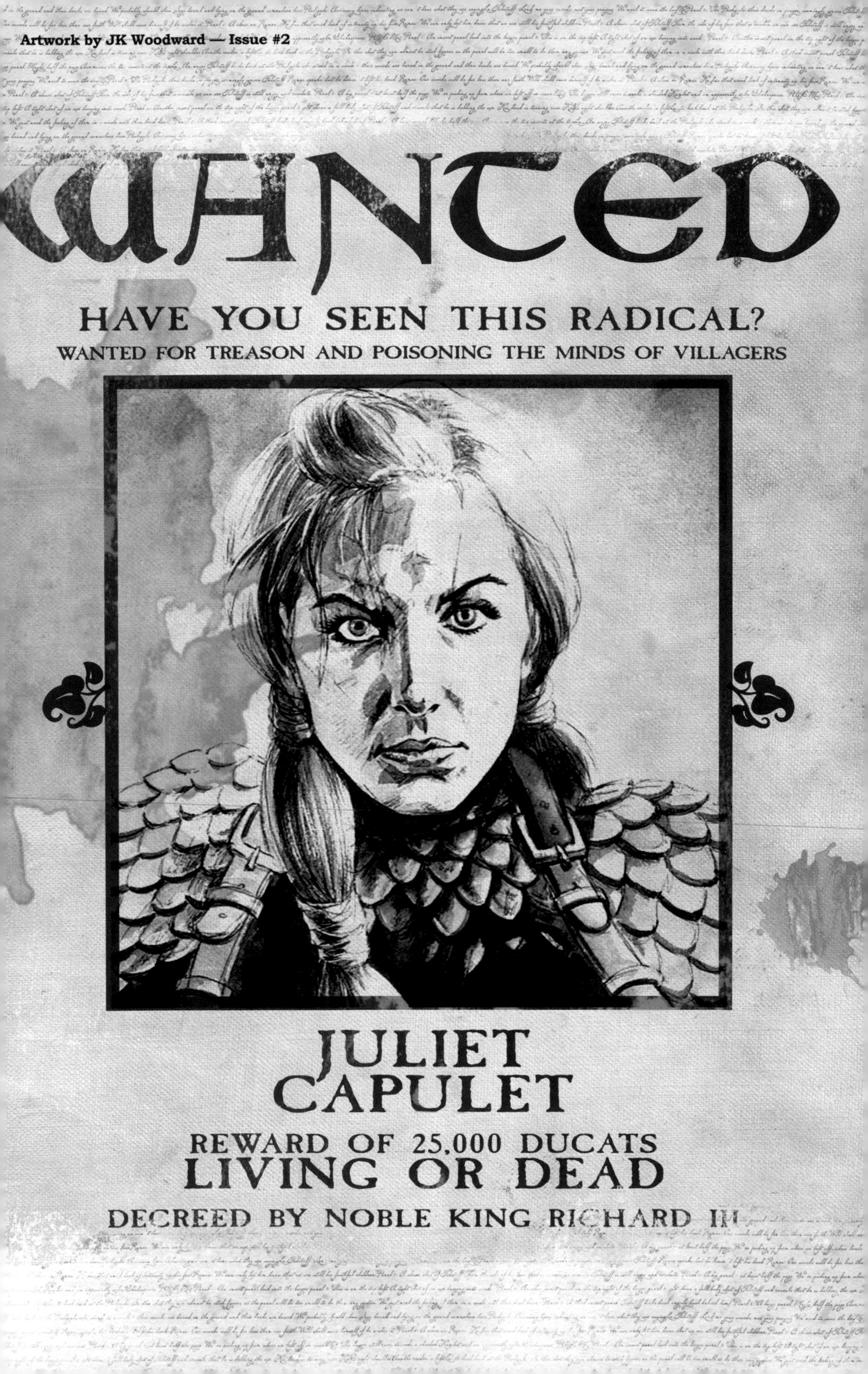
WANTED
HAVE YOU SEEN THIS RADICAL?
WANTED FOR TREASON AND POISONING THE MINDS OF VILLAGERS
JULIET
CAPULET
REWARD OF 25,000 DUCATS
LIVING OR DEAD
DECREED BY NOBLE KING RICHARD III
Artwork by JK Woodward — Issue #2

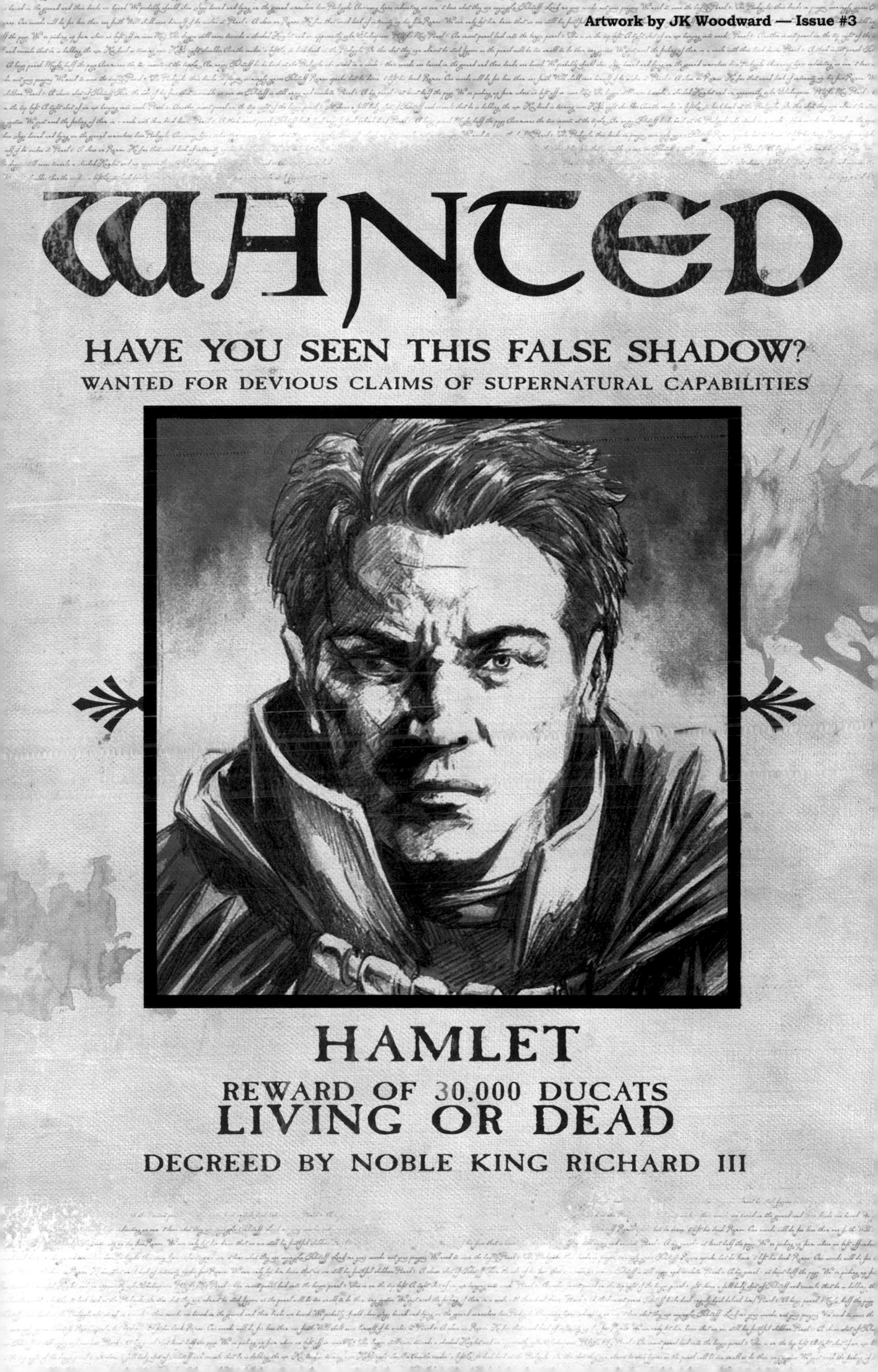
WANTED
HAVE YOU SEEN THIS FALSE SHADOW?
WANTED FOR DEVIOUS CLAIMS OF SUPERNATURAL CAPABILITIES
HAMLET
REWARD OF 30,000 DUCATS
LIVING OR DEAD
DECREED BY NOBLE KING RICHARD III

Artwork by JK Woodward — Issue #3

Artwork by JK Woodward — Issue #4

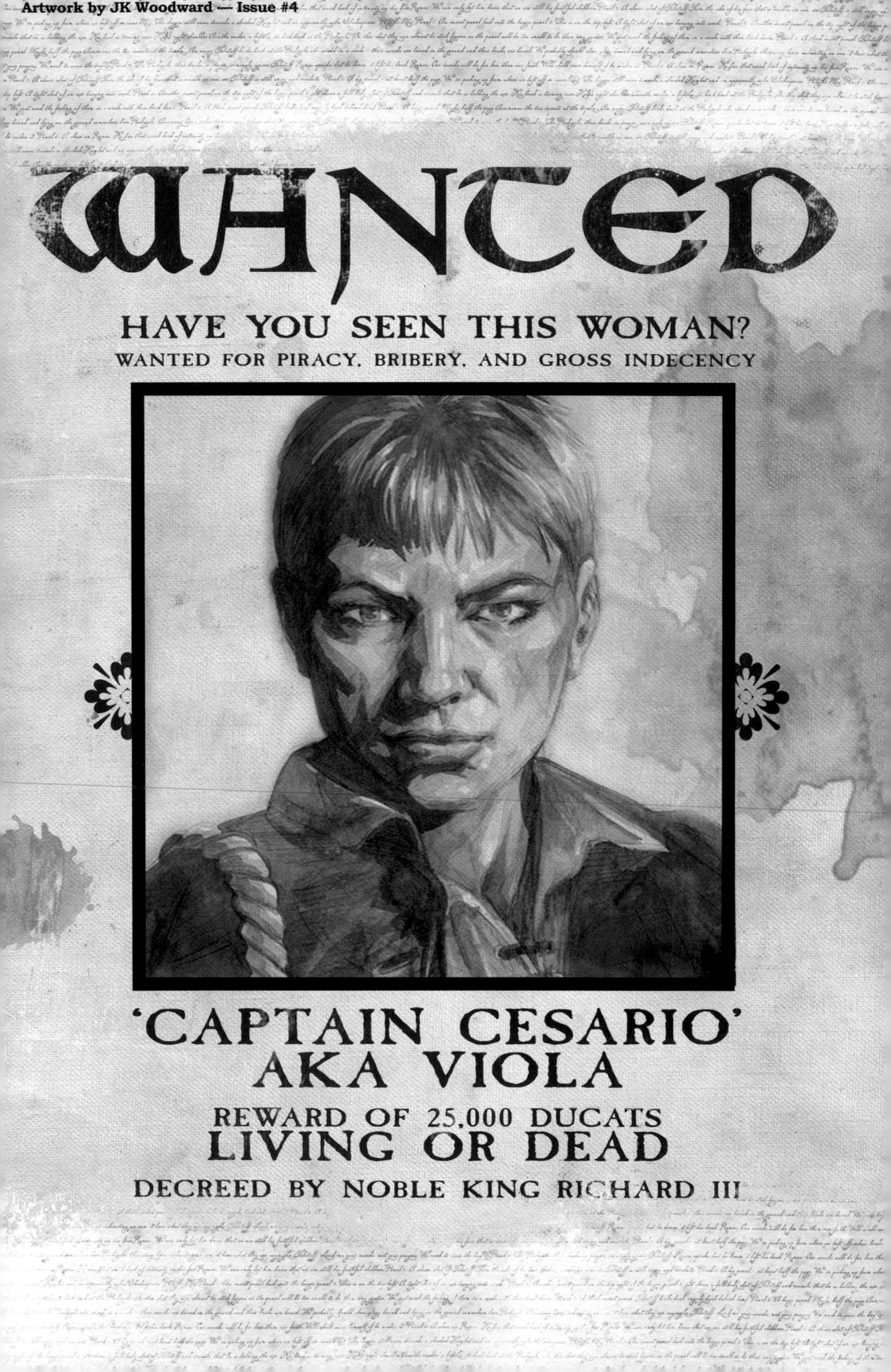
WANTED
HAVE YOU SEEN THIS WOMAN?
WANTED FOR PIRACY, BRIBERY, AND GROSS INDECENCY
'CAPTAIN CESARIO'
AKA VIOLA
REWARD OF 25,000 DUCATS
LIVING OR DEAD
DECREED BY NOBLE KING RICHARD III

Pin-up Artwork by Vivian Ng

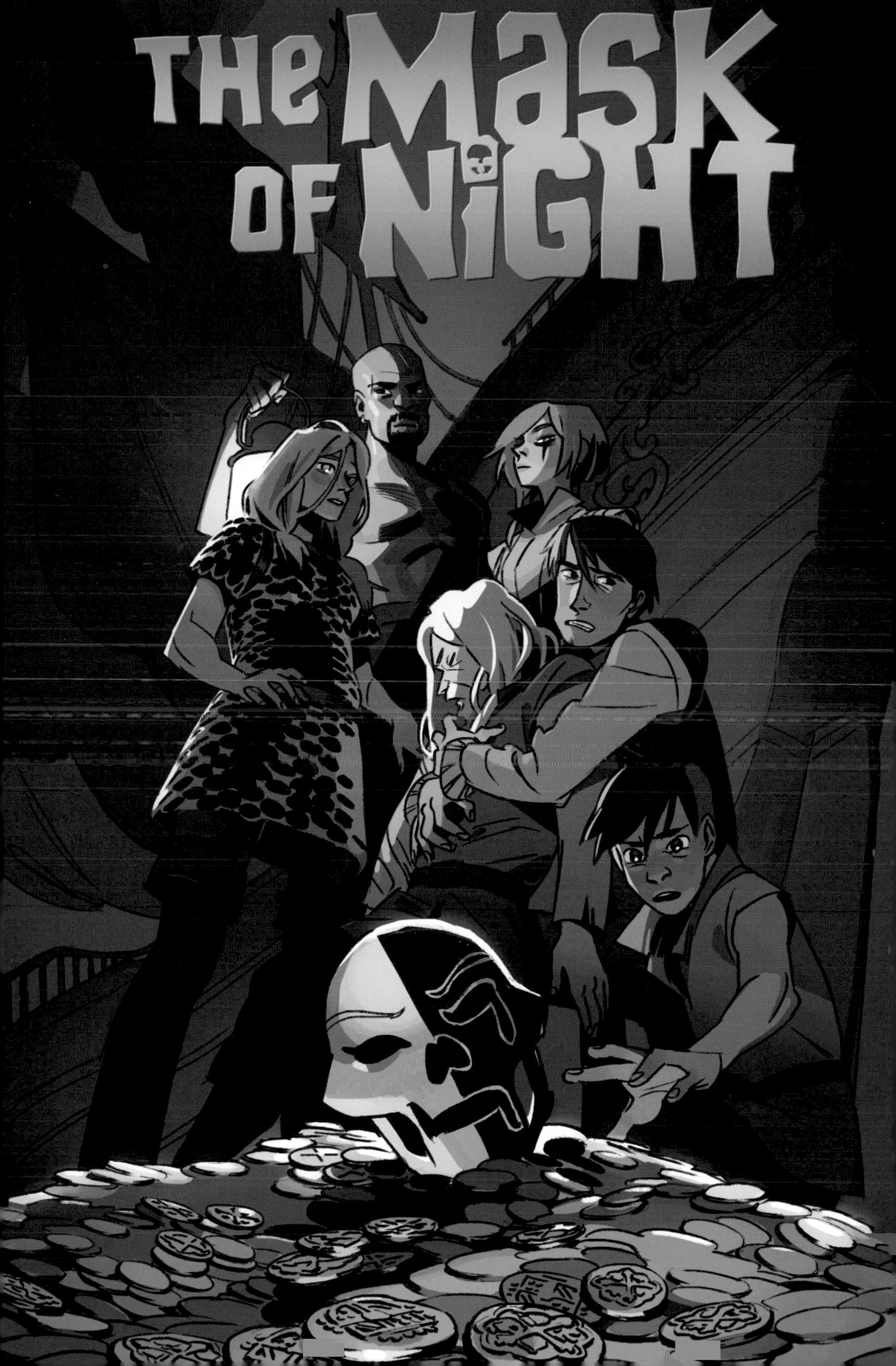
The Mask of Night

Winner of our Tumblr contest Ian Mahler.
kill-shakespeare.tumblr.com

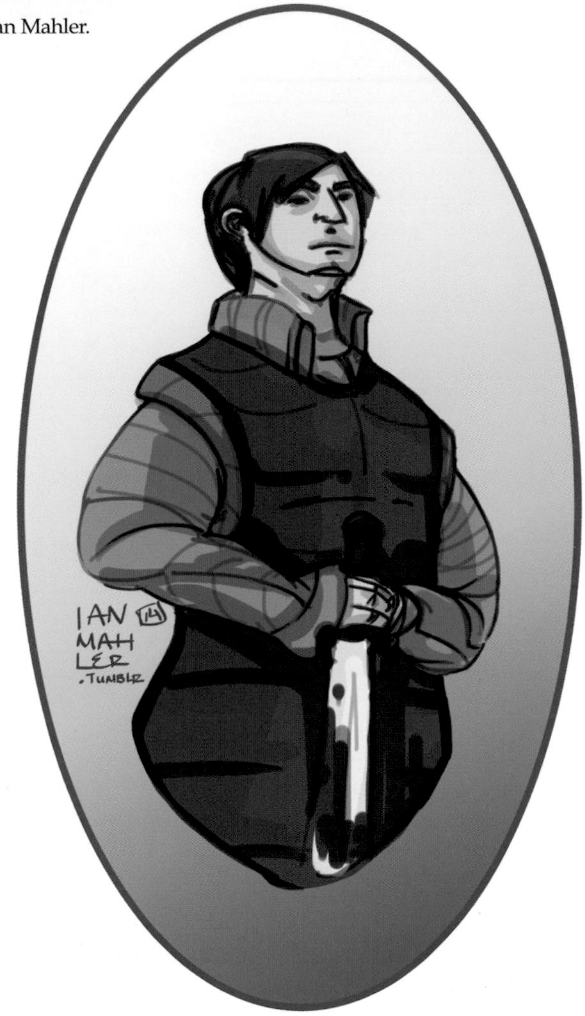
IAN MAHLER .TUMBLR

Second place our Tumblr contest STRAWBERI-CHAN.
kill-shakespeare.tumblr.com

Long gone, but not slain,
Set faraway like the sun, young Hamlet shall not return,
The promise of day means little more
Than the passing of a cloud
As the world rocks beneath his feet,
The waves are rough, the vast blue yonder
Is blissfully unaware of the poor prince
Puffs of wispy air peacefully at ease
In their kingdom of the sky
Yet they too, are misunderstood,
Too distant to recognize
The clouds are branded on perception,
It's a puppy. A wolf. A murderer.
The cloud never changed, but the perspective did.
Hamlet, too, has not changed
Yet the peoples' view have singed his name
In the toxic accusation of a murderer.
He must surpass the shackles that bind him,
Find himself as the clouds stroll onwards in their strife
Until one day he shall find
The sun will once again rise upon the dawn
Beyond the dark hauntings of grey infringing the mind
Of Lord Hamlet that once buried his future,
But now will set a blaze upon a new path
Kindled by the enticing need to eradicate his creator,
To take his life into his own hands.
Hamlet will kill Shakespeare.

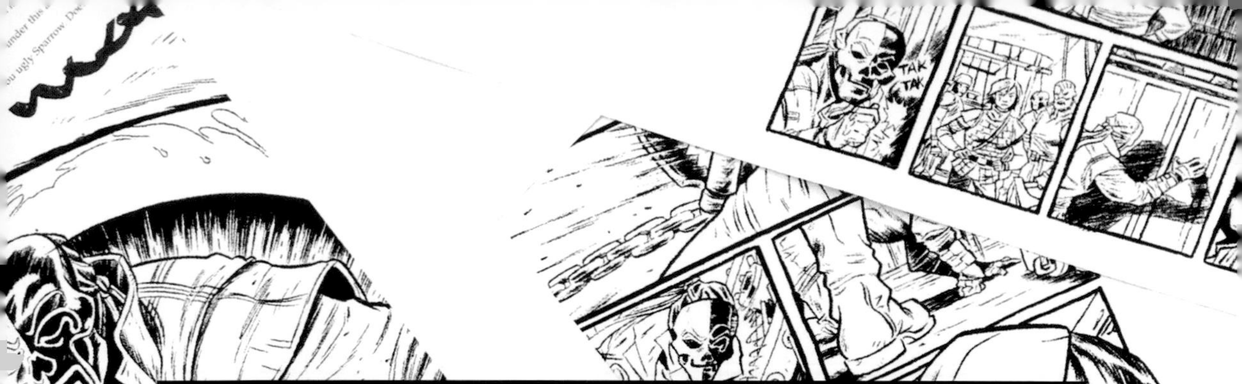

Story Breakdown

When we first started to work on *Kill Shakespeare* over four years ago we had absolutely no experience in the comics industry (other than Conor's stint working at The Silver Snail comics shop in Toronto, Canada). We had almost no idea what a comic script looked like or how the collaboration with an artist was supposed to work. Thankfully, by hunting online and digging through graphic novels we were able to piece together an idea of how to turn an idea into an actual comic.

So we want to pay it forward and provide you, dear reader, with an inside glimpse into the process behind the creation of an issue of *Kill Shakespeare* – from the script stage to the final inks (done amazingly by Andy Belanger). You'll have a chance to see how we put together the idea on paper and then see how Andy is able to capture our ideas – and then more – with the magic of his pencil and brushes.

So wander through this adventureland if you dare to see what really happens when you open the curtain…

Anthony & Conor
October, 2014

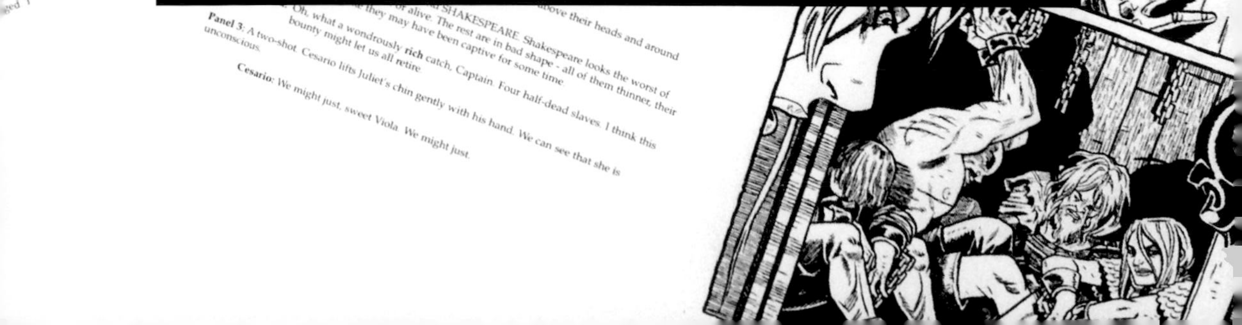

THE MASK OF NIGHT
"A MOST NOTORIOUS PIRATE"
Written by Conor McCreery & Anthony Del Col

April 22, 2014

Page One

Panel 1: A full-page panel.

In the DEAD OF NIGHT a PIRATE LEAPS at the reader. One hand holds a sword raised high in the air. In the other hand is a **classic dirk**.

This is CESARIO.

He wears dark padded leather clothing: black, brown or navy. The clothing is sleek, almost modern looking. This is not Jack Sparrow.

The most notable thing about him, though - in fact the thing that will stay with his enemies as long as they live - is the MASK he wears, a grotesque parody of the "Comedy" and "Tragedy" masks.

Half of the mask has the twisted grin of Comedy, the other the grimace of Tragedy. The mask might be two tones – Comedy could be white with a red smile, while Tragedy could be predominantly red, but with a white grimace.

The key is that the overall effect is both intimidating, yet somehow, slightly devil-may-care in the way that V from *V from Vendetta*'s mask is. Maybe one of the eyes, has a painted on eye-patch — our one wink (ha, ha) to pirate tradition?

Behind Cesario, we should be able to make out a BATTLE.

We are on board a PIRATE SHIP. Cesario's crew are FIGHTING RIVAL PIRATES. They wear make-up versions of his mask. Some mimic Cesario but most are of their own design. Have fun with these as well, Andy; they can be a mix of horrific, comic, and the absurd.

We won't see too much of them here. The focus is on Cesario but this helps contextualize where he is.

> **Cesario:** Cesario **never** dies!

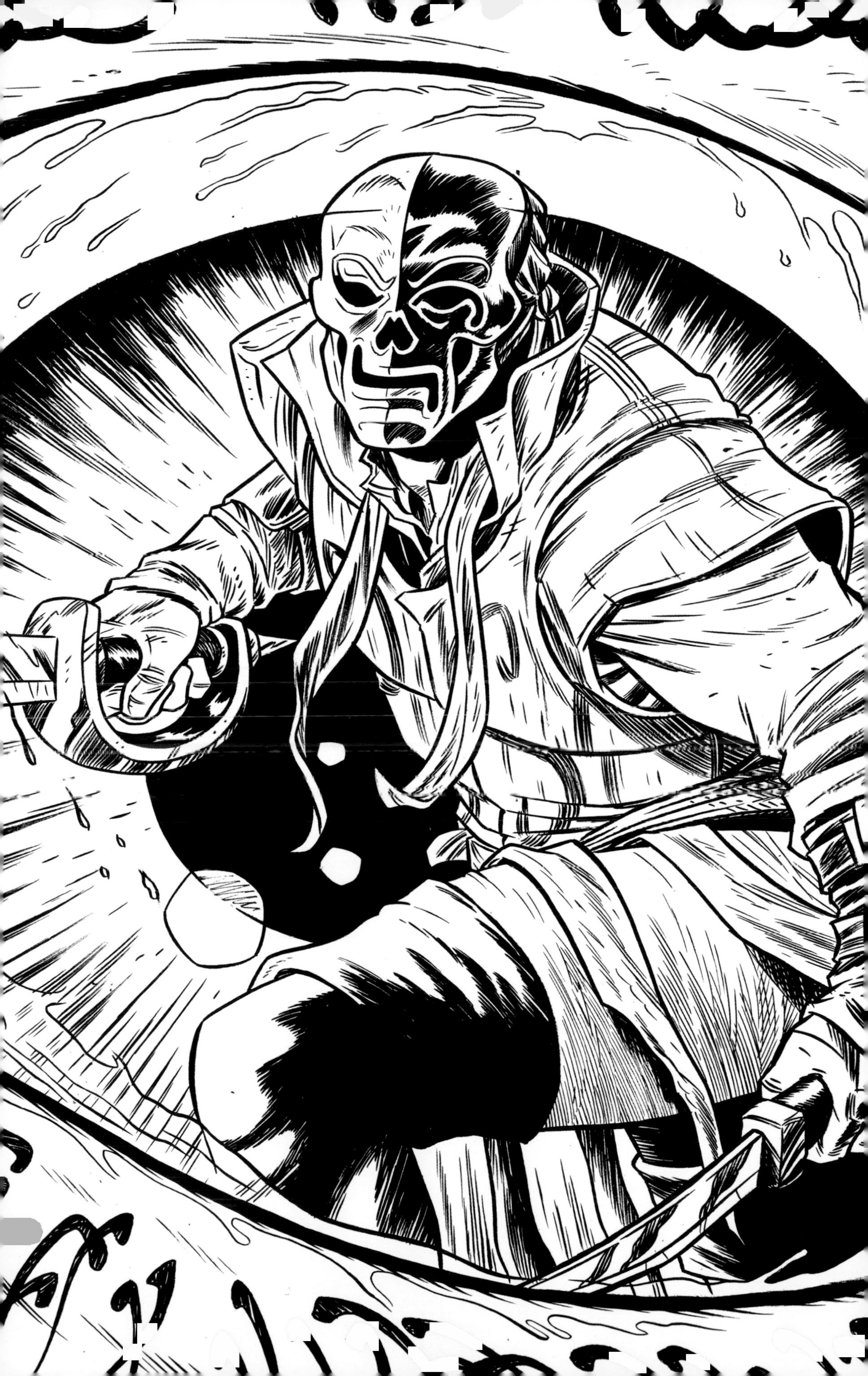

Page Two

Panel 1: An establishing shot of *The Boreas*, Cesario's ship, locked together with its prey, a rival pirate's vessel. These should both be sleek corsairs. This panel stretches across this page and Page 3.

Panel 2: I was imagining that panels 2-4 will be like a side-scrolling video-game. Each of the RIVAL PIRATES should fit a stereotype – a parrot on the shoulder, a bandana on the head, etc.

Cesario lands on his feet and runs through a RIVAL PIRATE with his sword. A second pirate, NEXT PIRATE, long flowing hair, is behind the first.

>   **Rival Pirate:** Urk!

Panel 3: Same angle. WHACK! Using his momentum, Cesario spins forward and slams the NEXT PIRATE in the side of the head with his elbow. We see a THIRD PIRATE, a real ugly brute, sword upraised, is next in line.

>   **Next Pirate:** Unh.

>   **Third Pirate:** Graaaaaa—

>   **Third Pirate:** —aaaa—

Panel 4: Same angle. Cesario, drops to a knee, blocking a CHOPPING STRIKE with his sword.

>   **Cesario:** Too **easy**, gentlemen. Too easy.

Panel 5: We get a good view of Cesario as he uses his dirk and stabs the THIRD PIRATE in the groin.

>   **Third Pirate:** —aaa-*ooooohhhhh!*

>   **Cesario:** You call yourself pirates?

Panel 6: Cesario stands and admires his handiwork, lying in a heap at his feet. We can't see his face because of the mask but his hands and body language signal disappointment.

>   **Cesario:** You **sully** my good name by mere association.

Page Three

Panel 1: FRIGHTENING FREAK stands at least 7 feet tall. He's broadly muscled, ugly as sin, and naked from the waist up, revealing a litany of scars that shows this guy has won fight after fight.

In his nose is a large gold ring. A chain runs from the nose ring to a large ear-cuff in his right ear. In his hands he has a strange weapon, the JAWS OF DEATH. It is like a bear-trap on a chain (kind of like what the one zombie-hick uses in "Cabin in the Woods").

Panel 2: A close-up of this ugly bastard.

    1a. Freak: Your **name** will soon be on the lips of the gravedigger.

    Freak: I shall snatch thee in one-half, **Cesario**, with these jaws of death!

Panel 3: The Jaws of Death smash into the deck — wood chips fly up…

Panel 4: But Cesario ROLLS under this attack.

    Cesario: Oh, you ugly Sparrow. Does not a man-jack of you <u>ever</u> listen?

Panel 5: And DRIVES his sword AND dirk deep into the monster's side.

    Cesario: Cesario…

Panel 6: The Freak snaps the weapons with his hands.

    Cesario: Never…

Panel 7: Cesario looks at the broken, jagged and bloody sword.

    Cesario: …

    (6) **Cesario:** Well, that was unfortunate.

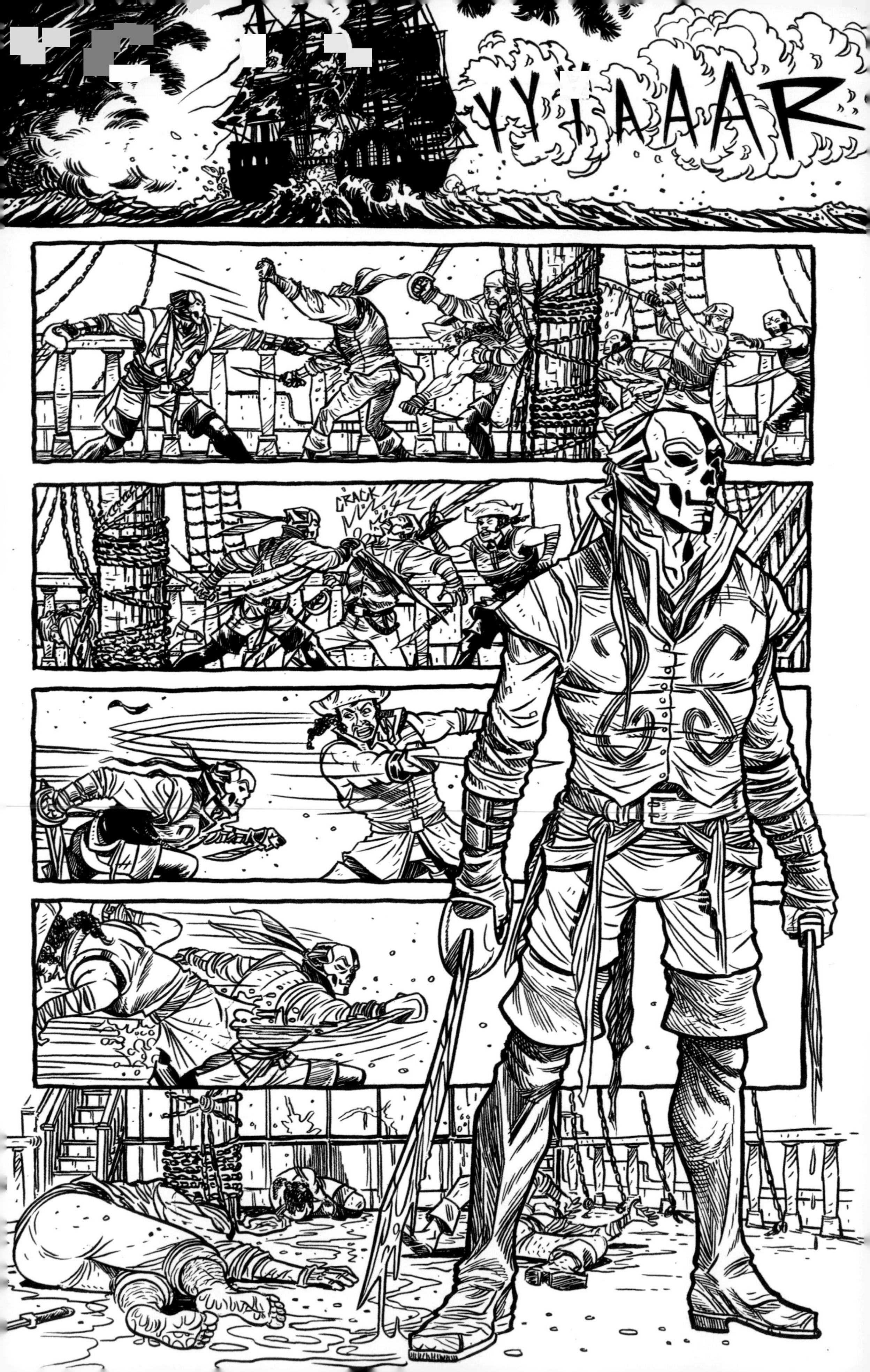
CRACK

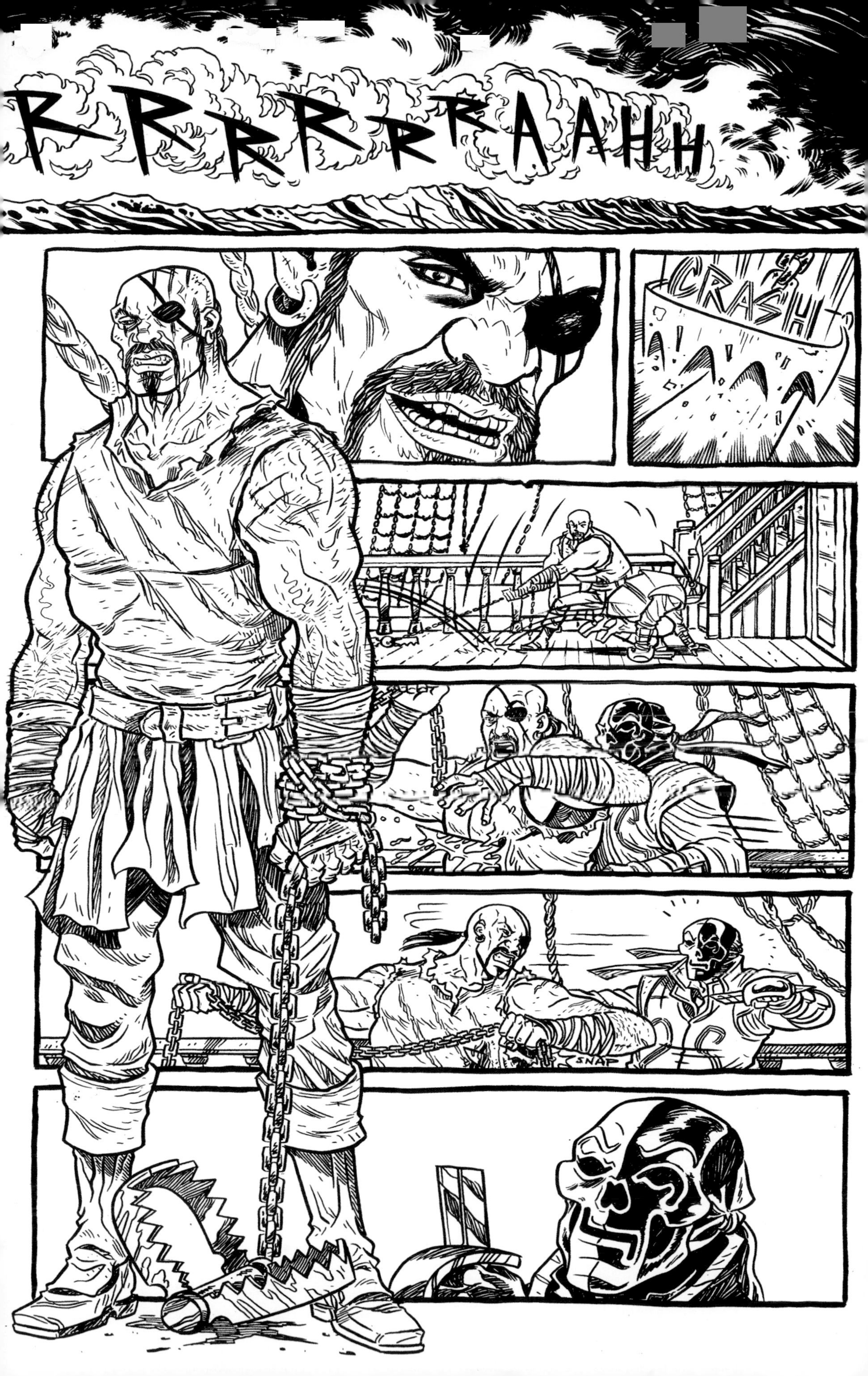
RRRRRRRAAHH
CRASH
SNAP

Page Four

Panel 1: SMACK! Cesario is smashed in the back of the headby the Jaws.

     1a. SFX: CRACK

Panel 2: He lands painfully, with his back against the wheel of the ship.

     1b. SFX: WHUMP

Panel 3: He painfully tries to rise to his feet.

Panel 4: The Freak is already on top of him. He's using the CHAIN of the Jaws of Death to try to choke Cesario. Cesario has one wrist in-between his neck and the chain. It's the only thing keeping him alive. He's bleeding from the wrist and it's only a matter of time before the Freak snaps it.

     Freak: The pangs of death will shake thee, Cesario.

     Freak: And then I'll have thy mask so **all** can see thy despised face!

Panel 5: Cesario's free hand is on the Freak's side, searching.

Panel 6: Cesario finds the fresh wounds… … slips his hand inside…

Panel 7: The Freak suddenly realizes what Cesario is doing.

     Freak: Guh?

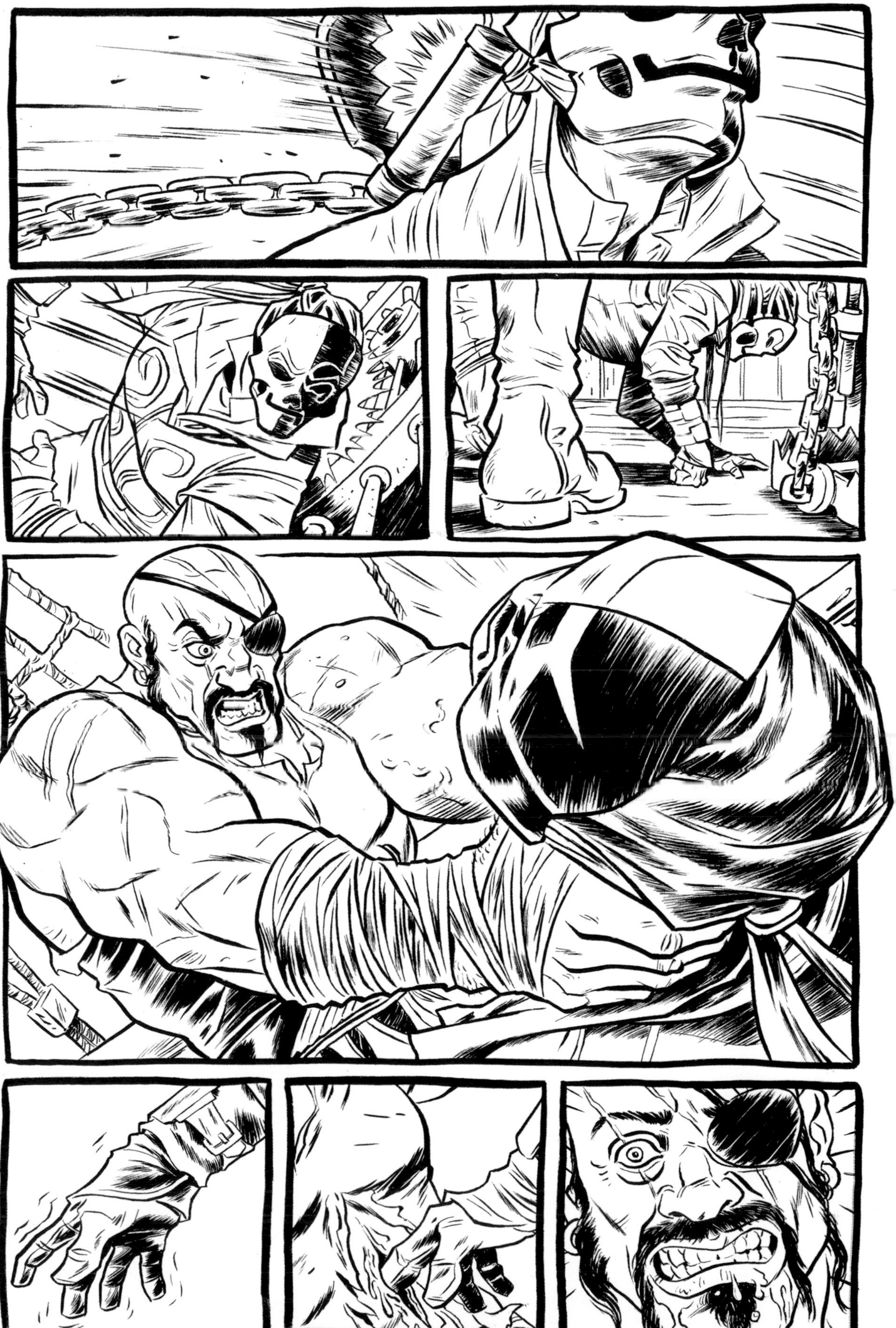

Page Five

Panel 1: Cesario is reaching into the Freak's guts.

    1A. **Freak:** Hraaaagggghhh!

Panel 2: His hand comes out bloody, with a CHUNK of intestine/guts. Nothing too graphic is needed, just a bloody hunk of meat.

Panel 3: In horrible pain the Freak rears back, looking at the bloody wound.

Panel 4: A piece of flesh drops into the deck.

    1B. SFX: SHLOP

Panel 5: Cesario loops the Jaw's CHAIN around the monster's neck…

Panel 6: … and pulls backs, toppling the Freak.

    1C. HRGK!

Panel 7: The Freak is on his back. Cesario has him in a rear-naked choke. He's now the one using the chain to try to snap the other man's neck.

One of the Freak's big hands should be behind Cesario's head, the Freak is trying to tear Cesario's head off, and it should look like he could do it.

    Cesario: Come now, chap. With all this talk of death you could kindly **accept** yours.

    Freak: Glrrgg…

    SFX: SNAP!

Panel 8: Cesario flops back, exhausted. The Freak's body lies limp on top of him, his neck at a strange angle to his head.

    SFX: Clap. Clap. Clap.

    Viola (off-panel): What performance, friend, was **that?**

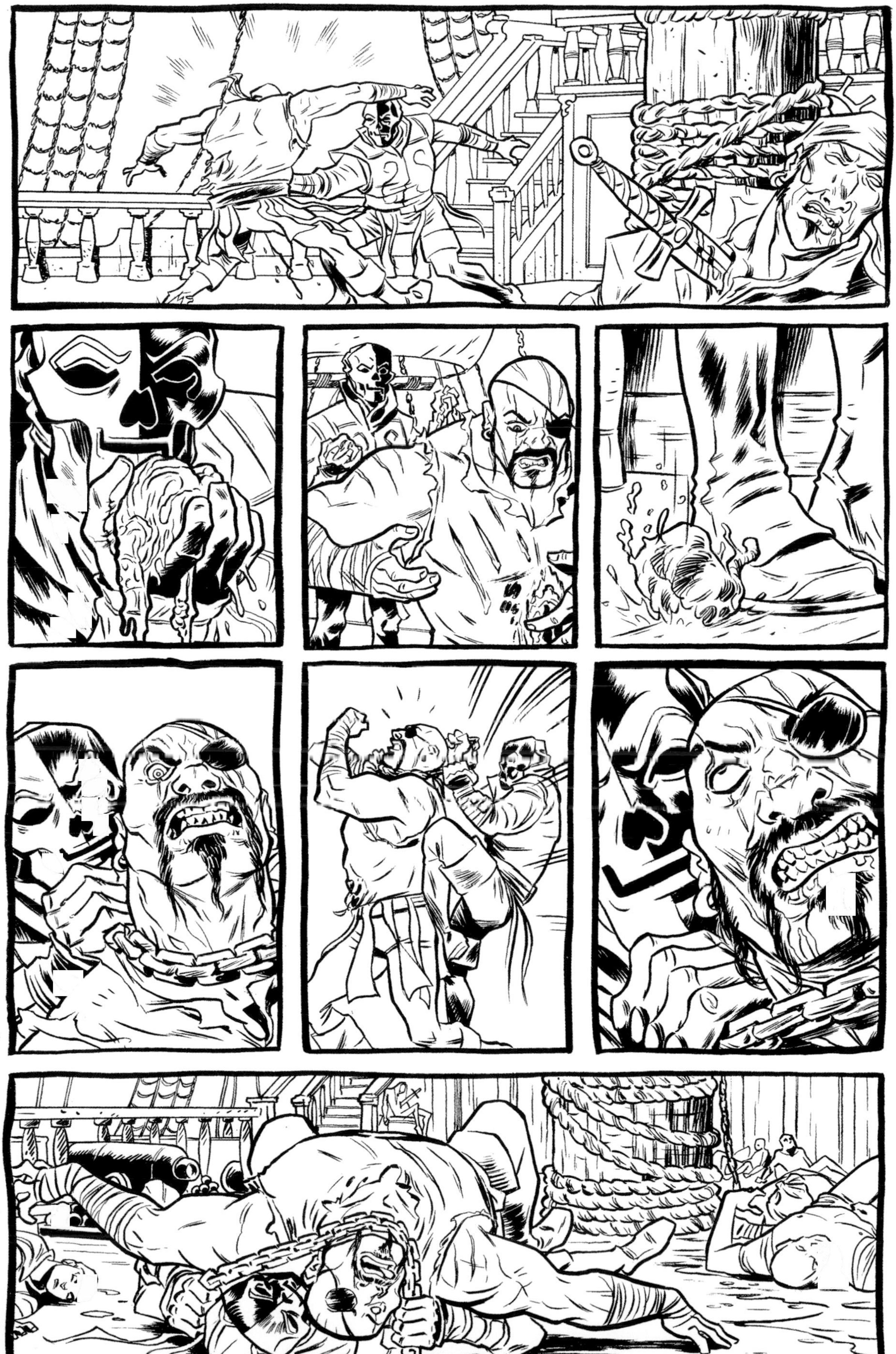

Page Six

Panel 1: Reveal a handful of CESARIO'S CREW, all of them with painted masks, standing around their leader.

Standing slightly ahead of them is VIOLA. She's a dangerous-looking woman with perhaps the most frightening face-paint. However her body-language and expression are mocking and insubordinate, with a large dash of affection.

> **Cesario (off-panel):** How long have you been standing and watching, Viola?

> **Viola:** Long enough to see that even if Cesario does not die…

Panel 2: A close shot of Cesario.

> **Viola (off-panel):** …he **falls** most amusingly.

> **Cesario:** >Sigh< Will no one save me from this woman's slings and arrows?

Panel 3: A two-shot. Viola grins as she helps pull Cesario up.

> **Cesario:** I fall amusingly, but with a **purpose**, woman.

> **Ceasrio:** While you lot ran all pell-mell about the deck, I cunningly ascertained that our frightful friend refused to be lured from this spot

Panel 4: Cesario has walked back to where he first faced the Freak. We can tell it is the same wall because of however you marked that wall (Page 3, Panel 1). Viola smirks as she walks behind him.

> **Cesario:** Protecting something of **great value**, undoubtedly.

> **Viola:** Oh, undoubtedly.

> **Viola:** But surely you would excuse *one* doubt over a treasure being concealed *exactly* where the stoutest guard stood.

Panel 5: Cesario starts to tap his knuckles along the wall. It might be fun to rake the angle here so all we can see is Cesario and the wooden wall.

Panel 6: Viola watches Cesario work with a grin.

> **Viola:** Is that not a trifle obvious, Captain?

Panel 7: Cesario knocks on another stretch of the wood. He's paying complete attention to this.

> **Cesario:** My dear, you are too intelligent to be a pirate. Most of us have barely the brains to swing a cutlass without cutting off our cock.

Panel 8: He knocks again, but this time the sound is different.

> **Cesario:** See? As dim as mollusks.

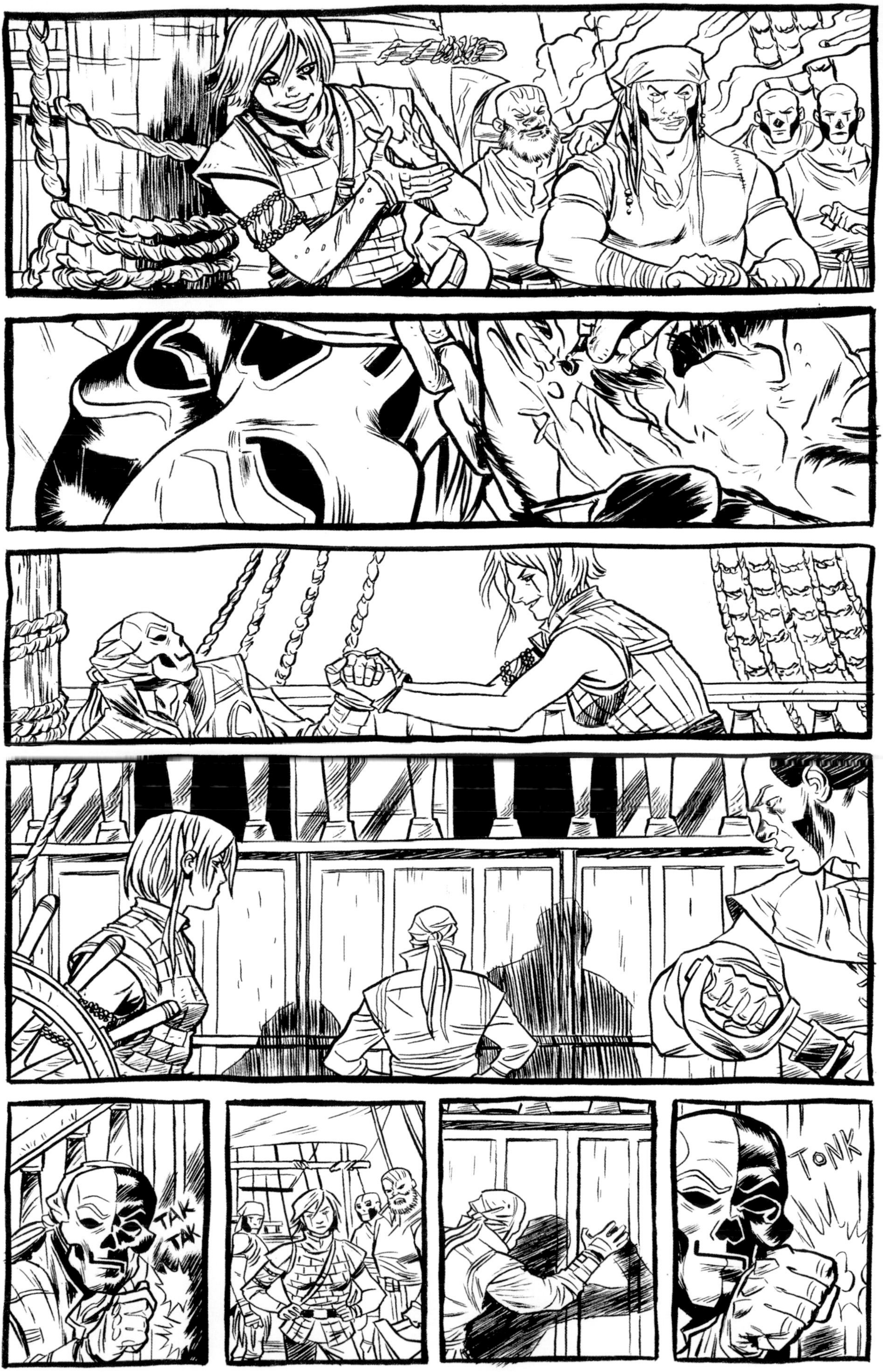
TAK
TAK
TONK

Page Seven

Panel 1: The wood panel springs open.

Panel 2: Inside we see four people hanging, their wrists bound above their heads and around some sort of pipe.

These are JULIET, HAMLET, OTHELLO and SHAKESPEARE. Shakespeare looks the worst of the bunch. We can't tell if he's dead or alive. The rest are in bad shape - all of them thinner, their clothes ragged. They look like they may have been captive for some time.

> **Viola:** Oh, what a wondrously **rich** catch, Captain. Four half-dead slaves. I think this bounty might let us all retire.

Panel 3: A two-shot. Cesario lifts Juliet's chin gently with his hand. We can see that she is unconscious.

> **Cesario:** We might just, sweet Viola. We might just.

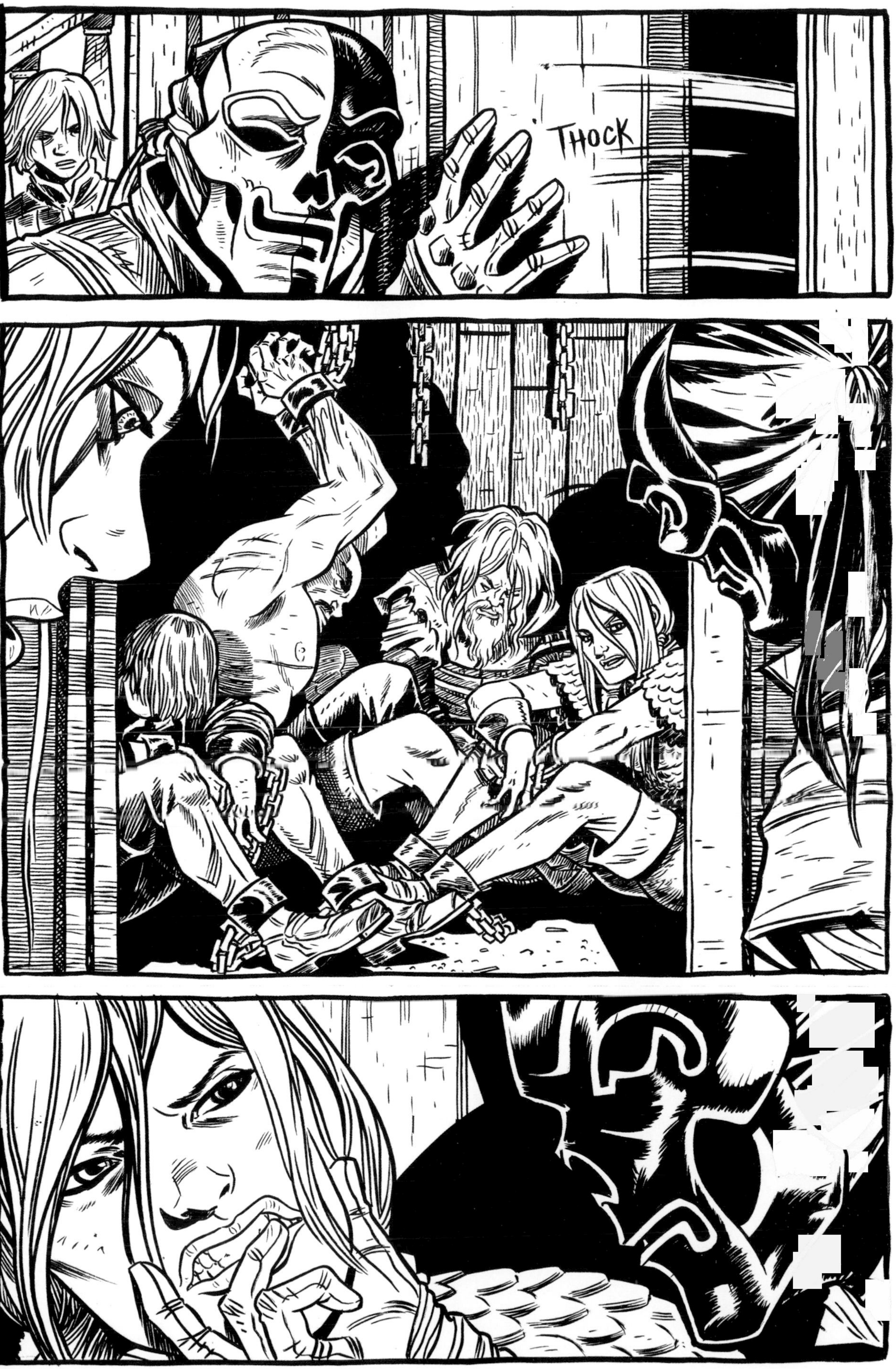
THOCK

Page Eight

Panel 1: An establishing shot of Cesario's ship racing through the sea. *The Boreas* is a classic pirate vessel - small, fast, agile; it's the *Black Pearl*-lite .

We can see a THICK FOG is starting to roll in. The morning sun is JUST starting to rise, so we're not totally in the dark anymore.

> **CAPTION:** *The Boreas.*

> **CAPTION – Viola:** "Do you not wish to **play** thy Viola?"

> **CAPTION – Cesario (let's use a different colour from Viola):** "Saucy wench. You are not tired from our exertions 'pon our enemies?"

Panel 2: Now we're on deck of *The Boreas*. The crew goes about their duties. A FIRST MATE yells at the men and women to prepare the ship. Gear is being stowed, sails tightened, etc…

> **CAPTION - Viola**: "Never. I pity the ladies who know nothing of the pirate way, nor of broil and battle. There is **nothing** like pillage to prepare one's passage for paradise."

> **CAPTION – Cesario:** "If mayhem be the food of love, then reave on, you say?"

Panel 3: We're below deck in Cesario's bedchambers. He and Viola are in the midst of MAKING LOVE. Cesario is on top. Viola is on the bottom, one hand around the back of Cesario's head, keeping him pulled close to her. She has a wicked grin on her face.

> **Viola:** O, Captain…

Panel 4: She pulls him in for a deep kiss.

> **Viola:** …my captain… It is **ravaging** that comes to mind.

Page Nine

Panel 1: They break apart. Viola has an amused expression on her face. Her arms are opened wide, inviting Cesario to again mount her.

> **Viola:** That lacked thy **usual** vigour. Come dance to your Viola's sweet tune.

> **Cesario:** You know I adore its country steps…

> **Viola:** But…?

> **Cesario:** Titus has smashed the Prodigal fleet at Ardea

Panel 2: Cesario is now sitting up, turned away from Viola. Viola lounges on the bed in a provocative feline-like manner, she's still looking for sex, although we don't want any nudity. She is still teasing her lover here and isn't actually offended.

Now we see Cesario's face. He has a beard, something rugged and manly (for some variety from all our other male characters). He smiles as he looks back at Viola – he's teasing her now too.

While we'll get a better look in the next panel, he's not the dashingly handsome man you might expect. He looks more like a professional rugby player. He has a plain face with a broken nose and a cauliflower ear. There is a scar on one cheek above the beard. He's not ugly, but he's rugged. This is not the face that turns the head of women in the tavern.

> **Viola:** So *The Lavinia* will hunt thee again. Is *that* reason to leave me cold?

> **Cesario:** I cannot let Young Lucius steal our newly seized prize.

> **Viola:** Prize? That girl? You offend me, Cesario, thinking 'pon another woman while I lie in your bed unfulfilled.

> **Cesario:** I could scarce *not* think 'pon the Prodigal's General.

Panel 3: Viola wraps herself around Cesario. Her head is on his shoulders – she is nuzzling his neck and ear – very pleased. Her naked body is mostly covered by the fact she's sitting behind the Captain.

> **Viola:** The Capulet? That girl is Juliet Capulet?

> **Viola: Oh!** Most clever Captain, play your Viola.

Page (off-panel): Captain! Captain Cesario!

Panel 4: Reverse angle on the young mate, WILLIAM PAGE, standing in the doorway. He's maybe 11 or 12, all gangly-limbs and bad skin. He's scandalized by seeing the naked Viola (who is off-panel) and so is looking away.

> **Cesario (off-panel):** Well? Page? **Speak**, boy!

Panel 5: Cesario turns over his shoulder to Viola, who is unashamed by her nakedness although, again, we don't really SEE anything here.

> **Cesario:** Oh, in Will's name, put on some breeches, Viola. You've rendered the boy dumb.

Panel 6: Viola is putting on her doublet with a smirk. Page looks at her shyly.

Page (small font, embarrassed and overwhelmed): I didn't know to look port or stern…

> **Viola:** They **never** do, boy.

Panel 7: Cesario is sliding his mask down as he looks at Page.

> **Cesario:** So what is it, Page?

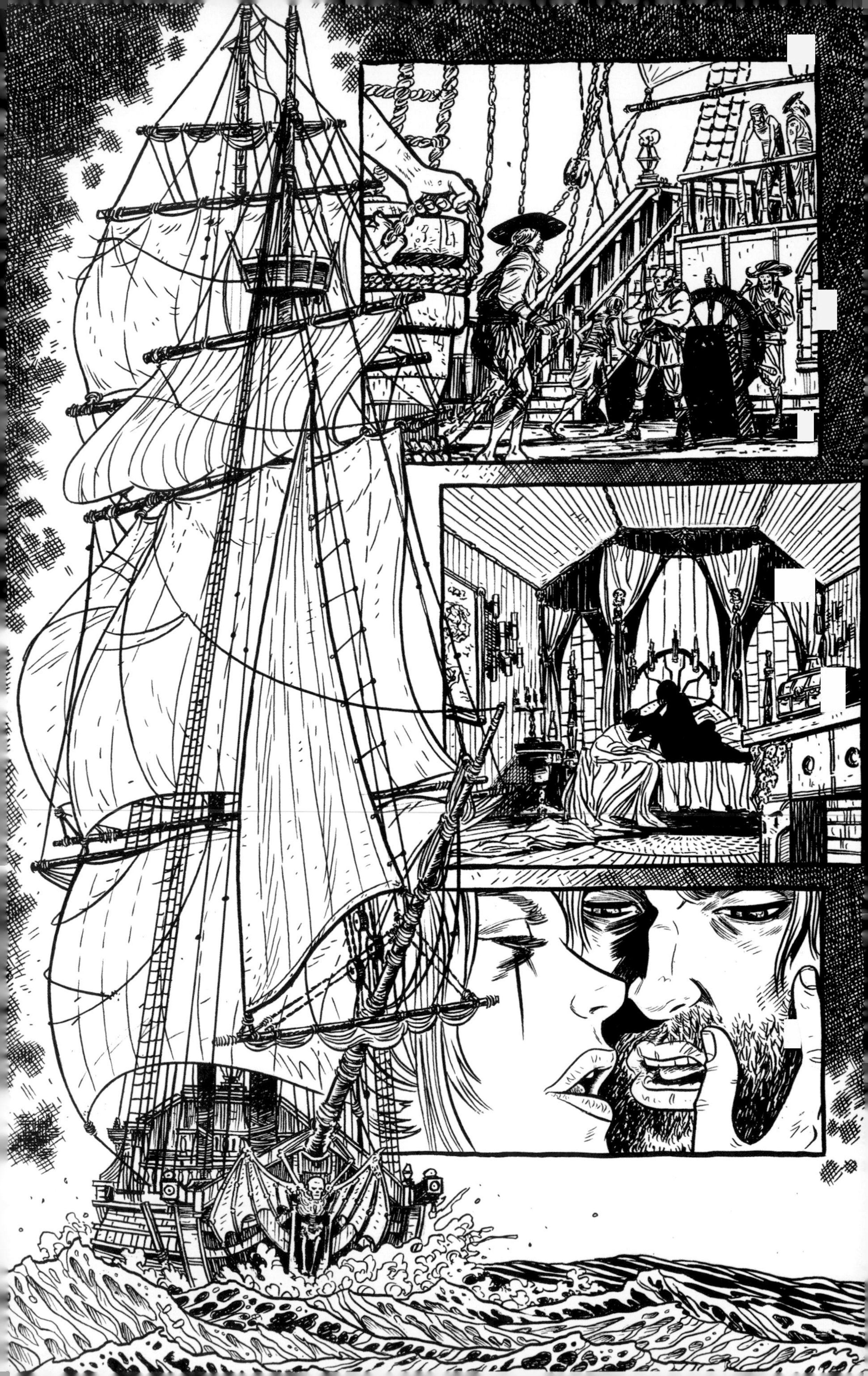

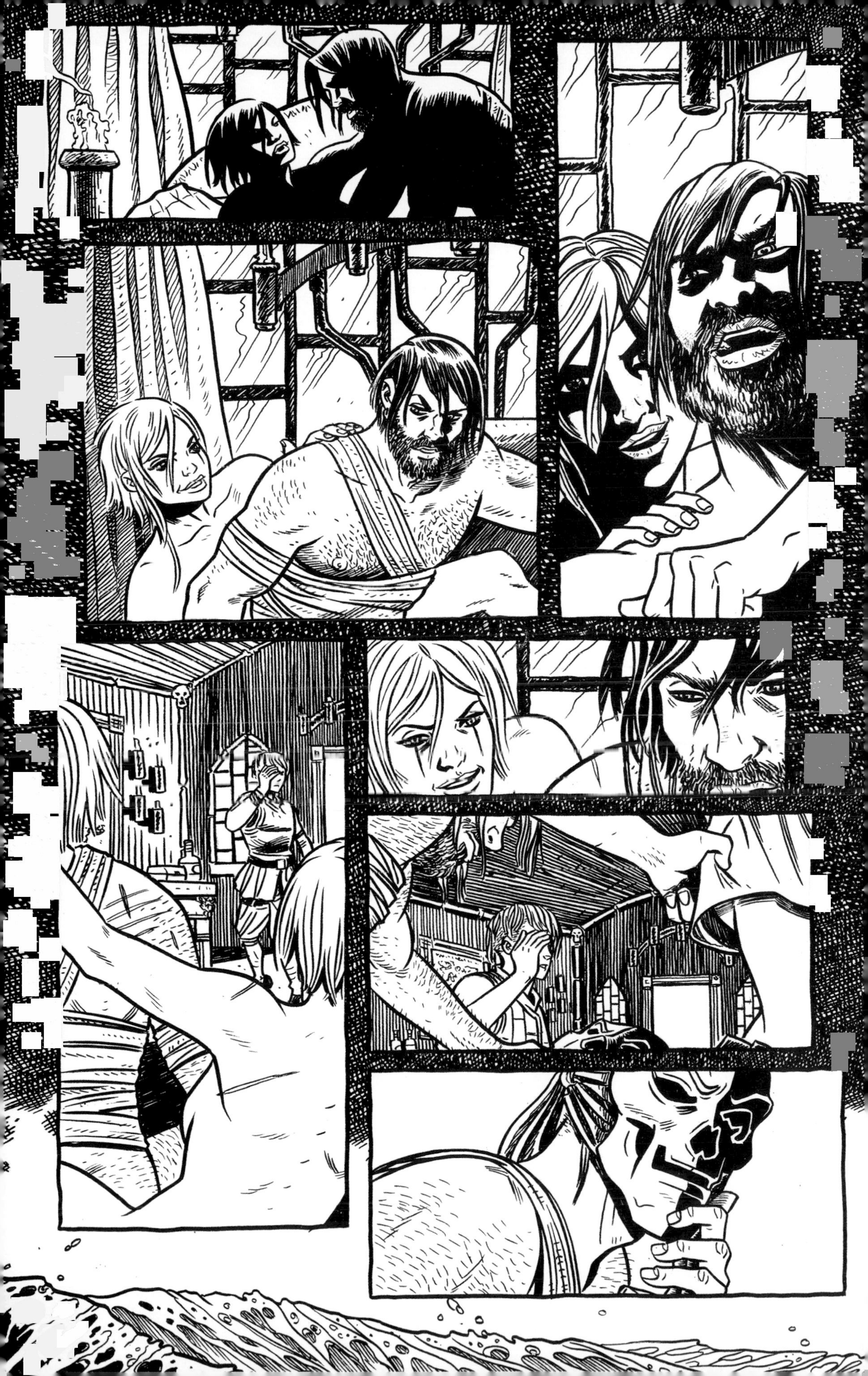

Page Ten

Panel 1: A PIRATE flies through a wooden wall.

>   **CAPTION – Page:** "It's the **Moor**, Captain…

>   **CAPTION - Page:** "…he's gone mad."

Panel 2: Reveal Othello freaking out! A pirate lies unconscious or dead at his feet. Juliet and Hamlet are in the frame, cautiously approaching their friend.

>   **Othello**: **Where is she!** Where have you taken my Desdemona?

Panel 3: Hamlet grabs onto Othello.

>   **Hamlet:** Peace, Othello! This is not real!

>   **Othello:** I saw her! She spoke to me!

Panel 4: Othello throws Hamlet off of him. In the foreground Cesario and Viola arrive.

>   **Othello:** Where hast thou hidden her?

Panel 5: Viola draws her sword.

>   **Othello (off-panel): Desdemona!** Come to me!

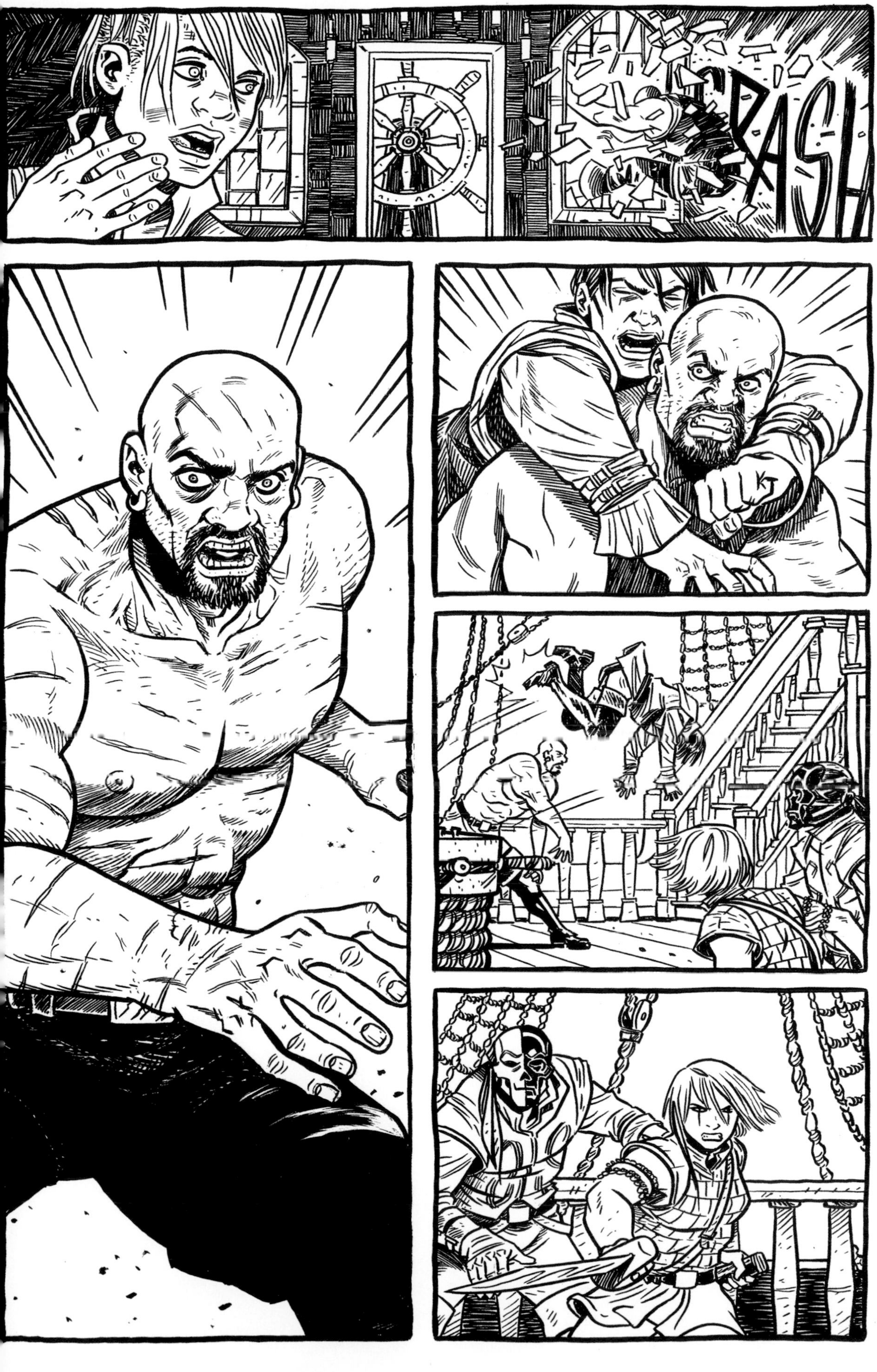

RASH

Page Eleven

Panel 1: Juliet grabs Viola's arm.

> **Juliet: Hold!** Othello is sick, but it will pass.

> **Viola:** Stand aside!

> **Juliet:** It is a fever of the mind. I can calm it.

Panel 2: Viola has wrenched her arm free, the sword raised threateningly above Juliet.

> **Viola: Stand aside!**

> **Cesario (off-panel):** Stay thy hand, Viola!

Panel 3: Viola looks at Cesario reproachfully but lowers her sword.

> **Viola:** She better be worth as much dead as she is alive.

Panel 4: Juliet approaches Othello slowly. Her face is calm, gentle. She is being matter of fact, but not unkind.

> **Juliet:** Othello, Desdemona is not here. She is gone. You **know** this.

Panel 5: Othello turns on Juliet. His face is filled with rage and sorrow. Juliet's face is also sad. She feels for Othello. Watching him lose it like this over Desdemona is hard for her.

> **Othello:** You lie…

> **Juliet:** You know I do not.

Panel 6: Othello grabs Juliet, pulling her up by her throat.

> **Othello: You lie!**

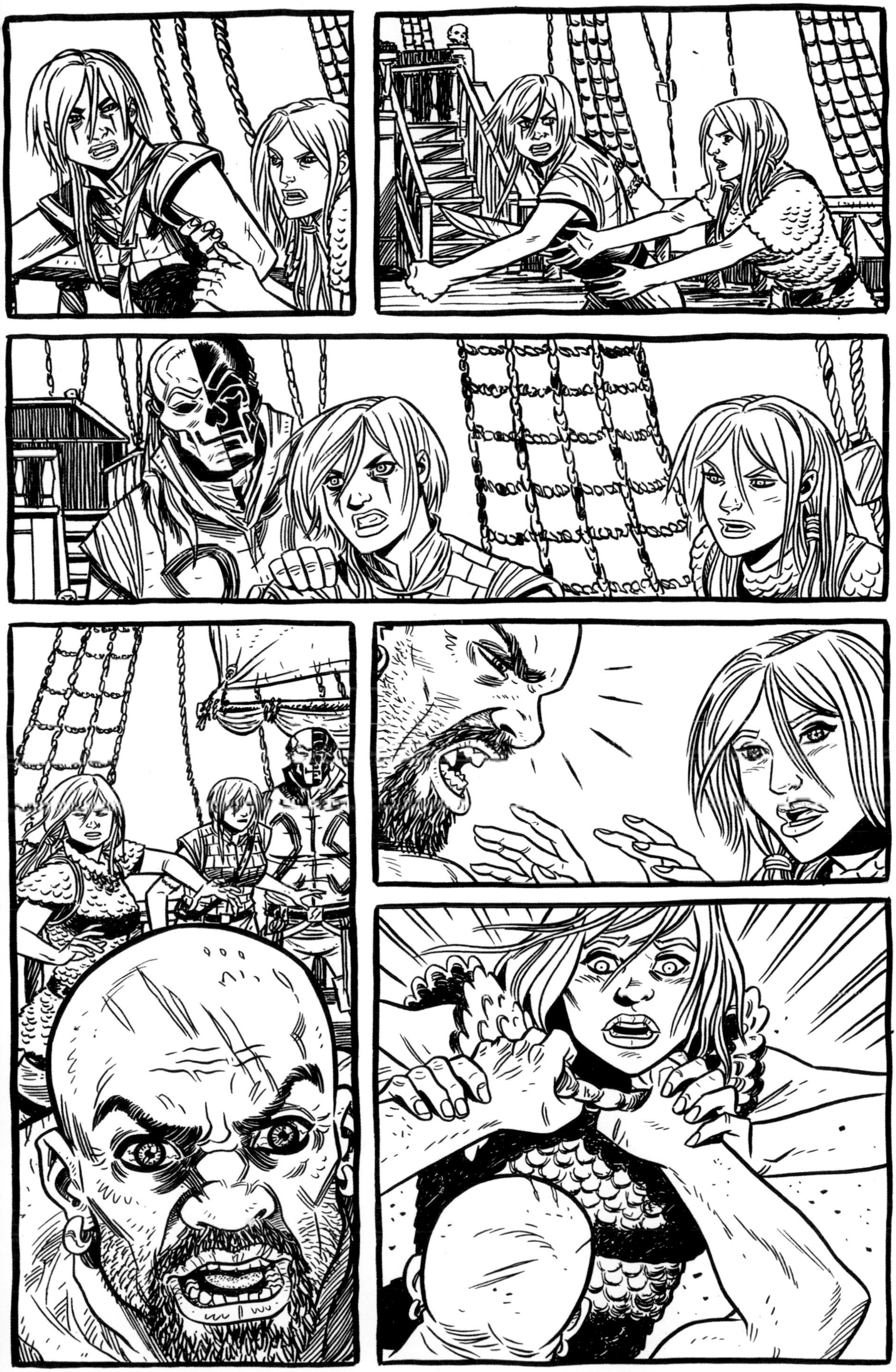

Page Twelve

Panel 1: Othello slams Juliet against the wall.

> **Othello:** Where is she?

Panel 2: Othello's face is wild.

> **Othello: Where is she?!**

Panel 3: He slams her into the wall again. Juliet stays calm as best she can.

> **Othello: Where is she?!!!**

> **Juliet:** She is **dead**, Othello!

Panel 4: Juliet looks at Othello gently. She's not trying to be cruel here.

> **Juliet:** She is dead.

Panel 5: Othello pauses, the truth of this registering with him.

> **Juliet (off-panel):** She cannot speak to thee any longer.

Panel 6: Othello pulls Juliet into a hug.

> **Othello (SMALL):** No, no, no…

> **Juliet:** *Shhhh, shhhh…* this will pass. It is just the island's **poison** working within thee.

> **Juliet:** It will pass.

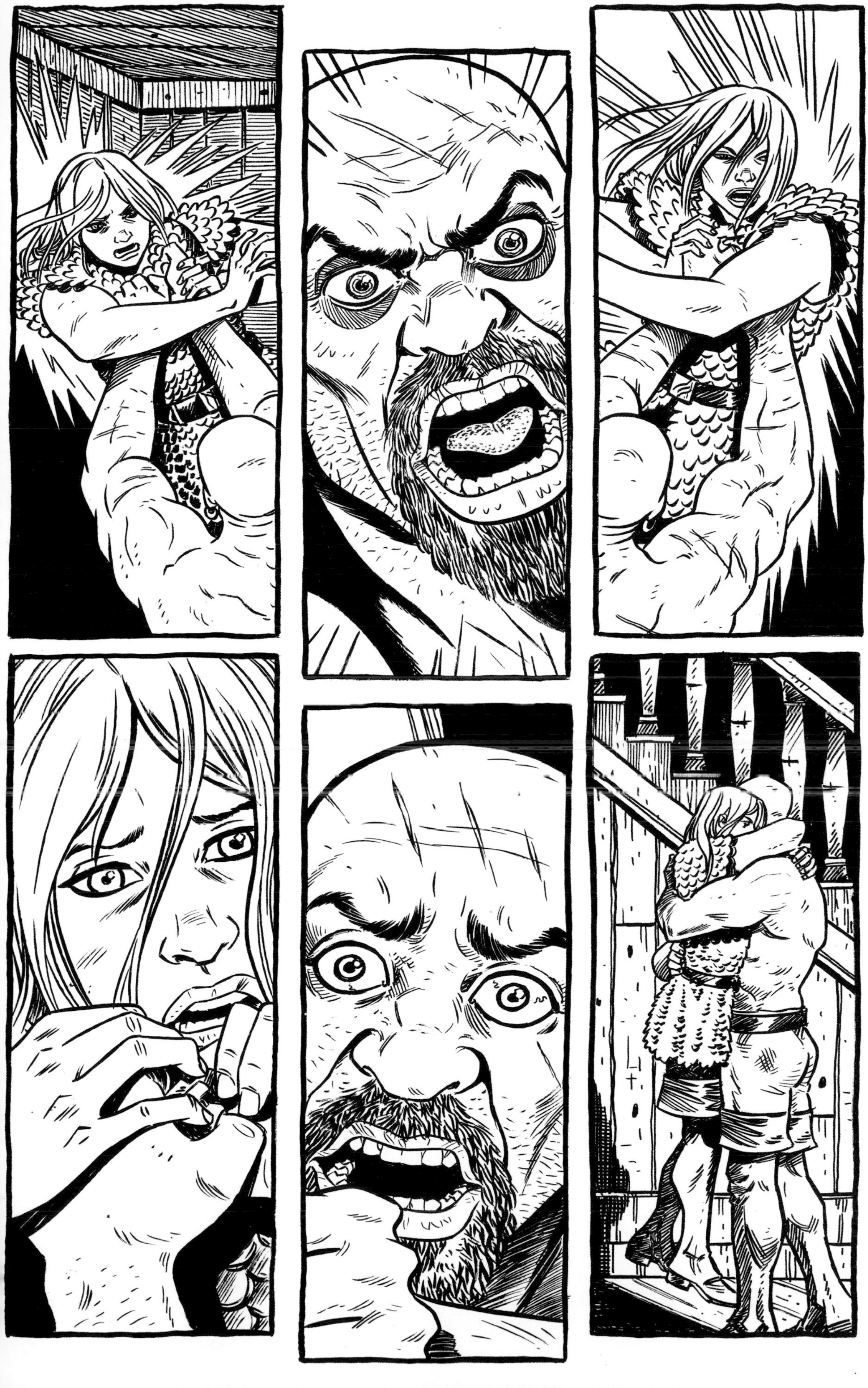

Page Thirteen

Panel 1: Viola and some of CESARIO'S crew separate Othello from Juliet. Juliet isn't fighting this, but she is concerned for Othello. Viola gives Juliet a hard look.

>**Juliet:** Be gentle with him, please. He—

>**Viola:** We shall be as harsh as we judge necessary.

Panel 2: Cesario offers his hand to Juliet. Exhausted, Juliet takes it. Viola is unimpressed. She's not jealous, she just doesn't get why Cesario is bending over backwards for a prisoner like this.

>**Cesario:** We will judge gently, I promise thee. But what ails him?

>**Juliet:** We were trapped 'pon a monstrous island. Its malice **infected** his mind. His ghosts… no longer give him up…

Panel 3: Suddenly, Juliet doubles over. She's trying not to vomit. Cesario stands above her.

>**Juliet:** Hhhk. Hhhhk.

>**Cesario:** My lady, your new friend Cesario has broad shoulders—lean upon them but a little.

>**Hamlet (off-panel):** Friend? I'd be wary if I were **thee**, Captain.

Panel 4: Hamlet is standing, holding his shoulder from where he landed when Othello threw him, but absent-mindedly. He's focusing on Juliet with a cold look.

>**Hamlet:** Ask her what happened to her dear "friend" Romeo.

>**Cesario:** Have a care, sir. She is unwell, and your words provide no medicine.

>**Hamlet:** It is her guilt-strung soul that makes her ill.

Panel 5: Still partially bent over, Juliet stares at Hamlet, the tension obvious. In the background Viola is watching this with great interest.

Panel 6: Cesario lightly helps Juliet stand. He's defusing the tension, but also clearly in Juliet's corner and finds Hamlet's outburst insulting.

>**Cesario:** My lady, you are too pretty for his ugly words.

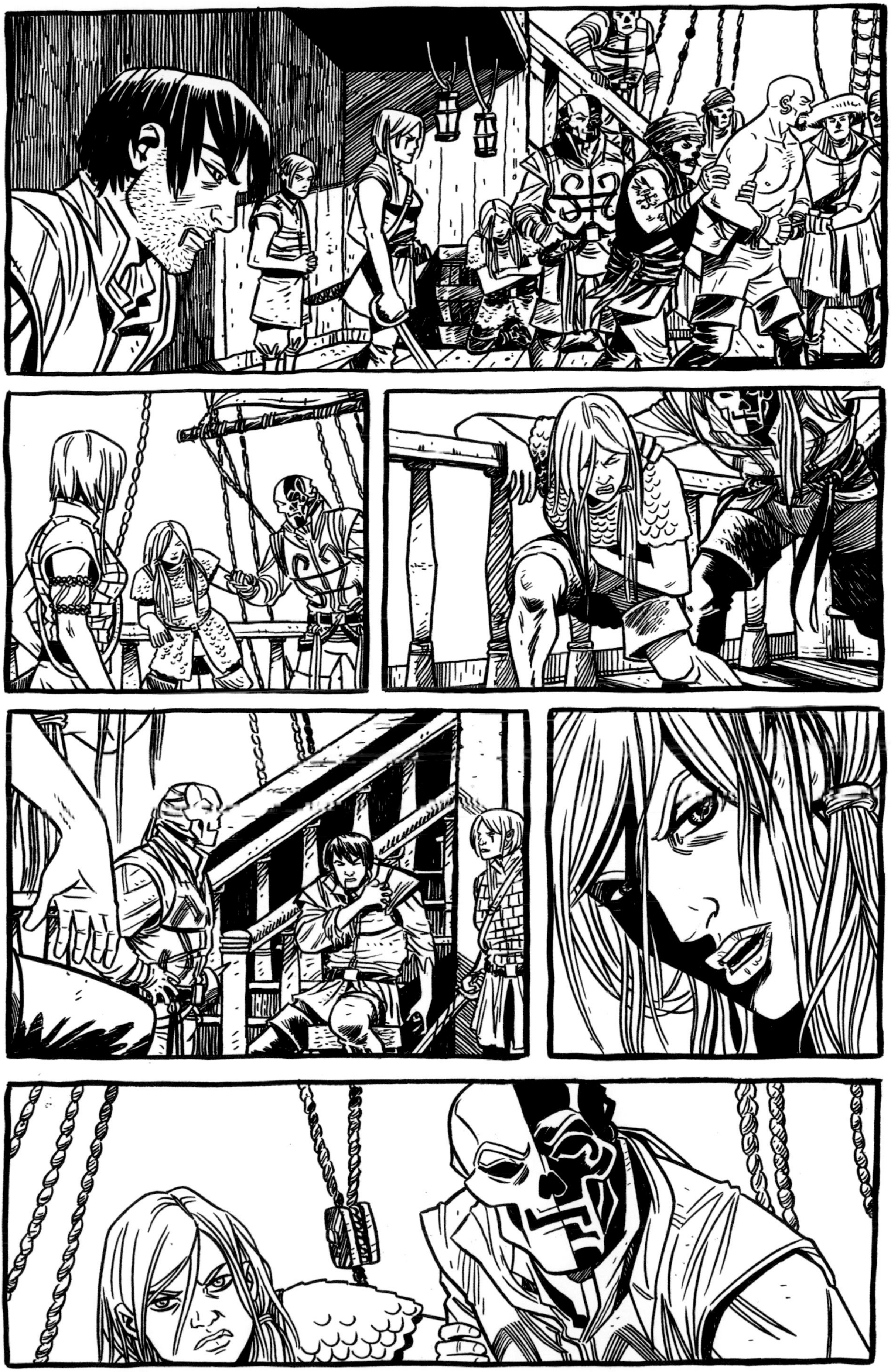

Page Fourteen

Panel 1: Cesario gestures towards Shakespeare who lies on a bed in the foreground, unconscious. He is badly bruised and beaten.

>**Cesario:** What of your man here? Is he **too** beset by phantoms?

>**Juliet:** He… he was already weak from lack of food and water and then Othello… was struck by one of his fevers…

>**Cesario:** Then I must insist we bind your Othello. At least 'til we come 'pon our destination. I cannot have a mad Moor wandering about my ship, can I?

>**Juliet:** Destination? So you already have a **price** for us, Captain. Who is it that has offered you the most gold? Titus? Philip? Lear?

Panel 2: Cesario gives Juliet an ornate half-bow.

>**Cesario:** Not at all, Juliet. You are not my prisoner.

>**Cesario:** I intend to join my ship to the Prodigal cause.

>**Viola (off-panel):** Cesario?

Panel 3: Furious, Viola stalks up to Cesario.

>**Viola:** Titus will pay good gold for these Prodigals. **More** than good gold! Have you gone craven?

Panel 4: It is clear Viola has gone too far. For the first time we see Cesario as an absolutely no-nonsense leader. He points at her.

>**Cesario:** You will address me as **Captain**, and the choice is not **yours!**

Panel 5: Cesario turns and strides away.

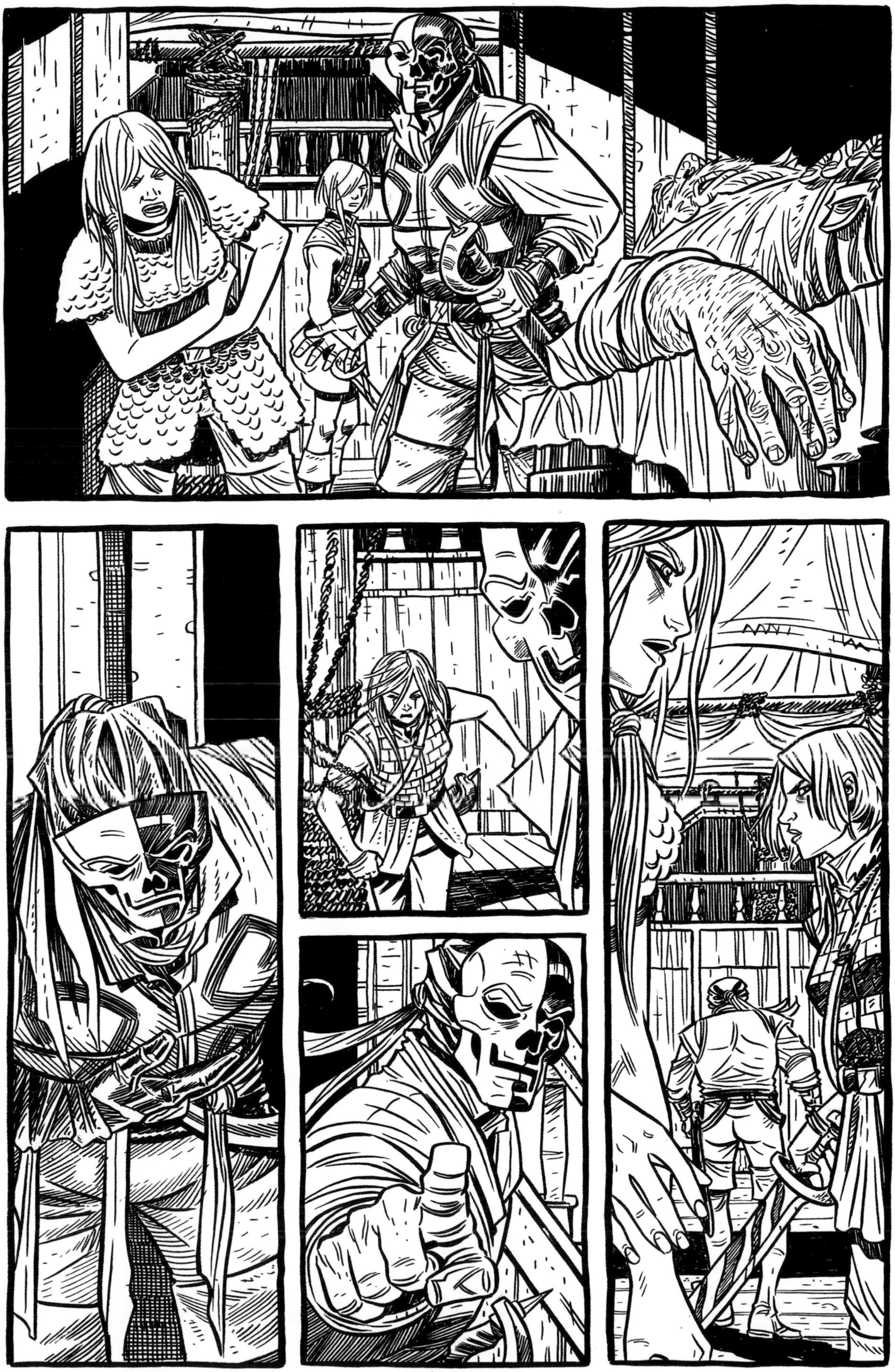

Page Fifteen

Panel 1: Still below deck, Cesario walks through the larder of the ship. Hanging on the wall are all manner of salted and cured meats.

Panel 2: He pushes the mask up on the top of his head. He looks tired.

Panel 3: He is slicing off a piece of salt-pork, when…

> **Viola (off-panel):** A word, "Captain".

Panel 4: Cesario wearily turns his head.

> **Cesario:** Viola…

Panel 5: A two-shot. This is a standoff.

> **Viola:** What is this? Turning *The Boreas* to the Prodigals? Giving up the Capulet for no gold at all?

> **Cesario:** It is the wisest course.

Panel 6: He steps forward and holds both of Viola's arms with his own.

> **Cesario:** I love thee, Viola. You know I do. I would marry thee, and have children with thee. *The Boreas* is **no place** for that.

Panel 7: On Viola, shocked.

Panel 8: Same shot. She bursts out laughing.

> **Viola:** Oh, would that Lucius and *The Lavinia* capture us. Many a good hanging prevents a bad marriage.

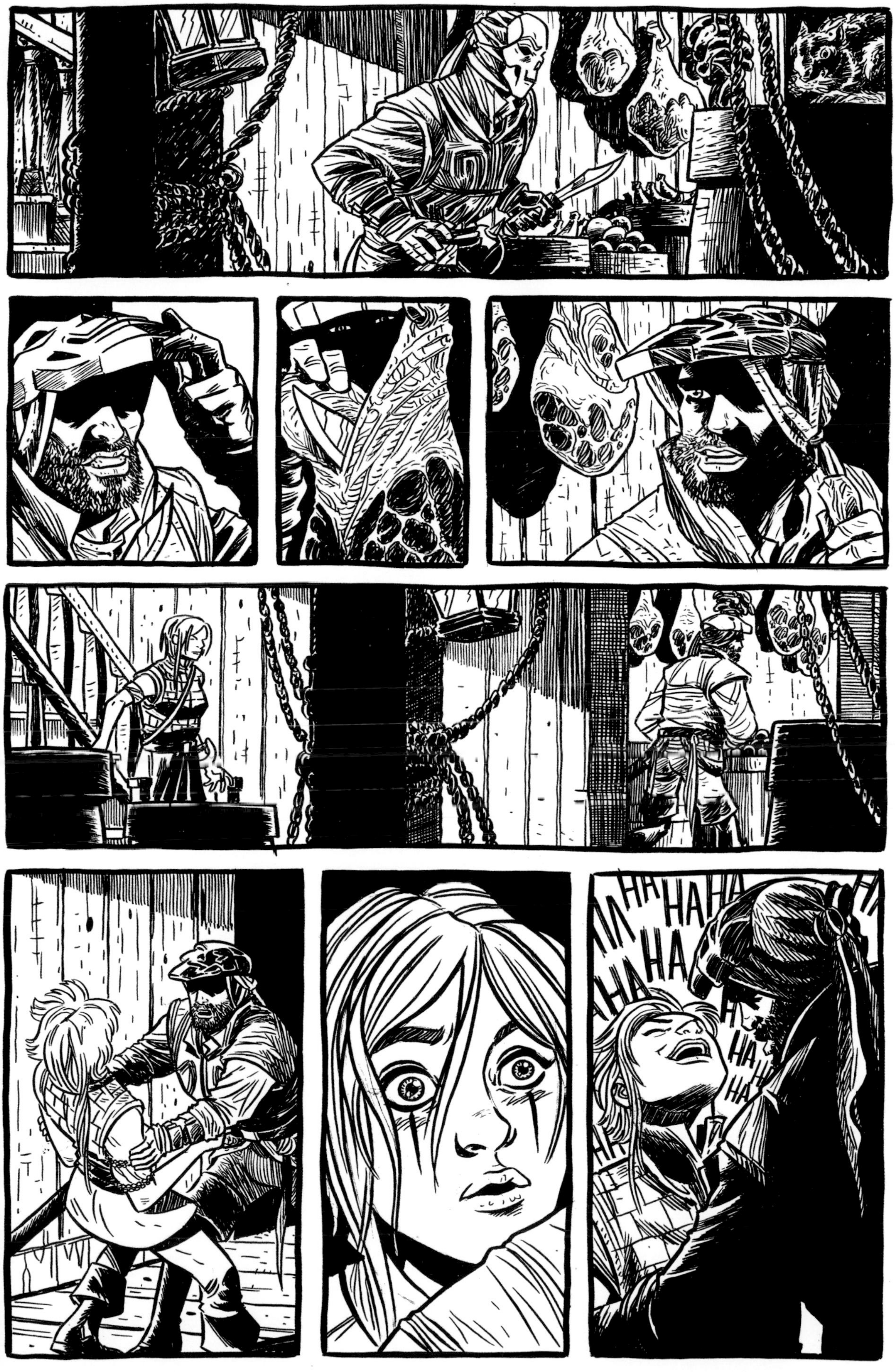
HA HA HA HA HA HA HA HA

Page Sixteen

Panel 1: Viola walks away from Cesario, heading for the ladder that leads above deck.

    Cesario: Spare me your poetry. If we lend our swords to the Prodigals we would have land, safety—

    Viola: Safety? What cares "Cesario, who never dies" for safety?

Panel 2: On Cesario.

    Cesario: Today I almost **did** die. Tomorrow, it could be you.

Panel 3: Viola looks at Cesario with contempt.

    Cesario: Marry me, Viola. We can fight for an honest cause and then grow fat and happy together.

    Viola: Marry thee? I cannot stand to **look** upon thee!

Panel 4: She reaches the ladder, and has her hands on it. She may even be a step up on it. Cesario may or may not be visible in this frame.

    Viola: Cesario, I loved thee for thy lean and hungry look.

    Cesario (off-panel): O, what a deal of scorn looks beautiful in the contempt and anger of your lip.

Panel 5: She stops on the ladder and turns angrily towards him.

    Viola: Now who plays at poetry? I **chose** this life! The sea and salt, the blood and treasure.

    Viola: You desire children? Whelp them with another wench, or have them with me here. The little bastards can swab the decks for all I care, but ask me not to give up who I am because your heart goes white.

Panel 6: Cesario lowers his mask.

    Cesario: I love thee, Viola.

    Cesario: But *The Boreas* is mine to take her as I will.

Panel 7: Viola, climbing up the ladder, looks down.

    Viola: *She* is. But *I* am not.

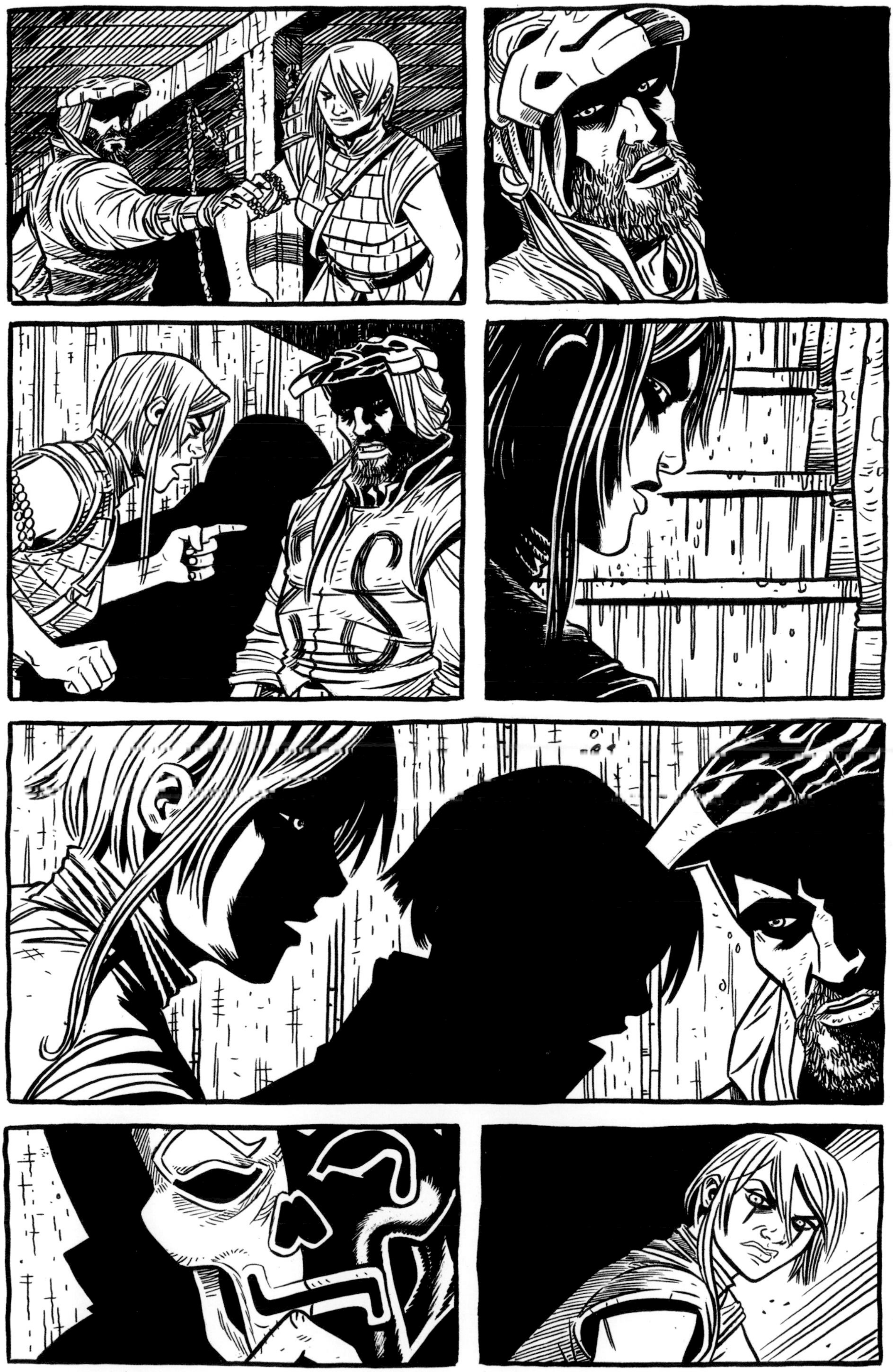

Page Seventeen

Panel 1: A long shot of *The Boreas* cutting through the water. The dominant feature of this panel should be the morning sun. We want to establish this for the morning sickness theme from below. We also want to show that the fog is still gathering so the sun may be somewhat obscured.

> **Juliet:** Hkkkk

Panel 2: On Juliet. She vomits over the side of the gunwale.

> **Juliet:** Hkkk.

Panel 3: Miserable, she wipes her mouth.

> **Viola (off-panel):** No taste for the sea, eh, girl?

Panel 4: Juliet looks up, in no mood for this. In the foreground we can see Viola's silhouette.

> **Juliet:** Leave me. Your captain said we were **free** to go about the ship. Unless he was a liar, leave me be.

Panel 5: On Viola, the mention of Cesario darkens her mood.

> **Viola:** My captain says **many** things about you. Now get up, you wretch. I won't have you befouling my decks.

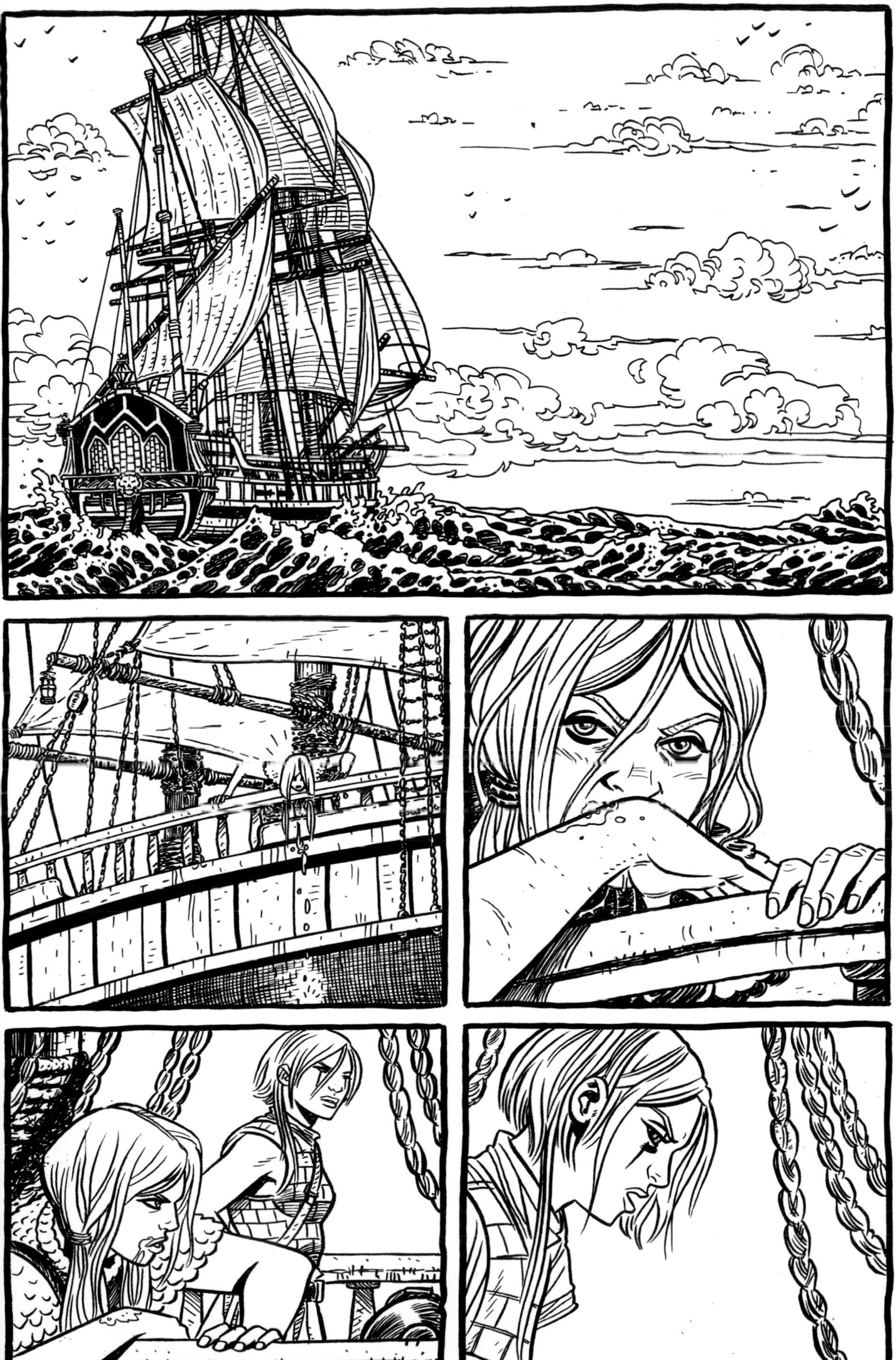

Page Eighteen

Panel 1: Juliet is sick again.

Panel 2: Viola reaches out to Juliet.

> **Viola:** I said on your feet!

Panel 3: Juliet shoves Viola away.

> **Juliet:** And I said **leave** me!

Panel 4: Viola shoves Juliet right back.

> 3a. **Juliet**: Unf!

Panel 5: Weakened, Juliet falls with a heavy thud.

Panel 6: Viola looks at Juliet appraisingly. She realizes what is going on here: morning sickness? Protecting her stomach?

> **Viola:** Sick at morning's first light.

> **Juliet:** No…

Panel 7: On Juliet, her face frozen, her secret discovered.

> **Viola (off-panel):** You hold thy belly carefully, girl.

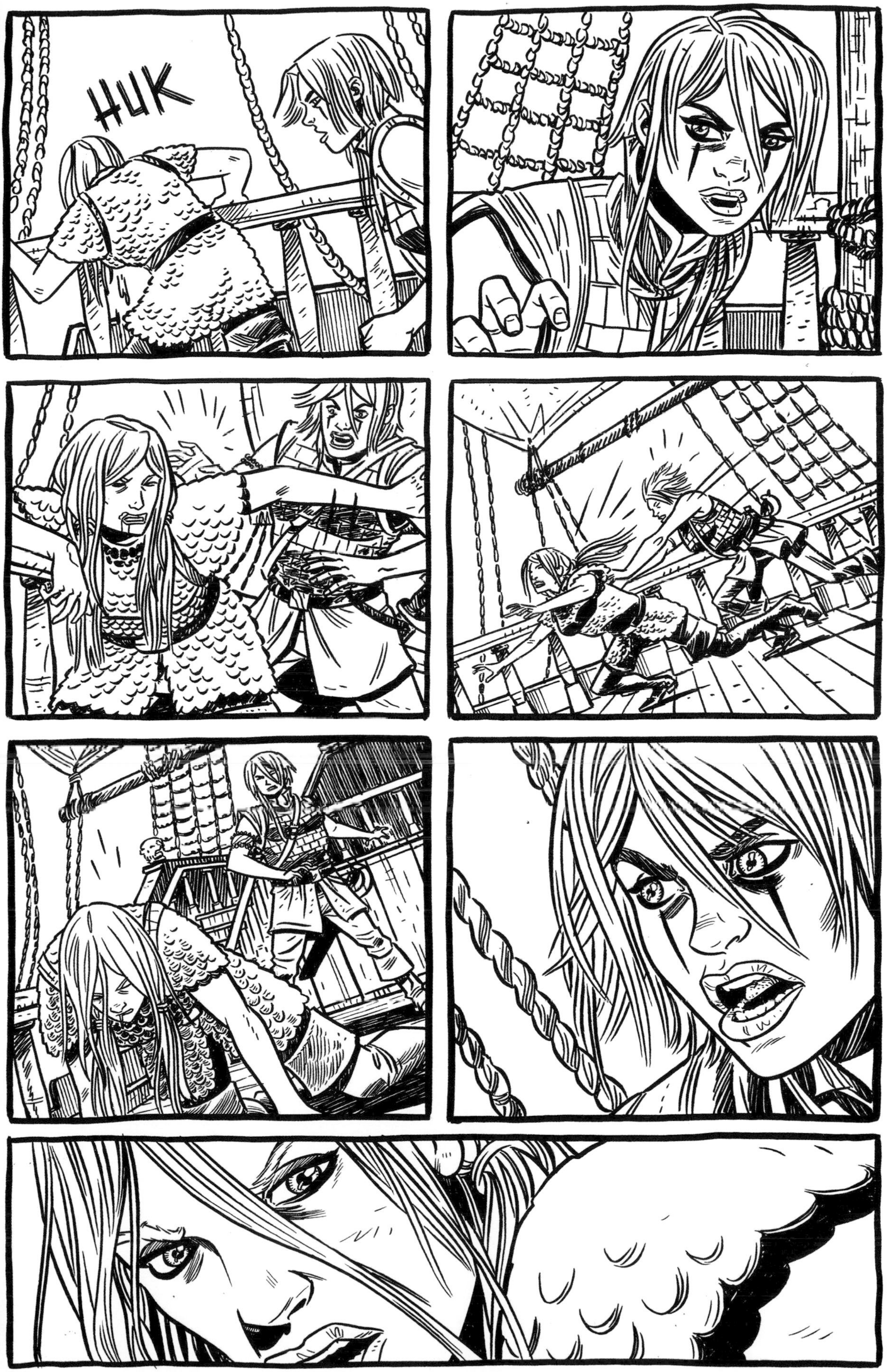
HUK

Page Ninteen

Panel 1: Viola tosses a water-skin at Juliet's feet.

> **Viola:** Drink it. You do **us** or that **child** within thee no good if you die.

> **Juliet:** There is no baby.

> **Viola:** You lie like a friar.

Panel 2: Viola, on her haunches beside Juliet, who has propped herself against the side of the ship. Viola has a questioning expression on her face, but this too is tinged with mockery.

> **Viola:** But why then is that lovely Shadow King so cross with thee? You'd think a suckling would make one like him all-a-flutter.

> **Juliet:** Say not one more word.

Panel 3: A tighter shot on Viola, who is enjoying this. She raises an eyebrow and puts a lascivious expression on her face.

> **Juliet:** Be silent.

> **Viola:** General Capulet, you keep secrets…

> **Juliet:** Be silent!

> **Viola:** Perhaps I will tell your Hamlet about his "blessing"

Panel 4: Juliet erupts, screaming at the leering Viola.

> **Juliet: BE SILENT!**

> **SFX (soft whistling):** thweeeeee

Panel 5: Viola looks at Juliet with raised eyebrows. She didn't think she was right.

Still sitting, Juliet has pulled her knees into her chest, she says nothing.

> **Viola:** I take back my words, General. You must be a fine liar.

> **SFX (soft whistling – growing louder):** thweeeeee

Panel 6: An explosion rocks the ship, knocking Viola off her feet.

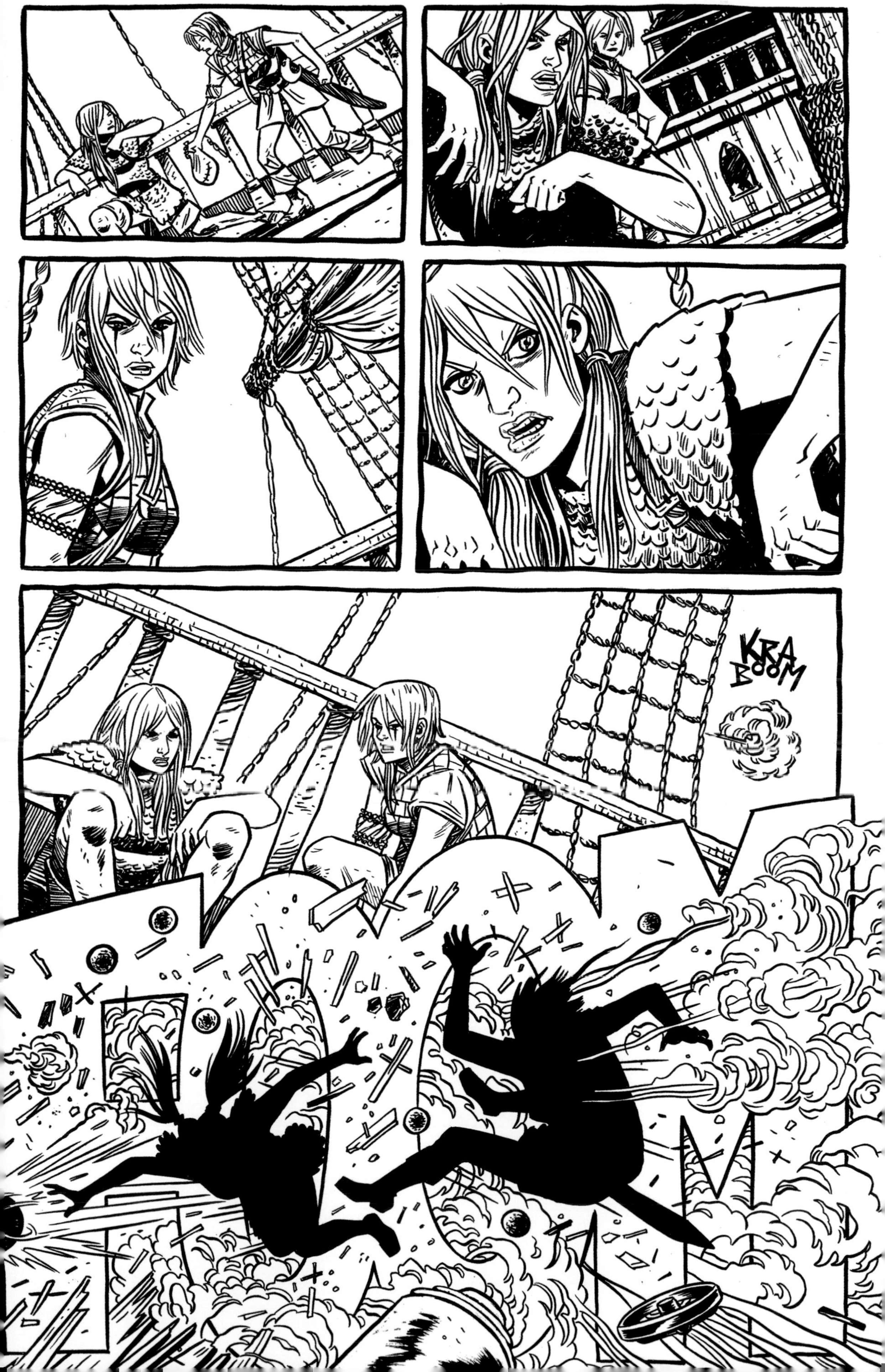
KRA BOOM
BOOM

Page Twenty

Panel 1: Viola struggles to her feet. Behind her Juliet has come out of her torpor.

> **Juliet:** What was that?!

> **Viola:** Pray for your bastard, Capulet.

Panel 2: Cutting through the fog is THE LAVINIA. This is Titus Andronicus' top ship-of-the-line. It is a massive war-machine and it is clear why a boat like this crushed the Prodigal fleet.

The sails are emblazoned with the RED HAND OF LAVINIA (we used these in issue #1 of The Tide of Blood.), which is disconcerting but what makes it truly terrifying is that the ship is designed to look like a KRAKEN.

The back of the ship is the head, and the tentacles snake alongside the outside of the ship ending as a twisted mass at the front of the ship. In practice these would be used by Titus' soldiers to get a better angle for boarding. They also serve as a devastating battering ram.

When *The Lavinia* sails at you head on you see that the prow has been shaped and painted to look like the sharp beak of the Kraken.

We see red flashes from *The Lavinia's* MANY canons.

> **CAPTION - Viola:** *"The Lavinia* has found us!"

> **CAPTION (TEXT):** To be continued…

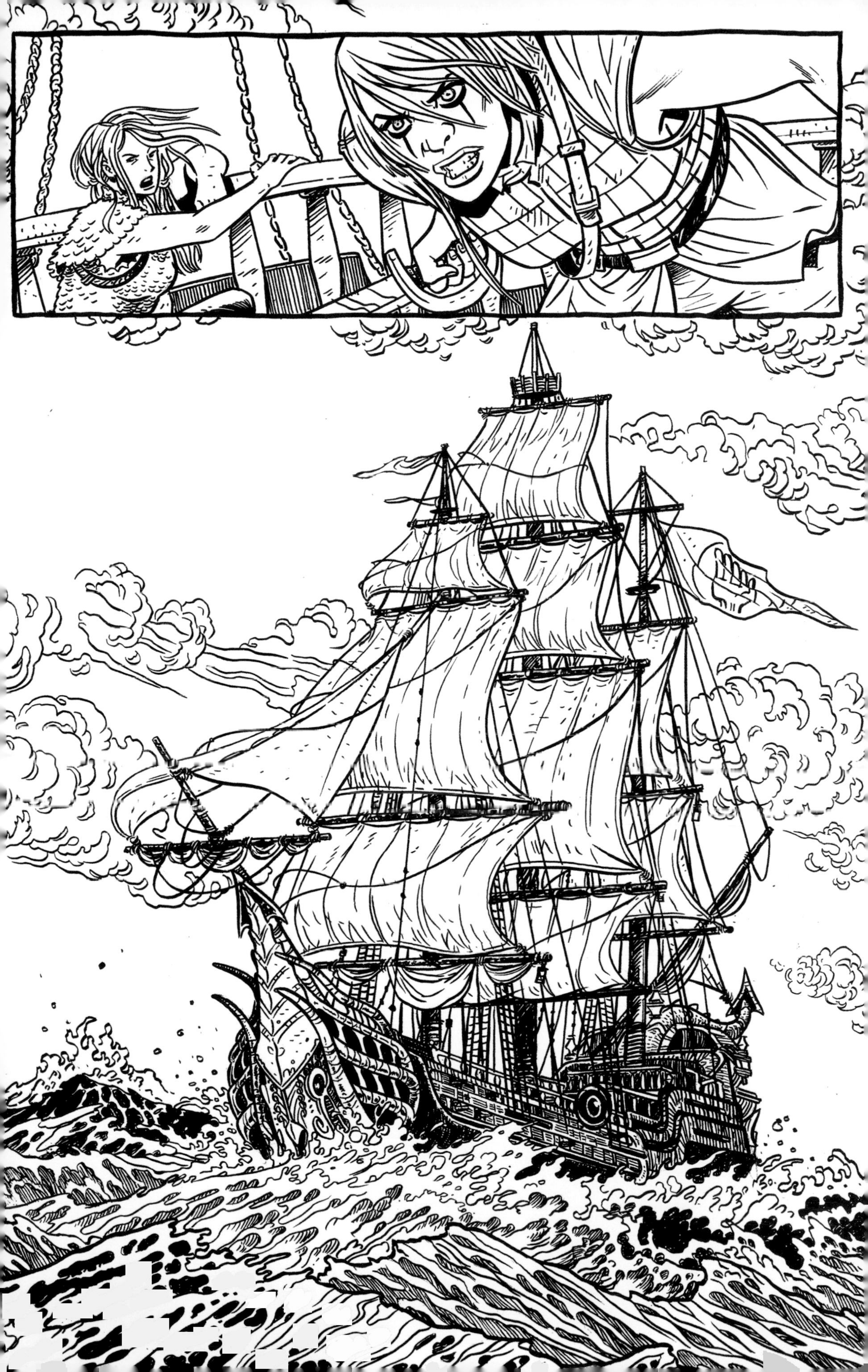

CREATOR BIOS

ANTHONY DEL COL (CO-CREATOR / CO-WRITER)

Prior to embarking on this epic quest to bash the Bard, Anthony successfully completed journeys in the film (producer of two independent feature films), music (served as a manager for international pop star Nelly Furtado), and television landscapes. He has helped to revive other well-known characters as the co-writer of *Sherlock Holmes vs. Harry Houdini* for Dynamite Comics.

CONOR MCCREERY (CO-CREATOR / CO-WRITER)

Conor has spent most of his career in film, television and journalism. He's covered everything from the NBA, to stock-market apocalypses, with a little dash of celebrity gossip for (questionable) taste. *Kill Shakespeare* is his first comic. He's looking forward to assassinating the character of Sherlock Holmes and Harry Houdini in his and Anthony's next project, *Holmes vs Houdini* for Dynamite Comics. He lives in Toronto with his wife Crystal and daughter Peregrine (who is lamentably weak at the whole "killing-a-pigeon-in-mid-air-thing").

ANDY B. (ARTIST AND COVERS)

Andy is a comic artist and commercial illustrator working out of Montreal-based Studio Lounak. He has worked on D.C.'s *Swamp Thing* as well as other projects with Marvel, Wildstorm and Boom! He is the creator of Zuda Comics' *Bottle of Awesome* and also self-publishes the awesomely gonzo medieval horror comic *Black Church*. His latest project is the Image Comics series *Southern Cross*, written by the award-winning Becky Cloonan.

SHARI CHANKHAMMA (COLOURS)

Shari hails from Thailand and has worked on such comic titles as *Kill Shakespeare: The Tide of Blood*, *Sheltered*, and *Fuse*. She previously worked on creator-owned titles such as *The Sisters' Luck*, *The Clarence Principle*, *Pavlov's Dream*, and short stories in various anthologies. When there's spare time, she enjoys wasting it on casual games and romance novels.